THE ROUTLEDGE COMPANION
TO THE AMERICAN CIVIL WAR ERA

'This well-conceived compilation of primary sources and concise biographical and historiographical essays on the period of sectional conflict, Civil War, and Reconstruction in the United States is a valuable reference and teaching tool.' – Professor James M. McPherson, *Princeton University*

'Tulloch's *Companion* is an invaluable resource for students, teachers, and anyone who wishes to begin or continue learning about what is perhaps the central event in the history of the United States.'– Natalie Zacek, *University of Manchester*

The American Civil War is a defining moment in the history of the United States. At least 600,000 Americans lost their lives in a conflict that merged elements of the Napoleonic era with the technologies of the Machine Age. In this indispensable reference guide, Hugh Tulloch examines the military aspects of the war alongside the political, constitutional, social and economic developments and trends that informed and were in turn informed by the turbulent events that took place during America's nineteenth century. As well as offering a unique examination of the literary and religious aspects of the era, key themes addressed include:

- emancipation and the quest for racial justice
- abolitionism and debates regarding freedom versus slavery
- Civil War military strategies
- presidential elections and party politics
- cultural and intellectual developments
- the Confederacy, secession and reconstruction
- industrial and agricultural changes

Including a full glossary, biographies of central figures, key documents, guides to further reading and illustrated with informative maps, this companion provides a comprehensive and essential guide for all those who study American history.

Hugh Tulloch was Senior Lecturer in American History at Bristol University from 1971 to 2003. He is author of *James Bryce's American Commonwealth* (1988), *Six British Travellers to the United States, 1919–41* (2000) and *The Debate on the American Civil War Era* (2000).

Routledge Companions to History
Series Advisers: Chris Cook and John Stevenson

Routledge Companions to History offer perfect reference guides to key historical events and eras, providing everything that the student or general reader needs to know. These comprehensive guides include essential apparatus for navigating through specific topics in a clear and straightforward manner – including introductory articles, biographies and chronologies – to provide accessible and indispensable surveys crammed with vital information valuable for beginner and expert alike.

The Routledge Companion to Medieval Europe
Baerbel Brodt

The Routledge Companion to Twentieth Century Britain
Mark Clapson

The Routledge Companion to Britain in the Nineteenth Century, 1815–1914
Chris Cook

The Routledge Companion to European History since 1763
Chris Cook and John Stevenson

The Routledge Companion to World History since 1914
Chris Cook and John Stevenson

The Routledge Companion to Fascism and the Far Right
Peter Davies and Derek Lynch

The Routledge Companion to the Crusades
Peter Lock

The Routledge Companion to Historiography
Alun Munslow

The Routledge Companion to Decolonization
Dietmar Rothermund

The Routledge Companion to Britain in the Eighteenth Century, 1688–1820
John Stevenson and Jeremy Gregory

The Routledge Companion to the Stuart Age, 1603–1714
John Wroughton

LIST OF MAPS, TABLES AND FIGURES

Maps

Tables

Figures

ACKNOWLEDGEMENTS

My thanks go, as ever, to Hugh Brogan and Anne Merriman, for their aid and support, and to my colleagues – Peter Coates, Brian Miller and Ken Thomas.

The Emily Dickinson poems are reprinted by permission of the publishers and Trustees of Amherst College from *The Poems of Emily Dickinson*, Thomas H. Johnson, ed., Cambridge, Mass.: The Belknap Press of Harvard University Press, © 1951, 1955, 1979, 1983 by the President and Fellows of Harvard College.

NOTE

Throughout the book, cross-references are shown in bold. They aim to help the reader navigate through the book. More information on such names and terms can be found under the respective headings in relevant sections.

You could not look upon the table but there were frogs, you could not sit down at the banquet but there were frogs, you could not go to the bridal couch and lift the sheets but there were frogs! ... this black question, forever on the table, on the nuptial couch, everywhere!

(Thomas Hart Benton, 1848)

INTRODUCTION

The American Civil War era continues to fascinate. Ken Burns's recent TV documentary, shown in the United States and in Great Britain, was hugely popular and made riveting viewing. This reference book attempts to cover not only the military conflict itself, but other facets of the era – political, economic, constitutional, social, literary, religious – ignored or given scant coverage by most compilers. Starting in 1831, with the publication of **Garrison**'s **abolitionist** *Liberator* and **Nat Turner**'s slave revolt in Virginia, and ending with the withdrawal of the last federal troops from the South and the end of **Reconstruction** in 1877, the book is held together by the central theme of emancipation and the quest for racial justice. In this, the war itself is vital, but has to be placed in the context of mid-nineteenth-century America where the roots of conflict lay within each individual's choice on the stark moral question of freedom or **slavery** or, indeed, the conscious choice of complete indifference to the issue. It was **Lincoln** who accused Senator **Douglas** of caring not whether slavery be voted up or voted down; but that, too, was a moral choice. So the book finds room not only for Lincoln and **Jefferson Davis**, **Grant** and **Lee**, but also the poet **Emily Dickinson**, for **Albert Brisbane**, the American apostle of utopian Fourierism, and **John Stuart Mill**, the English Liberal who championed the Northern cause.

The divisive issue of slavery was present in the United States from its beginnings in colonisation. With the arrival of the first Africans in Jamestown, Virginia, in 1619, imported to cope with an endemic labour shortage and a tobacco boom, they were initially granted the status of indentured servants like many of their white counterparts. But increasingly the fatal conjunction of race and slavery was established and legally codified. The African American was born into slavery, his or her status that of mere property whose duty it was to serve master or mistress for life. In his Declaration of Independence of 1776 Thomas Jefferson ringingly asserted that 'all men are created equal, that they are endowed by their Creator with certain unalienable Rights, that among these are Life, Liberty and the pursuit of Happiness'. Yet Jefferson was a Virginian slaveowner who had children by one of his female slaves, Sally Hemings, and who omitted any reference to slavery in his Declaration out of deference to his fellow Southerners, and Northerners who were profitably engaged in the slave trade. But the problem refused to go away. The **Missouri Compromise** of 1820 attempted a precarious balancing act between free and slave states and drew a line across the continent separating the two spheres. Jefferson issued a warning to his fellow citizens of 'a fire bell in the night … A geographical line, coinciding with a marked principle, moral and political, once conceived and held up to the angry

1

passions of men, will never be obliterated; and every new irritation will mark it deeper and deeper'.

This question played little part in the presidential election of 1832 which pitched the belligerent **Jackson**, who wanted to destroy the Bank of the United States, against horrified moderate **Whigs**, but positions on slavery were beginning to become more entrenched and embittered. Southerners such as **Calhoun** and **Fitzhugh** began to enunciate a doctrine of slavery as a positive good, while Garrison and his small band of abolitionists apologised for their former temporising and advocacy of colonisation and compensated emancipation, urging immediate emancipation instead. Most Southerners were not slaveowners and few Northerners were abolitionists; indeed, in many ways both sections were remarkably similar – the majority of both consisting of self-sufficient farmers enacting the Jeffersonian vision of a pure, agrarian republic. It was not Garrison's radical, religious anarchism or Calhoun's sophisticated defence of **states' rights** which stirred the majority into action, but the link with the West and land – America's preordained future – which dictated their response. 'Revisionist' historians, such as **J.G. Randall** and **Avery Craven**, have played down the moral issues of this period and argued that ambitious and manipulative politicians, a 'blundering generation', led Americans into a disastrous and avoidable civil war. But it could be argued, contrariwise, that politicians in this era of mass, participatory democracy responded all too well to the major concerns of their constituents. For Southerners the 'peculiar institution' must be federally protected and allowed to expand westwards, untrammelled, while to the Northerner the cry of '**free soil**, free labor, free men' led them to rally around a new, sectional party, the **Republicans**, and vote for **Frémont**, who, in 1856, failed to gain the presidency, and for Lincoln in 1860, who succeeded, and triggered off the civil war crisis.

Lincoln had achieved executive power constitutionally and his taking the nation to war following the **secession** of eleven Southern states was not just to re-establish an indissoluble Union but to reassert the democratic principle of ballots replacing bullets as the final arbiter. It is ironic that Lincoln had to resort to arms to reaffirm this principle; it is an even greater irony that, as **Alexander Stephens** said, it was impossible to imagine black emancipation while the South remained in the Union. Buttressed by an unassailable fifteen-state veto on any constitutional amendment to strike down slavery, emancipation came in war, ordered by the President not on moral grounds but predominantly because of military necessity. The irony does not end there, nor the disparity between American idealism and practice. The call for 'free soil' was supported by many Northern negrophobes to keep black labour out of the West. Lincoln himself, though always personally opposed to slavery, had no faith in racial equality: 'Your race', he told an African American delegation, 'are suffering, in my judgement, the greatest wrong inflicted on any people. But even when you cease to be slaves, you are yet far removed from being placed on an equality with the white race. You are cut off from many of the advantages which the other race enjoy. The aspiration of men is to enjoy equality with the best when free, but on this broad continent not a single man of your race is made the equal of a single man of

2

ours. Go where you are treated the best, the ban is still upon you ... It is better for us both, therefore, to be separated.'

Yet, briefly, under Reconstruction, a revolution occurred: 'the slave went free; stood a brief moment in the sun; then moved back again towards slavery' (**DuBois**). The long-term commitment emerging from the civil war crusade – the constitutional amendments which freed the slave, made him an equal citizen and gave the adult African American male the vote – was simply not there. Most Southerners were determined that the freedpersons have nothing save their freedom; Northerners, never deeply committed, grew weary of the intractable problems of Reconstruction and grew indifferent to the fate of the black. In a deal brokered by politicians following the disputed presidential election of 1876, the Northern Republican candidate, **Hayes**, gained the presidency, and the Southern, in turn, gained 'home rule'. Thereafter, by means of the judicial undermining of civil liberties, the informal disfranchisement of freedpersons and brute intimidation, the African American all but disappeared from American political life. America's brief engagement with racial justice was at an end.

Then the historians took over, beginning with contemporaries who attempted to write *apologias* for their actions. Ex-Confederates Jefferson Davis and Alexander Stephens wrote of the nobility of the lost cause in its fight for states' rights against democratic despotism: Grant and **Sherman** in their memoirs wrote of the tragedy of a bloody but inevitable conflict. Then, in an attempt to heal sectional wounds, a nationalist school of historians, personified in **James Ford Rhodes**, delivered a Solomonic judgement: 'All the right is never on one side, and all the wrong on the other.' Slavery was an evil, secession was wrong, but the utopian aim of Radical Reconstruction to revolutionalise the social order of the South was both vindictive and wrongheaded. The Progressive upsurge at the turn of the century led to a fresh reassessment of the civil war era, but tended to underplay the moral dimension. **Frederick Jackson Turner** believed that the western frontier overwhelmingly shaped the American character, not the relatively superficial sectional differences of North and South, free and slave. **Charles Beard**, an economic determinist much influenced by **Marx** and British Socialism, interpreted the conflict of Northern capital destroying the backward **Confederacy** in order to turn it into a dependent economic colony. Southerners were transformed into poor Jeffersonian farmers gallantly but vainly fighting the implacable juggernaut of Yankee trusts and corporations. **Vernon Parrington** found much to admire in an ante-bellum South which stood out against the sterile, atomistic social relations of a *laissez-faire* North. It was worth hanging on to Confederate currency: it was redeemable and the South seemed to be winning the historiographical Civil War.

Even more so with the emergence of a Southern cultural renaissance in the 1930s. The Southern Agrarians conjured up an essentially mythical rural South held together by harmonious, organic social relations; the plain folks of the South were the carriers of vital but increasingly depleted cultural values; the respectful slave fitted well into this complacent scheme and is reflected in the film *Gone with the Wind* and the scholarly writings of the Georgian, **U.B. Phillips**. This depiction was reinforced by 'revisionist' writers, both North and South, who considered the war a tragedy of unparalleled proportions and entirely avoidable. Slavery was slowly dying a natural death; was the sacrifice of 620,000 lives really worth it? Theirs was a reconstructed history of that which had not happened while the historical reactions against them from such historians as **Peter Geyl** and **Arthur Schlesinger** Jr had the advantage, at least, of dealing with what had happened. If they tended to overplay the moral card – 'To reject the moral actuality of the Civil War is to foreclose the possibility of an adequate account of its causes' (Schlesinger Jr) – they got slavery and race back into the narrative from which, because of racial assumptions, they had been carefully effaced. But this was very much a cold war history shaped by the events of the 1940s and 1950s: to work for perpetual peace and the avoidance of all conflict in a tragic and ideologically divided world was sentimentalism; appeasement of Southern sectionalist by Northern '**doughface**' politicians such as **Pierce** and **Buchanan** in the 1850s was as self-defeating as Henry Wallace's attempt to reach agreement with Stalin in the 1940s.

Then the Warren Court's *Brown v. Topeka* decision of 1954 changed everything. The second **Civil Rights** movement had begun and matters looked very different from before. In his groundbreaking *The Peculiar Institution* of 1956, **Kenneth Stampp** saw slavery as tragic for both white and slave, and profoundly evil. Abolitionists, previously depicted collectively as crackpots, were now sane idealists attempting, in the best reformist American tradition, to transform an unjust and insane society. Hitherto the tragedy of Reconstruction stemmed from its attempts at misguided social engineering: now the tragedy lay in its marked failure to achieve racial equality. The 1960s were intoxicating and euphoric days for American historians as well as for its youth.

Since then things have settled down a little. In the 1970s and 1980s computers facilitated the growing predominance of econometrics, or 'cliometrics', as it was called. Traditional, written evidence was dismissed as hopelessly impressionistic and only that which could be counted counted. In the case of **Fogel** and **Engerman**'s *Time on the Cross* (1974) the results appeared perilously close to depicting slavery as a 'happy institution' because the institution was measured in terms of profitability and thus inevitably interpreted through the eyes of the slavemaster. But the grafting of economics on to the new social history which concerned itself with those groups historians had tended to forget or ignore – slaves, misfits, rebels and minorities of all sorts – and the rich mining of gender studies has left a residue of more modest but subtler studies. Now we could read about the female slave and her relations with master and mistress, of runaway slaves and letters written by the common soldier to his family back home; of the early struggles of freedpersons to establish a degree of independence through such agencies as the **Freedmen's Bureau**, the Church and the schools. I hope this reference book will serve as an aid and guide in an adventure: to rediscover a tumultuous period in US history which engaged everyone at the time and continues to engage us today.

The survey begins with a chronological table giving an overview of the period and delineating the major relevant events of the era. A historiographical section will give brief summaries of major historians' conflicting interpretations of the period, ranging from contemporaries such as **Henry Wilson** to living historians such as **Eugene Genovese** and **Martin Duberman**. The section on founding documents points out the relevant aspects of the Declaration of Independence, Federal Constitution of 1787 and Confederate Constitution of 1861. The political section summarises the individual parties of the US and presidential elections between 1832 and 1876, with their profound consequences. A social and economic section deals with the tangible raw materials of the age such as land, population, cotton and wheat and an overall summary of civil war military strategy refers the reader to the most significant soldiers and battles of the conflict. A selection of contemporary documents, such as Garrison's first number of *The Liberator* and Lincoln's **Gettysburg** Address, attempts to capture the spirit of the age. This is followed by a biographical section, a glossary and an up-to-date annotated bibliography.

I
HISTORICAL BACKGROUND

CHRONOLOGICAL TABLE

1619

First African Americans in Virginia.

1776, 4 July

Declaration of Independence.

1787

Constitution of the United States of America.

1787

North-West Ordinances: **slavery** banned from North-West territory.

1816

American Colonisation Society established.

1820

Missouri Compromise: prohibited slavery north of 36°30′ in territory of Louisiana Purchase.

1831, 1 January

First number of **Garrison**'s *Liberator*.

1831, 13–23 August

Nat Turner's slave revolt, Southampton County, Virginia.

1831–32

Debates in Virginia legislature. Narrow defeat of **emancipation** and state **black codes** reinforced.

1832

South Carolina State Convention nullifies federal tariffs of 1828 and 1832.

1832, 5 December

Jackson re-elected president.

1832, 10 December

Jackson issues a proclamation to people of South Carolina against **nullification**.

1833

Oberlin, America's first co-educational college, established and, under **Theodore Weld**, became centre of north-west **abolitionism**; American Antislavery Society established in Philadelphia; slavery and slave trade ended in British Empire.

1834

Prudence Crandall's school for African American girls in Canterbury, Connecticut, closed by vandalism.

1835, 21 October

Mob attacks female Antislavery Society meeting in Boston, and Garrison is nearly killed.

1836, March

Texas declares independence from Mexico.

1836, 11 March

A '**gag rule**' introduced in Congress barring discussion of anti-slavery petitions (repealed 1844).

1837, May

Economic panic and depression; **Martin Van Buren** 8th President of the United States.

1837, 7 November

Abolitionist editor, Elijah Lovejoy, murdered by mob in Alton, Illinois; **Emerson**'s address at Harvard, 'The American Scholar', declaring American literary independence from Europe.

1838

Joshua Giddings (Ohio, **Whig**) first abolitionist in Congress; first American edition of **Tocqueville**'s *Democracy in America*.

1839

Theodore Weld's *Slavery as It Is; Armistad* slave mutiny.

1840

Harrison's 'Log cabin and hard cider' campaign; World Antislavery Convention held in London, and women denied seating on floor of hall; **Liberty Party** organised and nominated James Birney as presidential candidate.

1841

William Henry Harrison 9th President of the United States.

1841, 4 April

John Tyler (previously Vice President) becomes 10th President of the United States; Brook Farm, utopian communal experiment, established in Massachusetts by George Ripley.

1842

Prigg v. Pennsylvania.

1843

Baptist church split over slavery.

1844

James Polk stands on platform of annexation of Texas and acquisition of Oregon territory.

1845, December

Texas admitted as 28th state and 15th slave state; **Douglass**'s *Narrative of the Life of Frederick Douglass: An American Slave*.

1846, 13 May

Congress declares war on Mexico.

1846, 15 June

Settlement of Oregon boundary at the 49th Parallel.

1846, June

Frémont leads Bear Flag revolt in California against Mexico; David **Wilmot** (Pennsylvania, **Democrat**) **Proviso** excluding slavery from any territory acquired from Mexico fails in Senate.

1847, 23 February

General **Zachary Taylor** defeats Mexicans at Buena Vista.

1847, 14 September

Winfield Scott captures Mexico City.

1848, 24 January

Gold discovered at Sutter's Mill, California. Start of **California Gold Rush**.

1848, 2 February

Treaty of Guadalupe Hidalgo with Mexico.

1848, 19–20 July

First female rights' convention held at **Seneca Falls**, New York State; **Free Soil** Party established with Martin Van Buren as presidential candidate.

1848

Zachary Taylor elected 12th President of the United States.

1849

Thoreau, *Resistance to Civil Government.*

1850, 9 July

Death of Taylor. Vice President **Millard Fillmore** becomes 13th President of the United States.

1850, 9 September

California established as 31st and free state. Great **Compromise of 1850**.

1851

Melville, *Moby Dick.*

1852

Publication of **Harriet Beecher Stowe**'s *Uncle Tom's Cabin.*

1853

Franklin Pierce 14th President of the United States.

1853, July

Commodore Matthew Perry's mission to Japan.

1854

Kansas–Nebraska Act repeals Missouri Compromise.

1854, 28 February

Founding of **Republican Party** in Ripon, Wisconsin; Thoreau, *Walden or Life In The Woods;* **George Fitzhugh**, *Sociology for the South.*

1855

Civil war in '**Bleeding Kansas**'.

1855, 28 April

Massachusetts bans segregation in education; **Whitman**, *Leaves of Grass.*

1856

John Brown and 7 followers massacre 5 pro-slavers at Pottawatomie Creek; **Sumner**'s 'Crime against Kansas' speech, followed by assault upon him in Senate two days later.

1857

Buchanan 15th President of the United States.

1857, November

Buchanan accepts pro-slavery Lecompton Constitution for Kansas. **Douglas** rejects it. Democratic split.

1858, 16 June

Lincoln's 'House Divided' speech at Illinois Republican state convention.

1858, 21 August–15 October

Lincoln–Douglas Debates in Illinois; **Seward**'s 'Irrepressible Conflict' speech at Rochester.

1859, 16 October

John Brown's raid on Harper's Ferry. Executed 2 December.

1860, 6 November

Lincoln elected 16th President of the United States.

1860, 20 December

South Carolina secedes, followed rapidly by 6 other slave states.

1860, 31 December

Crittenden Amendment rejected by Senate Committee.

1861, 8 February

Confederacy of 11 states established at Montgomery, Alabama; **Davis** (Mississippi) provisional president and **Alexander Stephens** (Georgia) provisional vice president.

1861, 28 February

House of Representatives adopts proposed **13th Amendment** guaranteeing slavery against federal interference.

1861, 4 March

Lincoln's inaugural.

1861, 12–14 April

Confederates take **Fort Sumter**.

1861, 15 April

Lincoln calls for 75,000 militia to suppress 'insurrection'; Virginia secedes, along with 3 other slave states.

1861, 21 July

Battle of **First Bull Run** (Manassas).

1861, 20 December

Joint Committee on Conduct of War established; James Mason and John Slidell (Confederate agents) removed from *Trent* on way to England. Released by Seward, 26 December.

1862, 6–16 February

Grant captures **Forts Henry and Donelson**, Tennessee.

1862, 9 March

Naval battle in Hampton Roads, Virginia.

1862, March

Start of **McClellan**'s **Peninsula Campaign**.

1862, 6–7 April

Battle of **Shiloh**, Tennessee.

1862, 25 April

New Orleans captured by **Farragut**.

1862, 20 May

Homestead Act (cheap land for Western settlers).

1862, 2 July

Morrill Land Grant Act.

1862, 29–30 August

Second battle of Bull Run. General John Pope retreats to Washington.

1862, 7 September

Lee invades Maryland.

1862, 17–18 September

Battle of **Antietam** (Sharpsburg). Lee retreats into Virginia.

1862, 13 December

Battle of **Fredericksburg**. Burnside retreats.

1863, 1 January

Lincoln's **Emancipation Proclamation**.

1863, 25 February

National Bank Act.

1863, 3 March

First Union Conscription Act.

1863, 2–4 May

Lee defeats **Hooker** at **Chancellorsville**.

1863, 1–4 July

Lee defeated by **Meade** at **Gettysburg**.

1863, 4 July

Confederates surrender to Grant at **Vicksburg**.

1863, 13–16 July

New York City draft riots (1,000 dead).

1863, 19 November

Lincoln's Gettysburg Address.

1863, 23–25 November

Bragg defeated at **Chattanooga**.

1864, 9 March

Grant Commander-in-Chief of all Union forces.

1864, 4 May

Sherman leaves Chattanooga to start march into Georgia.

1864, 1–3 June

Grant versus Lee at Cold Harbor.

1864, 12 June

Grant's 9-month siege of **Petersburg** begins.

1864, 8 July

Lincoln pockets **Wade–Davis Bill**.

1864, 5 August

Naval battle of Mobile Bay, Alabama.

1864, 2 September

Sherman captures Atlanta.

1864, 8 November

Lincoln re-elected president.

1864, November–December

Sherman's march to sea.

1864, 15–16 December

Hood's army destroyed at Nashville.

1864, 22 December

Savannah surrenders.

1865, January–April

Sherman's march through the Carolinas.

1865, 3 March

Freedmen's Bureau established.

1865, 4 March

Lincoln's second inaugural.

1865, 2–3 April

Confederates retreat from Richmond and Petersburg, Virginia.

1865, 9 April

Lee surrenders to Grant at **Appomattox Court House**, Virginia.

1865, 14 April

Assassination of Lincoln (dies 15 April). Seward severely injured by assassin. **Andrew Johnson** becomes 17th President of the United States.

1865, 26 April

Johnston surrenders to Sherman at Durham, North Carolina.

1865, 10 May

Davis captured and imprisoned for 2 years.

1865, October

United States demands withdrawal of French troops from Mexico.

1865, 4 December

Joint Commission on Reconstruction established.

1865, 18 December

13th Amendment ratified. Black codes introduced in South.

1866, 9 April

Civil Rights Act passed by Congress over Johnson's veto.

1866, 16 June

14th Amendment passed by Congress.

1866, July

Freedmen's Bureau Bill passed by Congress over Johnson's veto.

1867, 2 March

First Reconstruction Act passed over Johnson's veto. South divided into 5 military districts.

1867, 21 March

Tenure of Office Act passed over Johnson's veto.

1867, 30 March

Alaska bought from Russia for $7.2 million.

1867, May

Ku Klux Klan formally organised in Nashville, Tennessee.

1868, 16 May

Senate impeachment of Johnson fails by one vote.

1868, 28 July

Ratification of the 14th Amendment.

1868, 3 November

Grant 18th President of the United States.

1869, 27 February

15th Amendment passed by Congress.

1869, 10 May

Completion of First Transcontinental Railroad.

1869, 10 December

Female suffrage in Wyoming territory.

1870

First African American in Congress (Senator Hiram Revels of Mississippi).

1870, 30 March

15th Amendment ratified.

1870, 31 May

First Enforcement Act to crush Klan.

1871, 8 May

Anglo-American Treaty of Washington to settle **Alabama Claims**; Whitman, *Democratic Vistas*.

1872, 4 September

Crédit Mobilier scandal exposed involving Cabinet members.

1872, 14 September

Geneva, Alabama Claims against Britain settled with payment of $15.5 million.

1872, 5 November

Grant re-elected over **Liberal Republican** nominee, **Horace Greeley**.

1873, 18 September

Financial panic on Wall Street; Supreme Court's **Slaughterhouse Case** undermines 14th Amendment.

1874

Women's Christian Temperance Union established in Cleveland, Ohio.

14

1875, 1 March

Civil Rights Act passed (invalidated by Supreme Court, 1883).

1875, 1 May

Exposure of Whisky Ring, again implicating Grant and his private secretary.

1876

Centennial Exposition in Philadelphia; disputed **Hayes–Tilden** presidential election.

1876, 25 June

Massacre of Custer and US cavalry by Sioux at Little Big Horn.

1877, 5 March

Hayes's inauguration as 19th President of the United States.

1877, 24 April

Last federal troops evacuate South.

HISTORIOGRAPHY/HISTORIANS

$$\boxed{A}$$

$$\boxed{B}$$

JOHN EMERICH EDWARD DALBERG ACTON (1834–1902) (Great Britain) Trip to United States of America, 1853. Civil War shaped his opposition to nationalism and democratic despotism. Strong supporter of southern **states' rights** and **Lee** became his personal hero. 'The North has used the doctrine of Democracy to destroy self-government. The South applied the principle of conditional federalism to cure the evils and to correct the errors of a false interpretation of Democracy.' This led him, inevitably, to support of 'the peculiar institution'. 'Slavery is the condition in which certain definitive rights are lost by the slave. Absolutism is the state in which no rights are assured to the subject … The decomposition of Democracy was arrested in the South by the indirect influence of slavery.' Regius Professor of Modern History, Cambridge University, 1895–1902.

HERBERT APTHEKER (1915–2003) (New York) Radical historian and early writer on the biracial nature of **abolitionism**. Author of *The Negro in the Civil War* (1938) and *Negro Slave Revolts in the United States* (1942), though criticised for exaggerating their nature and extent. Wrote, 1964, that 'part of the effort to cleanse the United States of racism is to cleanse its educational system of that blight. Certainly, an anti-racist educational system cannot have racist history books; integrated schools require integrated texts.'

GILBERT BARNES (1889–1945) (Nebraska) Head of Economics department at Ohio Wesleyan University, 1920. Later, University of Michigan at Ann Arbor. His *The Antislavery Impulse 1830–44* (1933) marks beginning of modern scholarship on abolitionism. Discerned its roots in religious revivalism in upstate New York and mid-West and stressed the vital axis of **Weld** in the West and the **Tappan** brothers in New York City in crusade. Highly critical of radicalism of **John Brown** and **Garrison**: 'The reputation of *The Liberator* was made by its enemies and not by its subscribers … Once he had tasted the heady wine of anarchism, Garrison drank deep.'

HOWARD BEALE (1899–1959) (Illinois) Educated at Chicago and Harvard. Wrote *The Critical Year 1866: A Study of Andrew Johnson and Reconstruction* (1930) and 'On Rewriting Reconstruction History' (1940), a Beardian interpretation which emphasised economic motives of **Radical Republicans**. Also explored biracial Granger's coalition in South in 1870s and 1880s aimed against Bourbon Democrats.

CHARLES BEARD (1874–1948) (Indiana) Progressive historian employing Marxist concepts of economics as prime engine of historical change and economic conflict – capital versus labour, wealth versus poverty, Jefferson versus Hamilton, etc. – as essence of American past. Graduated from De Pauw in 1898, then formative period at working man's Ruskin College, Oxford, 1899–1901. At Columbia in 1907, resigning in 1917 over question of academic freedom, and helped establish new Center for Social Research, New York. Two most famous books – *An Economic Interpretation of the Constitution* (1913) and *Economic Origins of Jeffersonian Democracy* (1915) but *The Rise of American Civilisation* (1927) written with wife, Mary Beard, and *America in Mid Passage* (1939) also highly influential. Following **Jefferson Davis**, argued Civil War was caused by Northern economic aggression to subdue South and reduce it to economic satellite of Northern capitalism, but concept of 'the Second American Revolution' has fared better. Abolition was 'the most stupendous act of sequestration in the history of Anglo-Saxon jurisprudence' (three trillion dollars by 1990 standards). But again 'revolution' interpreted here in narrow economic terms and the era emptied of its moral content. 'Nobody but agitators, beneath the contempt of the towering statesmen of the age, ever dared to advocate Abolitionism.' **Peter Geyl** criticised Beard's 'despiritualisation' and later historians – James MacPherson, Eric Foner – have employed 'the Second American Revolution' in broader, more suggestive, ways.

DANIEL BOORSTIN (1914–2004) (Georgia) Educated at Harvard and Oxford as Rhodes Scholar. The preeminent exponent of a 'consensus' school of history, which rejected Progressives' concept of intractable ideological conflict in American history. *The Genius of American Politics* included a chapter on the Civil War entitled 'The Spirit of Compromise'. Argued that both sides in war did not have fundamental differences but differed only in their interpretation of the Constitution (the Confederate Constitution was remarkably similar to the Federal Constitution), and there was no appeal beyond the Constitution to a higher law except among extreme abolitionists. Nevertheless,

'for us who boast that our political system is based on compromise, on the ability to organise varied regions and diverse institutions under a single federal union, it offers considerable embarrassment … From any point of view it is one of the grimmest, most inexplicable, and most discouraging events of the modern era'. It must be read, in particular, as a cold war document. Went on to write hugely popular trilogy emphasising practical empiricism of the American experiment. *The Americans, the Colonial Experience* (1958). *The National Experience* (1965) and *The Democratic Experience* (1973). Director of the Smithsonian in 1969; Librarian of Congress in 1973.

CLAUDE BOWERS (1878–1958) (Indiana) Journalist and orator, 'The Gatling Gun Orator of the Wabash'. *The Tragic Era* (1929) popularised the **Dunning** School interpretation of **Reconstruction** which attacked the **Radical Republicans**. 'Never have American public men, in responsible positions, directing the destiny of the Nation, been so brutal, hypocritical and corrupt … the Southern people were literally put to the torture.' His pro-**Democratic** leanings earned him Spanish Embassy from a grateful FDR.

JOHN WILLIAM BURGESS (1844–1931) (Tennessee) Born into slaveholding **Whig** Unionist family. Studied in Germany, 1871–73, Columbia University, 1876 and in 1880 established, and became Dean of, School of Political Science. *Reconstruction and the Constitution* (1902) intended to reconcile North and South and emphasise futility of extending suffrage to African Americans. **Reconstruction** was 'the most soul-sickening spectacle that Americans have ever been called upon to behold … The claim that there is nothing in the color of the skin from the point of view of political ethics is a great sophism. A black skin means membership in a race of men which has never in itself succeeded in subjecting passion to reason; has never, therefore, created any civilisation of any kind.' Racial prejudice confirmed by American imperialism and possession of the Philippines. Taught **Dunning**.

C

AVERY CRAVEN (1886–1980) (North Carolina) Pacifist, Quaker. Prominent member of 'revisionist' school which argues that war was repressible and caused by fanatical abolitionists who 'threatened to produce a race problem which in large part had been solved by the institution of slavery' and irresponsible politicians: 'Those who force the settlement of human problems by war can expect only an unsympathetic hearing from the future. Mere desire to do "right" is no defence at the bar of history.' Wrote *Edmund Ruffin: Southerner* (1931), *The Repressible Conflict* (1939), *The Coming of the Civil War* (1942) and *An American Historian and the Civil War* (1964), a collection of essays which modified some of his earlier opinions.

D

DAVID BRION DAVIS (1927–) (Colorado) Educated at Dartmouth, Harvard and Oxford. Professor at Yale since 1969. Major, ongoing trilogy on slavery and its abolition throughout history. Wrote *The Problem of Slavery in Western Culture* (1966) and *The Problem of Slavery in the Age of Revolution* (1975). The third in the series, *The Problem of Slavery in the Age of Emancipation*, has yet to appear. Also *From Homicide to Slavery* (1986), *Slavery and Human Progress* (1984) and *In*

the Image of God (2001), a collection of essays which also looks at fellow historians such as **Genovese** and **Van Woodward**. 'The inherent contradiction of slavery lies not in its cruelty or economic exploitation, but in the underlying conception of a man as a conveyable possession with no more autonomy of will and consciousness than a domestic animal.'

MARTIN DUBERMAN (1930–) (New York) Educated at Yale and Harvard, has taught at Yale and Princeton and, since 1971, at Lehman College, City University, New York. Biographies of *Charles Francis Adams* (1961) and *James Russell Lowell* (1967) and editing of *The Anti-slavery Vanguard* (1965), which rejected the conventional caricature of abolitionists as crackpots and fanatics. Suggested, rather, that dedicated commitment to reform could indicate inner strength and mental health: 'The very definition of maturity may be the ability to commit oneself to abstract ideals, to go beyond the selfish, egocentric world of children.' Went on to become one of the founders of gay and lesbian studies.

WILLIAM EDWARD BURGHART DUBOIS (1868–1963) (Massachusetts) African American leader and Marxist writer. Educated at Fisk and first African American to achieve a PhD at Harvard in 1895. Wrote 'Reconstruction and its Benefits' (*American Historical Review*, July 1910), the first study to question **Dunning** school view on Reconstruction, emphasising **Republican Party** and black voters collaborating, through churches, schools and **Freedmen's Bureau**, to create more equitable society. Taken up and expanded in major *Black Reconstruction in America: An Essay Towards a History of the Part which Black Folk Played in the Attempt to Reconstruct Democracy in America, 1860–80* (New York, 1936). In its Introduction: 'I am going to tell this story as though Negroes were ordinary human beings, realising that this attitude will, from the first, seriously curtail my audience.' In Appendix, 'The Propaganda of

History' is withering on distortions and mendacities of **Burgess**, **Dunning**, **Rhodes**, etc. For DuBois, **Reconstruction** was 'the dawn of freedom ... the slave went free; stood a brief moment in the sun; then moved back again towards slavery'. Highly influential study. Eric Foner: 'A frustrating, flawed but monumental study ... replete with insights, revolutionary in its implications, for the scholarship of the 1930s, that have become almost commonplace today.' Also political activist: opposed Booker T. Washington's accommodationalism, helped create NAACP (National Association for the Advancement of Colored People), briefly arrested and imprisoned during McCarthy witch hunt in 1950s. In 1961 joined Communist Party and, in 1962, accepted Nkrumah's invitation to settle in Ghana and edit *Encyclopaedia Africana*.

DWIGHT DUMOND (1895–1976) (Ohio) Assistant to **Barnes** at University of Michigan at Ann Arbor, 1930. Wrote *Antislavery Origins of the Civil War in the United States* (1939) and *Antislavery: Crusade for Freedom in America* (1961). Discovered and published **Weld–Grimké** correspondence (1934) and James Birney correspondence (1938). Switched excessive attention from **Garrison** and Boston to **Weld** and **Finney** in the mid-West as source of **abolitionist** crusade.

WILLIAM ARCHIBALD DUNNING (1857–1922) (New Jersey) Taught by **Burgess** at Columbia, where he held chair from 1903. Wrote *The Constitution of the United States in Civil War and Reconstruction, 1860–67* (1885), *Essays on the Civil War and Reconstruction* (1898) and *Reconstruction Politics and Economics, 1865–77* (1907), whose Preface sums up his view on **Reconstruction**: 'Few episodes of recorded history more urgently invite thorough analysis and extended reflection than the struggle through which the Southern whites, subjected by adversaries of their own race, thwarted the scheme which threatened permanent subjugation to another race.' Huge influence on his pupils – 'the Dunning School' – in propagating conventional racial stereotypes on Reconstruction.

E

STANLEY ELKINS (1925–) (Massachusetts) Educated at Harvard and Columbia. Author of audacious and highly controversial *Slavery: A Problem in American Institutional and Intellectual Life* (1959). Employed psychological, anthropological, sociological and comparative methods to explore psyche of slaves and **abolitionists**. From Anglo-American comparisons he adduced that abolitionists failed because they pursued **Garrison**'s anarchic **transcendentalism**. From US–Latin-American comparisons he concluded that the United States had a uniquely 'closed system', which psychologically infantalised the slave and made him 'a sambo' incapable of revolting, unlike his Latin-American counterpart: 'The Negro was to be a child for ever.' His notorious concentration camp analogy was intended to test an extreme case of power and powerlessness and apply it, modified, to the antebellum South. His implicit condemnation of slavery was harsh and made its impact felt indirectly in the 1960s on President Lyndon Johnson and his Great Society Programme.

F

ROBERT FOGEL (1926–) (New York) and Stanley Engerman (1936–) (New York) Joint authors of highly controversial *Time on the Cross: The Economics of American Negro Slavery* (1974), whose aim, by econometrics – 'cliometrics' – was to 'strike down the view that black Americans were without culture, without achievement and without development for their first 250 years on American soil'. Argued, against 'neo-abolitionists' such as **Stampp** and **Elkins**, that slaves were hard working, that the system worked by incentive and not coercion and, overall, slave plantations were 35 per cent more efficient than their free Northern counterparts. Conclusions heavily criticised by fellow cliometricians. Fogel won the Nobel Prize for Economic Science in 1993. Fogel modified his thesis somewhat in *Without Consent or Contract* (1989).

SHELBY FOOTE (1916–2005) (Mississippi) University of North Carolina 1935–37. Published highly popular 3-volume *The Civil War, a Narrative* (1958–74), and even greater fame as commentator for Ken Burns's PBS series on the American Civil War. Emphasised lethal combination of new weapons – the rifle – and old methods of warfare. The two great sins committed in American history were slavery and emancipation; the latter was granted without any further help – social, political and economic – to support and sustain the freedperson.

JOHN HOPE FRANKLIN (1915–) (Oklahoma) Graduated from Fisk in 1935; Harvard PhD in 1941. Member of Southern Historical Association, 1949, but refused to attend its segregated hotels at their Louisville conference. University of Chicago in 1964. Wrote *From Slavery to Freedom* (1947), *The Militant South* (1956), and *Reconstruction after the Civil War* (1961), which emphasised African Americans' contribution and issued damning indictment: 'Southerners defied, ignored and worked against every conception of equality laid down in the 14th Amendment and subsequent legislation.' Author of *The Emancipation Proclamation* (1963), *George Washington Williams* (1985) and *Runaway Slaves: Rebels on the Plantation* (1999, with Loren Schweminger). In 1953 helped provide

historical background to NAACP and Justice Thurgood Marshall in *Brown v. Topeka* case and in 1997, aged 82, appointed by President Clinton to chair advisory board on President's Initiative on Race.

DOUGLAS SOUTHALL FREEMAN (1888–1953) (Virginia) Military historian. Accompanied father to Confederate reunions when young. PhD from Johns Hopkins, 1908, and then editor of Richmond newspaper 1915–53. His 4-volume biography of *Lee* (1934–35), won Pulitzer Prize, and helped canonise him: 'What he seemed he was – a wholly human gentleman, the essential elements of whose positive character were two, and only two, simplicity and spirituality.' *Lee's Lieutenants*, 3 volumes (1942–44), followed.

MAJOR-GENERAL JOHN FREDERICK CHARLES 'BONEY' FULLER (1878–1966) (Great Britain) Army commission 1898. Served in Boer War and First World War. Became advocate of tanks and mobility to break trench warfare deadlock. Wrote *The Foundations of the Science of War* (1925). In 1933 retired, disgruntled, from army. Wrote *The Generalship of Ulysses S. Grant* (1929) and *Grant and Lee* (1933). Stressed importance of rifles and the defensive in Civil War conflict. Dismissed myth that **Grant** was a 'butcher' and deflated **Lee**'s undeserved reputation. Lee had tactical flair but lacked overall strategic intelligence. Foresaw coming of total warfare.

G

EUGENE GENOVESE (1930–) (New York) Graduated from Brooklyn College 1953 and studied at Columbia University. Taught at Rutgers and Rochester University. Currently distinguished scholar in residence at the

University of Georgia, Atlanta. Wrote series of important studies on antebellum South. *The Political Economy of Slavery* (1965), *The World the Slave Holders Made* (1969), *In Red and Black* (1971), culminating in *Roll Jordan Roll* (1974), which recreated the complex world of the slave and 'their demonstration of the beauty and power of the human spirit under conditions of extreme oppression'. Employed **Phillips**'s concept of 'paternalism' and interdependence of slave and master, Marx on class and the solvent power of capitalism, and Gramsci, the Italian Marxist, on the hegemonic power of the master class, who were both profit-making capitalists and aristocrats. Later collaborated with wife, Elizabeth Fox-Genovese, on economic aspects of antebellum South. Later writings – *The Southern Tradition* (1994), *The Southern Front* (1995) and *A Consuming Fire: The Fall of the Confederacy in the Mind of the White Christian South* (1998) – hark back to Southern agrarian school of the 1930s celebrating a section 'that has resisted bourgeois society, its atavistic culture and its marketplace morality'.

PIETER GEYL (1887–1966) (Holland) In 'The American Civil War and the Problem of Inevitability' (reprinted in *Debates with Historians* [1962]) challenged revisionist assumptions along with **Schlesinger Jr.** Accused revisionists of playing down moral dimension and the tragic element which led to conflict. J.G. **Randall** 'belittles what had real greatness; it ignores the tragedy of that struggle with an overwhelming moral problem, slavery'.

HERBERT GUTMAN (1928–85) (New York) Labour historian and 'cliometrician'. Wrote *The Black Family in Slavery and Freedom, 1750–1925* (1976). Strikingly asserted, by innovative use of plantation records, kin names, formalising of marriages by **Freedmen's Bureau** and court testimony, that the African American family survived slavery. In his *Slavery and the Numbers Game* (1975) he savaged the methodology, accuracy and conclusions of **Fogel** and **Engerman**'s *Time on the Cross*.

H

BASIL LIDDELL HART (1895–1970) (Great Britain) Studies at Cambridge interrupted by First World War, fighting at Ypres and Somme. Invalided out of army in 1927. Military correspondent for *The Times* and the *Telegraph*. *Sherman* (1930) emphasised Sherman's march through Georgia and the Carolinas as confirming his own concepts of deep strategic penetration, surprise attacks, living off the land and mobility as solution to the fatal immobility of the First World War. 'Without mobility an army is but a corpse – awaiting burial in a trench.' His rehabilitation of **Grant** and **Sherman** had immense influence on Second World War strategy on both sides.

JOHN HAY (1838–1905) (Indiana) Served as private secretary to **Lincoln** during Civil War. Eulogistic 10-volume *Life of Lincoln* written in collaboration with John Nicolay completed 1894, with full access to papers in keeping of Robert Todd Lincoln, son of the President, who then locked them away until 1947. Hay to Robert Todd Lincoln: 'I need not tell you that every line has been written in the spirit of reverence and regard. We are Lincoln men all through.' Depicted President as respectable **Whig** and cautious emancipator and intended to counter Herndon's *Life of Lincoln* (1889), who depicted him as all too human. Later Hay became influential Secretary of State under McKinley and Theodore Roosevelt.

COLONEL G.F.R. HENDERSON (1854–1903) (Great Britain) Trained at Sandhurst, 1876. Served in Egypt. In 1883 went to US to examine battlefields of Civil War. Appointed Instructor at Sandhurst 1890. Wrote *Stonewall Jackson and the American Civil War* (1898). Turned attention of military historians away from the Franco-Prussian War of 1870–71 to the American Civil War as precursor of modern twentieth-century warfare involving entire populations. Great admirer of **Jackson** and his impalpable qualities of leadership: 'The higher art of generalship, that section of military science to which formations, fire and fortifications are subordinate … has neither manual nor textbook.'

RICHARD HOFSTADTER (1916–70) (New York) Studied, then taught, at Columbia from 1937 onwards. Perhaps the most influential historian of his generation, though his main field of enquiry was post-**Reconstruction** history. Nevertheless early writings markedly innovative. Article in *The American Historical Review* (October 1938) questioned **Beard**'s economic interpretation of Civil War origins. Paper in *Journal of Negro History* (29 April 1944) highly critical of **Phillips**'s overemphasis on large plantations in studies of **slavery** and of seeing the institution almost exclusively from the point of view of the slaveowner. *The American Political Tradition and the Men who Made It* (1948) assumed to reflect 'consensus' history of post-war America, but study of **Wendell Phillips**, 'a patrician as agitator', among the first to rehabilitate **abolitionists**: 'The historical reputation of Wendell Phillips stands very low … The agitator is necessary to a republican commonwealth; he is a counterweight to sloth and indifference.'

L

JOHN LYNCH (1847–1939) (Louisiana) Born slave on Louisiana plantation and freed, 1863, with arrival of Union troops. Appointed JP by Governor Adelbert Ames of Mississippi at the age of 21. Speaker of Mississippi House of Representatives, 1872. First African American in Federal House of Representatives, 1875. Keynote speaker at **Republican** National Convention in 1884 – last black before 1968. Wrote *The Facts of Reconstruction* (1913), aimed at **Rhodes**'s crude racial stereotyping, and insisted that Republican **Reconstruction** governments in the South were excellent.

M

KARL MARX (1818–83) (Germany) Covered American Civil War for *Die Presse* of Vienna and *New York Daily Tribune*. Interpreted war as inevitable struggle between feudal and bourgeois orders, slave against free, which would issue in bourgeois triumph in which proletariat would arise and conquer: 'From the commencement of the titanic American strife the working men of Europe felt instinctively that the star-spangled banner carried the destiny of their class.'

JOHN STUART MILL (1806–73) (Great Britain) Utilitarian and major liberal theorist. Wrote *Liberty* (1859). The Civil War presented him with a dilemma. European liberals identified with nationalism and self-determination and thus, theoretically, with Southern **states' rights**. But, identifying Northerners as an enlightened middle class, and the South as feudal and aristocratic and based on an abhorrent system of slavery, became a strong Unionist. 'War, in a good cause, is not the greatest evil which a nation can suffer. War is an ugly thing, but not the ugliest of things. The decayed and degraded state of moral and patriotic feeling which thinks nothing worth a war is worse.'

N

ALLAN NEVINS (1890–1971) (Illinois) Popular and highly productive historian, graduated from Urbana 1912. Taught at Cornell, 1927, and from 1929 at Columbia. *The Emergence of Lincoln* (2 vols, 1950), *The War for the Union* (4 vols, published collectively as *The Ordeal of the Union*, 1947–60). Remarkably even-handed treatment of Civil War issues. If the South was inflexible, the North was indifferent to the African American. Unlike the 'revisionist historians', believed politicians of the era reflected rather than whipped up the racial question and that **slavery** was central to the debate. 'The main root of the conflict (and there were minor roots) was the problem of slavery with its complementary problem of race adjustment. It was a war over slavery and the future position of the Negro race in North America.'

O

FRANK LAWRENCE OWSLEY (1890–1955) (Alabama) Graduate studies at University of Chicago under William Edward Dodd, 1916. Vanderbilt University, 1920. University of Alabama, 1949. *State Rights in the Confederacy* (1925) argued that excessive deference to this doctrine undermined the Southern war effort. *King Cotton Diplomacy* (1931) insisted that Britain remained neutral during conflict to make war profits. *Plain Folk of the Old South* (1949) explored hitherto neglected class of non-slaveholding farmers in South. Insisted agrarianism, and not slavery – which was largely irrelevant – defined the South. In 1930 contributed 'The Irrepressible Conflict' to Southern Agrarians' *I'll Take my Stand*. Adopted **Beard**'s theory that war caused by Northern capital's determination to colonise the South economically: 'The South had to be crushed out; it was in the way; it impeded the progress of the machine. So Juggernaut drove his car across the South.' Wrote to fellow Southern Agrarian, Allen Tate: 'The purpose of my life is to undermine by "careful", and "detached", "well-documented", "objective" writing, the entire Northern myth of 1820 to 1870.'

P

VERNON LOUIS PARRINGTON (1871–1929) (Illinois) 'Progressive historian'. Went in 1877 with family to Kansas. College of Emporia. Graduated from Harvard 1893 and taught at the University of Washington, 1908. Travelled in Europe 1903–04. First two volumes of *Main Currents in American Thought* published in 1927. Won Pulitzer Prize. Third volume published posthumously 1930. Greatly influenced by English socialist, William Morris, and American populism. Progressive belief in ceaseless struggle of democratic spirit against evil, reactionary forces, and that ideas were rooted in political and economic soil. Admired **abolitionists** for their moral integrity and rejection of crass materialism. But also admired Southern opposition to big government and big business. **Calhoun**, for example, 'erected a last barrier against the progress of middle-class ideas, consolidation in politics and standardisation in society; against a universal cash-register evaluation of life'.

ULRICH BONNELL PHILLIPS (1877–1934) (Georgia) Born in the year of Southern 'redemption', he studied under **Dunning** at Columbia and taught at the University of Michigan, Wisconsin (along with **Turner**), Tulane, and from 1929 onwards at Yale. First to apply scholarly research on slavery in *American Negro Slavery* (1918) and *Life and Labor in the Old South* (1929). In same way as Turner had emphasised the West, Phillips reaffirmed a Southern viewpoint against New England's domination of the historical profession. 'The history of the United States has been written by Boston and largely written wrong.' Phillips paints an essentially benign picture of **slavery**. American culture had little impact on the slave; the institution was not profitable but intended as a means of social control; the slave was child-like, the master paternal and the North was incapable of understanding the true nature of their relationship. The central theme of Southern history was not agrarianism or **states' rights** but 'its common resolve, indomitably maintained, that it shall be, and remain, a white man's country'. Phillips's writings remained unquestioned until **Hofstadter** and **Stampp** criticised them in the 1940s and 1950s.

DAVID POTTER (1910–71) (Georgia) Studied at Emory, and wrote PhD under **Phillips**'s supervision. Wrote *Lincoln and his Party in the Secession Crisis* (1942), *The South and the Sectional Conflict* (1968) and *The Impending Crisis, 1848–61*, published posthumously 1976. Replaced nostalgic view of Southern agrarianism with agribusiness, commerce and cash crops – much like the North – and gave increasing weight to moral issue of slavery, 'which presented an inescapable ethical question which precipitated a sharp conflict of values … a transcendent issue in its own right, and a catalyst of all sectional antagonisms'. Most famous book *People of Plenty* (1954) emphasised material abundance as the most formative factor in creating the American character.

R

JAMES GARFIELD RANDALL (1881–1953) (Indiana) 'Revisionist' historian and Wilsonian internationalist. Wrote *Constitutional Problems under Lincoln* (1926), *Civil War and Reconstruction* (1937) and 4-volume *Life of Lincoln* (1945–55, completed by Richard Current). His wife, Ruth, wrote Life of *Mary Todd Lincoln*. His influential address of 1940, 'The Blundering Generation', reprinted in *Lincoln: The Liberal Statesman*, forcefully argued the war not predetermined but brought about by manipulative politicians. 'If one word or phrase were selected to account for the war, that word would not be slaves, or economic grievance, or states' rights, or diverse civilisations. It would have to be such a word as fanaticism (on both sides), misunderstanding, misrepresentation or perhaps politics.' Was particularly harsh on the **Radical Republicans** and their **Reconstruction** strategy: 'The triumph of the Union was spoiled by the manner in which victory was used.'

JAMES FORD RHODES (1848–1927) (Ohio) Son of wealthy industrialist connected to **Stephen Douglas**. Retired early from family firm to dedicate himself to writing history in 1884. Settled in Cambridge, Massachusetts. In 1892–1922 wrote multi-volumed *History of the United States from the Compromise of 1850* continuing up to William McKinley and Theodore Roosevelt. Nationalistic and conciliatory between North and South: 'All the right is never on one side, and all the wrong on the other.' **Slavery** was the cause of war and the **Confederacy** was wrong to secede. But Northern 'Cotton Whigs' had collaborated with slavery and **Republicans** were wrong to impose harsh **Reconstruction** and grant franchise to African Americans. 'What idea could barbarism thrust into slavery obtain of the rights of property?' Excoriated by Marxist **DuBois** for capitalist principles and indifference to black aspirations.

S

CARL SANDBURG (1878–1967) (Illinois) Poet, author and journalist. Wrote 2-volume *Abraham Lincoln: The Prairie Years* (1926) and *Lincoln: The War Years* (4 vols) which won Pulitzer Prize 1940. Highly imaginative, sentimental and nostalgic and identified closely with President: 'Like [Lincoln] I am a son of the prairie, a poor boy who wandered over the land to find himself and his mission in life.' Very popular, but dismissed by American critic Edmund Wilson as the worst thing to happen to **Lincoln** since being shot by Booth.

ARTHUR SCHLESINGER JR (1917–) (Ohio) Educated at Harvard. Wrote 'The Causes of the Civil War: A Note on Historical Sentimentalism' (1949, reprinted in *The Politics of Hope*), the first to attack the 'revisionist' school head on. Influenced by theologian Reinhold Neibuhr on original sin and the tragic element in history, argued for irrepressible moral dimension in conflict and sentimentality of assuming wars could always be avoided. A cold war document – **Douglas**'s appeasement of South in 1850s, paralleled Henry Wallace's **'Doughfaced'** appeasement of Soviet Russia in 1940s: condemning **abolitionists** in 1850s was like condemning anti-fascists in 1930s or anti-communists in 1940s – but a necessary corrective. 'A society closed in the defence of evil institutions thus creates moral differences far too profound to be solved by compromise. To reject the moral actuality of the Civil War is to foreclose the possibility of an adequate account of its causes.' Special assistant to President Kennedy, 1961–64.

KENNETH STAMPP (1912–) (Wisconsin) Historian. Studied at University of Wisconsin, and taught at University of Arkansas, University of Maryland and Berkeley, California, 1946–83. Wrote *And The War Came: The North and the Secession Crisis 1860–61* (1950) and *The Peculiar Institution* (1956), the first study of **slavery** to question **Phillips** and his racial assumptions. Stated in Preface 'the slaves were merely ordinary human beings, that innately Negroes *are*, after all, only white men with black skins, nothing more, nothing less'. Stampp also shifted responsibility. 'Not the Negro but slavery was the old South's great affliction – the root of its tragedy.' Also argued that slavery was profitable, if inefficient, that it was a mobile system which systematically broke up families, that slaves were unable to revolt openly but could prove a 'troublesome property', that the slave lived in a cultural vacuum and that 'cruelty was endemic in all slave holding communities'. *The Era of Reconstruction* (1965) overturned the **Dunning** school entirely by arguing that **Radical Republicans**' tragedy lay not in its aim to aid the African American but in its ultimate failure to do so. Wrote *The Imperiled Union* (1980), a collection of essays on the Civil War era, and *America in 1857: A Nation on the Brink* (1990).

T

FREDERICK JACKSON TURNER (1861–1932) (Wisconsin) 'Progressive' historian but conservative on matters of race. Educated at University of Wisconsin and Johns Hopkins.

Returned to Wisconsin as professor 1885–1910, then Harvard 1910–24, then research at the Huntington Library, California. Published *The Significance of Sections in American History* (1932) and *The United States, 1830–50* (1935), but best known for 'The Significance of the Frontier in American History' (1893). This replaced the prevalent 'germ' theory of history (the genetic European characteristics immigrants carried with them to shape America) by the determining impact of the surrounding environment on the individual. America, and the frontier in particular, shaped Americans, not Europe. Reflecting turn-of-the-century conflict of populist West versus capitalist East, Turner emphasised the democratic impulse of the West and played down the traditional North–South divide. He also de-emphasised the significance of slavery – 'When American history comes to be rightly viewed it will be seen that the slavery question is an accident' – and criticised **Von Holst** and **Rhodes** for dwelling on this institution. The West had been the source of American renewal and 'if the negro were removed it seems not unlikely that the unity of the Mississippi valley would once more have free play'.

V

HERMANN EDUARD VON HOLST (1841–1904) (Russia) German parents. Moved in 1867 to United States of America. Professor at Chicago University, 1892–1900. *Constitutional and Political History of the United States* (8 vols, 1876–92) depicted slavery, the **slave power** and **states' rights** as obstacles in the way of inevitable Bismarckian centralisation of state, and **Confederacy** had to be providentially defeated.

W

ERIC WILLIAMS (1911–81) (Trinidad) Prime Minister of Trinidad and Tobago 1962–81. Influential *Capitalism and Slavery* (1944) argued that economic factors rather than humanitarian concern led to the British ending the slave trade and slavery in the West Indies. 'The capitalists had first encouraged West Indian slavery and then helped to destroy it … The rise and fall of mercantilism is the rise and fall of slavery.' Subsequent modification of model – the assumption that free labour would create greater economic efficiency – still influential.

GEORGE WASHINGTON WILLIAMS (1849–91) (Pennsylvania) Lied about age to enlist in Union army. Wounded. Baptist minister, journalist. Ohio House of Representatives, 1879, where he tried to repeal state laws against interracial marriage. Attempted as historian to portray blacks positively, actively working for their freedom. Wrote 2-volume *History of the Negro Race 1619–1880: Negroes as Slaves, as Soldiers and as Citizens* (1882–83) – 'not as a blind panegyrist of my race, nor as a partisan apologist, but for love for "the truth of history"'. Wrote *A History of the Negro Troops in the War of the Rebellion* (1888). In 1890 took trip to Congo and denounced Leopold III of Belgium's exploitation of black labour.

HENRY WILSON (1812–74) (New Hampshire) Senator for Massachusetts and President **Grant**'s vice president during his second term. In final years wrote definitive and partisan *History of the Rise and Fall of the Slave Power in America* (3 vols, 1872–77), in which he traced the emergence of Democratic pro-Southern control of government and the symbolic election of the slaveholding **Jackson** over the New Englander **John Quincy Adams** in the election of 1828 to its demise in war. 'After aggressive warfare of more than two generations upon the vital and animating spirit of Republican institutions, upon the cherished and hallowed sentiments of a Christian people, upon the enduring interests and lasting renown of the Republic, organised treasonable conspiracies raised the standard of revolution, and plunged the nation into a bloody contest for the preservation of its threatened life.' A **Republican Party** tract, it also condemned **Garrison** and other **abolitionists** for their anarchistic, moralistic apolitical stance.

THOMAS WOODROW WILSON (1856–1924) (Virginia) Elected 28th President of the United States, the first to emerge from the South since the Civil War. His early career was academic. PhD from Johns Hopkins in 1886, then taught at Bryn Mawr, Wesleyan and, in 1890, Princeton, of which he became president in 1902. Wrote *Congressional Government* (1885), *Disunion and Reunion 1829–89* (1893) and a 5-volume *History of the American People* (1902). Wilson praised the nobility of the fighting South, but Confederate success would have led to two separate, weak states and the extension of **slavery**. But was entirely Southern in his condemnation of 'the damnable cruelty and folly of reconstruction'. His stereotypical interpretation influenced Thomas Dixon's fictional trilogy, the second, *The Clansman: The Historical Romance of the Ku Klux Klan* (1905), being made into one of the first great epics of American cinema, D.W. Griffiths's *Birth of a Nation* (1915). Wilson had a private screening in the White House and commented: 'It is like writing history with lightning. And my only regret is that it is all so terribly true.'

CARTER WOODSON (1875–1950) (Virginia) Son of share cropper and former slave. Graduated from Berea College, Kentucky, in 1903, just before state prohibited interracial education. Went on to University of Chicago and PhD from Harvard 1912. In 1915 founded Association for the Study of Negro Life and History, and from then onwards edited *Journal of Negro History*. *The Negro in our History* (1922) employed census data, slave testimony and oral history to create a popular textbook. Received medal from NAACP in 1926.

COMER VANN WOODWARD (1909–99) (Arkansas) Educated at Emory, Chapel Hill and Columbia. Johns Hopkins 1946–61. Appointed professor at Yale 1961. Main area of research was post-Reconstruction South. *Tom Watson: Agrarian Rebel* (1938) revealed real if brief biracial populist alliance in the South. *Origins of the New South 1877– 1913* (1951) and *Reunion and Reaction: The Compromise of 1877* (1951) explored the sectional deals struck which ended **Reconstruction** and created the ascendancy of a wealthy, conservative white supremacist Democratic party order in the South. *The Strange Career of Jim Crow* (1955) suggested Southern segregation was of relatively recent origins and therefore, by implication, transient. Hailed by Martin Luther King Jr as 'the Bible of the civil rights movement'. In collected essays – *The Burden of Southern History* and *American Counterpoint* (1971) – suggested South unique in American terms, given its tradition of loss, failure and defeat and that it has tended to become the scapegoat for all America's social ills, and that racism is not a uniquely Southern phenomenon. 'It has served its country much as the Negro has served the White Supremacist – as a floor under self-esteem.'

PART II
DOCUMENTS AND RESOURCES

FOUNDING DOCUMENTS

THE DECLARATION OF INDEPENDENCE

Although the bulk of Jefferson's Declaration of 1776 is a histrionic indictment of George III's despotic enslavement of the American colonies, the opening paragraph is a more abstract rationale for independence. 'We hold these truths to be self-evident, that all men are created equal, that they are endowed by their Creator with certain inalienable Rights, that among these are Life, Liberty and the pursuit of Happiness. That to secure these rights, Governments are instituted among Men, deriving their just powers from the consent of the governed. That whenever any Form of Government becomes destructive of these ends, it is the Right of the People to alter or to abolish it, and to institute new Government, laying its foundation on such principles and organising its powers in such form, as to them shall seem most likely to effect their Safety and Happiness.' Although Jefferson was himself a Virginian slaveowner and his indictment of the slave trade was omitted out of defer-ence to both North and South (many Northerners being traders), its ringing assertion of human equality was an inspiration to the **abolitionists**, the African Americans and the feminists who, at the **Seneca Falls Convention** of 1848, adapted the document to further female rights. The Declaration also crucially affirms the necessity of gov-ernment by consent and the legitimacy of revolution. The former commitment was acted on when the thirteen states ratified the Constitution of 1787 and in the 'Revolution of 1800' when a peaceful, domestic transfer of power occurred and the Republican Jefferson replaced the Federalist John Adams in that election year; but it was rejected by eleven Southern states which seceded from the Union rather than accept the legitimacy of **Lincoln**'s election in 1860. The latter principle – the right of revolution – was adopted by the **Confederacy** to legitimise its cause.

THE CONSTITUTION OF THE UNITED STATES

The Constitution of 1787 is the fundamental law of the United States which all other laws are judged by and have, ultimately, to conform to. This task is assigned to the federal Supreme Court (Art. 3) consisting of a Chief Justice and eight Associate Justices. Delicate checks operate between the three branches of federal government – legislative (Art. 1), executive (Art. 2) and judicial – and the Constitution is a feder-ation: a coming together of separate states in which the distribution of powers between state and central government is carefully balanced. In a very real sense the causes of the Civil War and the consequent fighting was a battle over clashing constitutional interpretations. Only those articles especially relevant to the period will be touched on in this summary.

- **Preamble**: 'We the people of the United States, in order to form a more perfect Union, establish justice, insure domestic tranquillity, provide for the common defence, promote the general welfare, and secure the blessings of liberty to ourselves and our posterity, do ordain and establish this Constitution for the United States of America.' Here the consensual compact promised by Jefferson in the Declaration of Independence is made explicit with a contract forged between a sovereign people and their government. In the struggle between Federalists (strong central government) and anti-Federalists (weak central government and the primacy of states), the Federalists achieved a major coup by insisting upon a direct compact between citizens and government rather than the anti-Federalist formulation of 'We the States of the United States'. Art. 7 required the ratification of the Constitution by nine state legislatures or convened conventions, and this was formally achieved by 21 June 1788, although the last of the original 13 states, Rhode Island, did not ratify until 29 May 1790.
- **Art. 1** deals with the legislative powers of Congress, which comprises a Senate (two Senators for each state, irrespective of size, out of deference to **states' rights**) and a House of Representatives based on population. Thus, for example, in 1860 the small state of Rhode Island had only two representatives while New York State had 33.
- **Art. 1, Sec. 2.13**: The **three-fifths rule** which referred to slaves as 'other persons' – a cynical compromise whereby three-fifths of all slaves were counted voters and thus subject to federal taxation. The votes were, of course, exercised by the slaveowners, and contributed to the phenomenon of the **slave power**.
- **Art. 1, Sec. 2.15**: The House of Representatives has the sole power of initiating impeachment proceedings on grounds of 'Treason, Bribery or other high crimes and misdemeanours' which, if voted by a two-thirds majority, would then be tried by the Senate presided over by the chief justice if the trial involved the president. During **Reconstruction**, President **Johnson** was formally impeached but spared by a single vote.
- **Art. 1, Sec. 7.12**: Congressional bills become law if passed by a simple two-thirds majority of both houses. The president has the right of veto, but this can be overturned by a further two-thirds majority of both houses. This led to legislative–executive struggles, particularly during Reconstruction, when Lincoln clashed with Congress over the **Wade–Davis Bill** and, when the crisis deepened, between Johnson and the **Radical Republicans**, the President imposing 29 vetoes, 8 of which he pocketed (bills which emerged towards the end of Congressional Sessions and left unsigned by the President), and 15 of which were passed over his veto.
- **Art. 1, Sec. 8.15**: Congress has power to call out the militia, execute the laws of the Union, suppress insurrection and repel invasion.

- **Art. 1, Sec. 8** enumerated the powers specifically granted to Congress, ending with 18: 'To make all laws which shall be necessary and proper for carrying into execution the foregoing powers'. This was another ploy for extending the powers of the federal government beyond those powers – such as borrowing money on the credit of the US – specifically enumerated in the Constitution. It was used by the Federalist Hamilton, for example, to establish a Bank of the United States which Jefferson opposed on the strict grounds that establishing the Bank was unconstitutional because not expressly enumerated in the Constitution.
- **Art. 1, Sec. 9.1**: 'The migration or importation of such persons as any of the States now existing shall think proper to admit' is a constitutional euphemism for the slave trade from which both South and North (as traders) benefited. A tax not exceeding $10 was to be imposed for each slave and the trade was not to be ended before 1808.
- **Art. 1, Sec. 9.12**: 'The privilege of the writ of habeas corpus shall not be suspended, unless when in cases of rebellion or invasion the public safety may require it.' Highly relevant to both Lincoln and **Davis** and their struggles with courts and legislatures during the Civil War: cf. *Ex parte* **Merryman** and *Ex parte* **Milligan**.
- **Art. 2**: Concerning the Presidency. The **Electoral College** was a device of the Founding Fathers to filter and control public opinion and sustain states' rights. Instead of direct popular election, each state was granted a certain number of electoral college votes (equivalent to two senators for each state plus that state's number of representatives: in 1860 Rhode Island had 4 votes and New York State 35). Initially the body of electors, appointed by state legislatures, voted individually, but with the intensification of party conflict, the emergence of mass participatory politics and a wide, white male electorate, a mere popular majority of votes in any state gave the party candidate all the electoral college votes of that state (the 'Unit Rule'). Consequently it was (and is) possible to carry the presidency without a popular majority, and this period was replete with first-past-the-post minority presidents: **Polk** (1844: 49 per cent), **Taylor** (1848: 47.4 per cent), **Buchanan** (1856: 45.3 per cent), Lincoln (1860: 39.8 per cent), **Hayes** (1876: 48 per cent).
- **Art. 2, Sec. 1.5**: 'In case of the removal of the President from office, or of his death, resignation, or inability to discharge the powers and duties of the said office, the same shall devolve on the Vice President.' This was a period in which vice presidents frequently succeeded following the death of the president: **Tyler** succeeded **Harrison** (1841–45), **Fillmore** succeeded Taylor (1850–53), Johnson succeeded Lincoln (1865–69).
- **Art. 2, Sec. 1.7**: The incoming president is required to make the following oath or affirmation: 'I do solemnly swear (or affirm) that I will faithfully execute the office of President of the United States, and will to the best of my ability, preserve, protect and defend the Constitution of the United States.' In fulfilment of this oath Lincoln took the nation to war in 1861.

- **Art. 2, Sec. 2.1**: The president is also commander in chief of the army and navy, and the state militia – of huge significance in time of war.
- **Art. 2, Sec. 2.2**: The president requires 'the advice and consent' of the Senate in appointing ambassadors, public ministers and consuls, judges of the Supreme Court and all other federal officers. This was to be a major bone of contention in the struggle between Johnson and Congress over **Edwin Stanton**'s tenure as Secretary of War and the Tenure of Office Act.
- **Art. 3** defines the third and final branch of federal government – the Supreme Court. The Court's task was to preserve the Constitution and interpret all cases arising from it, reinforced by Art. 6 which affirms that 'this Constitution, and the laws of the United States … shall be the supreme law of the land'. John Marshall (Chief Justice 1801–35), in the seminal case of *Marbury v. Madison* (1803), asserted the principles of judicial review and judicial sovereignty – the right to strike down congressional legislation when deemed unconstitutional by the Court. Marshall's successor, **Taney**, in the **Dred Scott Decision** of 1857, for example, declared the **Missouri Compromise** of 1820 unconstitutional, so that slavery could theoretically be extended into all Western territories.
- **Art. 4, Sec. 2** defines citizenship and declares that citizens of all states share the same 'privileges and immunities', but that 'Persons held to service or labour' (i.e. fugitive slaves) were to be returned to their rightful owners. This was codified in the Fugitive Slave laws of 1793 and tightened further during the **Compromise of 1850**; cf. *Prigg v. Pennsylvania*.
- **Art. 5** concerns constitutional amendments. Two-thirds of Congress and three-quarters of all states – either through their state legislatures or specially convened conventions – are required to ratify any amendments. Behind this impregnable fortress the 15 slave states were able to resist any substantive change to their 'peculiar institution'.
- **1st 10 Amendments** (ratified 1791) were urged by the Anti-Federalists and accepted by the Federalists in order to balance the might of the new federal government with the rights of individuals. The 5th Amendment, which stated that no one could be deprived of 'life, liberty or property, without due process of law', was particularly relevant. It was deployed by Taney in Dred Scott to insist that freeing a slave was tantamount to depriving a slaveowner of his property, but was also the seedbed from which the three Civil War Amendments grew.
- **The three Civil War Amendments**, 13, 14 and 15, which comprehensively extended the federal commitment to the freedperson, were the direct result of Union victory and the moral crusade for **abolitionism** and social justice which accompanied it.
- **13th Amendment**: 'Neither slavery nor involuntary servitude … shall exist within the United States, or any place subject to their jurisdiction.' **Lincoln's Emancipation Proclamation**, which had been based on his emergency wartime powers, did not apply to large areas of the **Confederacy**, and the **border states** had rejected compensated emancipation. A Republican majority in the November

1864 elections led to Congressional approval on 31 January 1865 and its ratification by 27 states (New Jersey was the only free state to reject it), including 8 states of the former Confederacy, on 18 December 1865. President **Johnson** made its acceptance a precondition for rebel states re-entering the Union. Post-Reconstruction attempts to depict racial discrimination as a 'badge of servitude', and therefore unconstitutional, were rejected by the Supreme Court.

- **14th Amendment**: The core of the civil rights revolution following the war. Its first section reads: 'All persons born or naturalized in the United States, and subject to the jurisdiction thereof, are citizens of the United States and of the State wherein they reside. No State shall make or enforce any law which shall abridge the privileges or immunities or citizens of the United States; nor shall any State deprive any person of life, liberty, or property, without due process of law; nor deny to any person within its jurisdiction the equal protection of the laws.' Intended to protect the freedpersons from discrimination and grant them equal rights as citizens, this clause was systematically undermined by the Supreme Court in **Slaughterhouse Case** (1873), **Civil Rights Cases** (1883) and the *Plessy v. Ferguson* case of 1896. Instead the clause was used during the post-Reconstruction era by personalised business corporations to immunise themselves against federal economic regulation. The second section explicitly abrogated the three-fifths rule but its attempt to reduce Southern state representation in proportion to inhabitants denied the right to vote was never enforced, nor was the bar, in Sec. 3, against all those engaged in rebellion from holding office, which was mainly removed by the Amnesty Act of 1872. The Amendment passed Congress on 16 June 1866, but President Johnson led opposition to it, as did 10 Southern legislatures between 1866 and 1867, and it was not finally ratified until July 1868.

- **15th Amendment** granted the suffrage to the freed adult male. Passed by Congress 27 February 1869 and ratified 30 March 1870. Hitherto black suffrage had only been granted in 5 Northeastern and 4 Midwestern states which, in total, constituted only 1 per cent of the Northern electorate. The ending of the three-fifths rule increased Southern representation in the House of Representatives by up to 12 or 13 seats, and the Republicans' aim – a combination of calculation and idealism – was to swell the party ranks with the support of grateful freedmen. The black vote assisted **Grant** in 1868, but the proliferation of escape clauses and evasive measures – literacy tests, poll taxes (not abolished until the 24th Amendment, 1964), property requirements, grandfather clauses and white-only primaries (declared unconstitutional only in 1944) – effectively undermined the Amendment. In the medium term the black was informally disenfranchised, the South became a white, one-party Democratic section, while the Republican Party appreciated that a Northern white backlash against blacks' voting, combined with the knowledge that the party could achieve victory without the freedman's vote, could allow for a strategy of neglect and concessions to Southern 'Home Rule'.

CONFEDERATE CONSTITUTION

Adopted 11 March 1861 and implemented 18 February 1862. Remarkably similar to Federal Constitution of 1787, from which it was breaking away. Cancelled 'general welfare' and 'more perfect Union' in Preamble to 'We, the people of the Confederate states, each state acting in its sovereign and independent character'. President to serve six years without re-eligibility. Cabinet members could sit in Congress to discuss departmental matters, but not vote (this clause was never implemented). Slave trade prohibited, to mollify Britain, but full protection of slaveowners' property rights and their extension into territories. Religious tinge added to original, 'invoking the favour and guidance of Almighty God', and the word 'slavery', absent from the Federal Constitution, specifically used.

POLITICS

AMERICAN PARTIES

American or 'Know-Nothing' Party

Meteoric, nativist, xenophobic, anti-Catholic response to mass immigration to America in the 1840s and 1850s. A total of 2.9 million poor immigrants – mainly Irish and German – arrived between 1845 and 1854, settling mainly in the Eastern cities and the mid-West. Opposition to a revived papacy under Pius IX and a visit of the Papal Nuncio – Cardinal Bedini – led to riots. Highly secretive and members told, when asked, to reply: 'I know nothing.' Urged extension of naturalisation laws from five to twenty years and opposed taxes for parochial schools. Ex-President **Fillmore** ran in 1856, gaining 21 per cent of popular vote, though only carrying Maryland. Thereafter split over slavery – most Northern voters identifying new immigrants with **Democrats** – led many Northern voters to be absorbed into **Republican Party**, abandoning nativism for anti-Southernism, although its principles were opposed by **Lincoln**: 'How can anyone who abhors the oppression of negroes be in favour of degrading classes of white people?'

Anti-Masonic Party

First third party in American history and first to hold national convention (in Baltimore, September 1831), issue platform to elect William Wirt as presidential candidate aimed against **Jackson** (himself a Mason) and all secret orders. Carried Vermont in 1832, but thereafter absorbed into **Whig Party**.

Constitution Union Party

Response to sectional crisis of 1860. Comprised old-line **Whigs**, **Know-Nothings** and Southern Unionists dedicated to maintenance of Constitution and Union. Met in Baltimore, May 1860, and elected John Bell (Tennessee) as presidential candidate and Edward Everett (Massachusetts) as vice-presidential candidate. Gained 12.6 per cent of popular vote in 1860 but carried only Kentucky, Virginia and Tennessee.

Democratic Party

Oldest formal political party in the world. Created 1828 by **Jackson** and **Calhoun** in opposition to **Whigs** – **John Quincy Adams** and **Henry Clay**. Enshrined

Jeffersonian principles of **states' rights**, economic *laissez-faire*, hard money (coins as opposed to paper money) and popular grass-roots democracy. The dominant national party prior to the Civil War, it embraced subsistence farmers, urban working men, Irish and German immigrants, yeoman farmers and slaveowners in the South and ritualistic forms of religion (Catholics, for example). But the question of slavery led to a split in 1860 between North (**Douglas**) and South (**Breckinridge**) wings and loss of election to **Lincoln** (**Republican**). Further split during war itself between War Democrats (generally in favour of Lincoln's war) and Peace Democrats or '**Copperheads**', who sought mediation with South, and were accused of treason. **McClellan** was Democratic candidate in 1864, gaining 45 per cent of the vote. Following war the tinge of rebellion survived, as did its appeal to immigrant minorities. Hence the accusation of 'rum, Romanism and rebellion' by which Republicans waved the bloody shirt. But declining commitment to civil rights for freedpersons in the North, and their informal disfranchisement in the South, led to a solid Democratic South and popular majority for the 1876 Democratic candidate, **Samuel Tilden**.

Free Soil Party

Third party formed in Buffalo (1848) opposing the extension of slavery, supporting the **Wilmot Proviso** (1846) and urging 'free soil, free speech, free labour, free men'. Combined elements from **Democrats**, 'conscience' **Whigs** and members of **Liberty Party**. Ran ex-President **Van Buren** and **Charles Francis Adams** in 1848. Gained 10 per cent of the popular vote and defeated the Democrats in New York, Massachusetts and Vermont. John Hale ran in 1852 but gained only half of the 1848 vote. Thereafter absorbed into **Republican Party** which took up 'free soil' banner following the **Kansas–Nebraska Act** of 1854.

Liberal Republicans

A party which broke from the **Republican** mainstream in 1872 to merge with the **Democrats** in opposition to **Grant**'s corruption, federal intervention in Southern **Reconstruction**, high tariffs and inflationary 'greenbacks'. Also urged civil service reform against the traditional spoils system. The anti-Grant forces gained 44 per cent of the vote but **Greeley**, the Liberal Republican candidate, died shortly after the election and his votes were divided among minor candidates.

Liberty Party

Established 1830s in New York State under candidacy of James Birney. First entry of anti-slavery opinion into mainstream politics. Moderate and opposed **Garrisonian** extremism. Against **Mexican War** and extension of **slavery**. Ran 1840 and 1844, when Birney gained just over 2 per cent of the popular vote and helped swing the election from **Clay** (**Whig**) to **Polk** (**Democrat**). Thereafter absorbed into **Free Soil** and **Republican** parties.

Republican Party

Emerged following **Kansas–Nebraska Bill** and **Dred Scott Decision**, both of which nullified the **Missouri Compromise** of 1820. Powerful combination of 'free soil', non-extension of **slavery**, economic programme of federal support and sound money, and opening of West to homesteads inherited from **Whigs**. Against **Democrats'** tradition of **states' rights** and economic *laissez-faire*. Absorbed a wide spectrum of voters – **Whigs, abolitionists**, nativists, negrophobes and former members of **Free Soil** and **Liberty** Party. In 1856 first national convention met at Pittsburg. In 1856 ran **Frémont** against **Buchanan (Democrat)**, gaining 11 of the 16 Northern states and 33 per cent of the popular vote. Election of **Lincoln** in 1860 and again in 1864 transformed the American party system, which is essentially unchanged to this day. Clash with President **Johnson** led to radical **Reconstruction**, but recognition that party could carry election with Northern votes alone and fears of Northern backlash led to growing neglect of African American rights.

Whigs

Created in 1820s in opposition to excessive executive power of 'King Andrew' **Jackson** and his destruction of the Bank of the United States, *laissez-faire* economic policies and advocacy of **states' rights**. In contrast Whigs pursued **Clay**'s American system of high tariffs, internal improvement and encouragement of wealth which accrued from the market, and Western expansion, along with strict Protestant regulation of morality such as temperance. **Lincoln** and **Alexander Stephens** both began their political careers as Whigs, indicating its national character. Its two leading politicians, Clay (in the West) and **Webster** (from New England), were sectional and never gained presidency, which went instead to military heroes – **Harrison** (in 1840) and **Taylor** (in 1848). The slavery question led to a split between 'conscience' anti-slavery Whigs and 'cotton' pro-slavery Whigs. But growing defection of Southern wing and impact of mass Northern immigration who generally identified with **Democrats** led to its terminal decline in the 1850s.

PRESIDENTIAL ELECTIONS, 1832–76, WITH POPULAR ELECTORAL COLLEGE VOTE AND PERCENTAGE OF POPULAR VOTE

Election, 1832

The **Nat Turner** revolt and the publication of the first issue of **Garrison**'s *Liberator* in 1831 had little impact on mainstream party politics and the 1832 election. The clash with **Jacksonian Democrats** over the rechartering of the Bank of the United States led to the formation of the **Whig Party**, led by **Clay** and **Webster** and supported by Biddle, director of the Bank of the United States. Biddle distributed 30,000 copies of **Jackson**'s Bank veto message in the hope of unseating the incumbent President. This strategy backfired. This was the first election when a national nomination convention was held and the first in which a third party participated – the

Anti-Masonic Party – which nominated William Wirt (both Jackson and Clay were Masons). Wirt only carried Vermont but helped to split the anti-Jacksonian coalition. Jackson was re-elected, with support mainly from the South and West, with 55 per cent of the popular vote (though down on his 1828 vote) and Jackson took this as a popular mandate to destroy the Bank of the United States.

Year	Number of states	Candidate	Parties	Popular vote	Electoral vote	Percentage of popular vote
1832	24	ANDREW JACKSON	Democratic	687,502	219	55.0
		Henry Clay	National Republican	530,189	49	42.4
		William Wirt	Anti-Masonic ⎤		7	
		John Floyd	National Republican ⎦	33,108	11	2.6

Note: Candidates receiving less than 1 per cent of the popular vote have been omitted. For that reason the percentage of popular vote given for any election year may not total 100 per cent.

Election, 1836

Martin Van Buren (New York) became **Jackson**'s heir apparent following the President's split with **Calhoun**. A brilliant party organiser, he remained evasive on the issue of **slavery**, but there was an 18 per cent drop in slave states' voting for the **Democrats** and an increase in Southerners voting **Whig**. The Whigs, in contrast, were highly fragmented and fielded four candidates – **Harrison**, White, **Webster** and Mangum. Collectively they gained 10 states (higher than 1832), the Democrats 15.

Year	Number of states	Candidate	Parties	Popular vote	Electoral vote	Percentage of popular vote
1836	26	MARTIN VAN BUREN	Democratic	765,483	170	50.9
		William H. Harrison	Whig ⎤		73	
		Hugh L. White	Whig ⎟	739,795	26	49.1
		Daniel Webster	Whig ⎟		14	
		W.P. Mangum	Whig ⎦		11	

Election, 1840

An election notorious for its packaging and carnival atmosphere and conspicuous absence of substantive issues. White manhood suffrage existed in all but three states

(Rhode Island, Virginia and Louisiana) and literacy rates were over 90 per cent. The voting turnout, 80 per cent, was equalled only by the elections of 1860 and 1876. Northern African Americans could vote only in Maine, New Hampshire, Vermont and Massachusetts; nine-tenths were excluded. **Van Buren (Democrat)** was badly hit by the 1837 Depression though managed to achieve the two-thirds vote required for the first time in a Convention supporting his candidacy. The Democrats also issued a party platform, which included the protection of **slavery** and warned of 'the alarming and dangerous consequences' of **abolitionism**. James Birney (New York) stood as the **Liberty Party** candidate but was in England during the campaign and only gained 0.3 per cent of the popular vote. Despite the **Whigs'** 'log cabin and hard cider campaign', **Harrison** was actually born on a substantial estate in Virginia and, resident in Ohio, could carry the fourth largest state in the Union as its 'favourite son'. His vice-presidential running mate, **John Tyler**, was from Virginia, the third largest state in the Union, and together they provided a winning North–South balance. Although Harrison carried 19 states to Van Buren's 7, the actual margin of the popular vote was only 6.1 per cent.

Year	Number of states	Candidate	Parties	Popular vote	Electoral vote	Percentage of popular vote
1840	26	WILLIAM H. HARRISON	Whig	1,274,624	234	53.1
		Martin Van Buren	Democratic	1,127,781	60	46.9

Election, 1844

Clay's (Whig) initial opposition to the annexation of Texas was predicated on the assumption that **Van Buren** would be the **Democratic** candidate. Instead the Democrats elected **Polk**, who was pro-annexationist, and Clay's equivocation thereafter may have lost him a close-fought election. The Whigs, more urban based and cosmopolitan, stood for a sound currency, tariffs, the sale of public land, a single presidential term and an end to presidential 'usurpation'. Birney and the **Liberty** Party gained 2.3 per cent of the popular vote. Polk personified the expansionist mood and the belligerency of '54°40′ or fight' with regard to the Oregon question.

Year	Number of states	Candidate	Parties	Popular vote	Electoral vote	Percentage of popular vote
1844	26	JAMES K. POLK	Democratic	1,338,464	170	49.6
		Henry Clay	Whig	1,300,097	105	48.1
		James G. Birney	Liberty	62,300		2.3

Election, 1848

Although better organised than the **Whigs**, the **Democrats** faced drawbacks: Northern Democrats were displeased by the Oregon settlement, the '**free soil**' doctrine was growing and the '**Know-Nothings**' opposed the party's close connections with immigrant groups. **Cass, Buchanan** and Levi Woodbury were the chief contenders at the Democratic Convention in Baltimore, and Cass won with his compromise solution of '**popular sovereignty**' with regard to **slavery**. The **Free Soil** Party met at Buffalo and elected **Van Buren** and **Charles Francis Adams** as their candidates, standing for free labour 'against the aggression of the Slave Power'. They gained 10 per cent of the popular vote and deprived Cass of New York, which went to **Taylor**, who reflected the Whig penchant for running military heroes. Taylor was a Southerner but also a Unionist, who polled about 60 per cent of Northern Electoral College votes and about 40 per cent of Southern votes. He was opposed to the expansion of slavery. His running mate, **Fillmore**, was from New York and balanced the ticket.

Year	Number of states	Candidate	Parties	Popular vote	Electoral vote	Percentage of popular vote
1848	30	ZACHARY TAYLOR	Whig	1,360,967	163	47.4
		Lewis Cass	Democratic	1,222,342	127	42.5
		Martin Van Buren	Free Soil	291,263		10.1

Election, 1852

The national basis of the **Democratic** Party was becoming increasingly sectionalised. **Van Buren** opposed the annexation of Texas, the Southern wing insisted upon non-interference with **slavery**, while the Moderates – **Buchanan**, Macy, **Cass** and **Douglas** – just wanted to win the election through compromise. At a chaotic Convention at Baltimore the 'dark horse', **Pierce** (New Hampshire) won on the 49th ballot. John Hale (New Hampshire) and George Julian (Indiana) ran on the **Free Soil** ticket and tended to take votes from the **Whigs**. Its platform stated that slavery 'is a sin against God and a crime against man, which no human enactment nor usage can make right; and that Christianity, humanity and patriotism alike demand its abolition'. **Fillmore**, **Webster** and **Scott** were Whig candidates and Scott, another military hero, won on the first ballot but gained only four states – Massachusetts, Vermont, Kentucky and Tennessee – and an overall fall in the popular vote from 48 per cent in 1848 to 44 per cent in 1852. The Whig Party was in terminal decline.

Year	Number of states	Candidate	Parties	Popular vote	Electoral vote	Percentage of popular vote
1852	31	FRANKLIN PIERCE	Democratic	1,601,117	254	50.9
		Winfield Scott	Whig	1,385,453	42	44.1
		John P. Hale	Free Soil	155,825		5.0

Election, 1856

The repercussions of the **Kansas–Nebraska Bill** (1854) dominated this election year. Despite the efforts of **Douglas** and **Pierce, Buchanan** was elected on a platform that supported the Kansas Nebraska Bill, the **Compromise of 1850**, with its fugitive slave laws, and reiterated that there was to be no intervention in 'the domestic institutions of states'. Ex-President **Fillmore** led the '**Know-Nothing' Party**, gained over 21 per cent of the popular vote, but carried only Maryland. The candidate for the new **Republican** Party, **Frémont**, had the advantage of being a popular hero and apolitical, unlike his radical rivals, **Chase** and **Seward**. He carried 11 out of 16 free states and was within 35 Electoral College votes of winning the election.

Year	Number of states	Candidate	Parties	Popular vote	Electoral vote	Percentage of popular vote
1856	31	JAMES BUCHANAN	Democratic	1,832,955	174	45.3
		John C. Frémont	Republican	1,339,932	114	33.1
		Millard Fillmore	American	871,731	8	21.6

Election, 1860

A critical election which triggered the Civil War and was, in reality, two elections taking place simultaneously – **Lincoln** against **Douglas** in the North, and **Breckinridge** versus Bell in the South. Sectionalism dominated. Lincoln fought off opposition at the Chicago **Republican** Convention from McLean (Ohio), Simon Cameron (Pennsylvania), **Seward** (New York) and **Chase** (Ohio) to gain the nomination. **Douglas** was only able to secure the **Democratic** nomination by a two-thirds majority only after Southern Democrats rejected 'popular sovereignty', defected and elected **Breckinridge**. The electorate was faced with stark issues: the Republicans offered the non-extension of slavery, the Democrats 'popular sovereignty', the Southern Democrats the extension of slavery and the **Constitution Unionist Party** 'no political position other than the Constitution of the country, the union of the States and the enforcement of the Laws'. Lincoln carried every Northern state except New Jersey but was not even on the ballot of ten slave states. He won only 40 per cent of the popular vote but 54 per cent of the Northern vote. Combined, his opponents achieved 2.8 million votes against his 1.8 million. Douglas did well overall, but his popular votes did not convert into Electoral College votes: he carried only Missouri and New Jersey. Breckinridge carried all the South except Tennessee and Bell did well in the **border states**. Lincoln and Douglas together gained over 90 per cent of the Northern vote but less than 15 per cent in the South. Breckinridge and Bell between them gained over 85 per cent of the Southern vote. It is perhaps tragic that the combined votes for the moderate candidates – Douglas and Bell – were greater than that for the two more radical candidates – Lincoln and Breckinridge.

Year	Number of states	Candidate	Parties	Popular vote	Electoral vote	Percentage of popular vote
1860	33	ABRAHAM LINCOLN	Republican	1,865,593	180	39.8
		Stephen A. Douglas	Democratic	1,382,713	12	29.5
		John C. Breckinridge	Democratic	848,356	72	18.1
		John Bell	Constitutional Union	592,906	39	12.6

Election, 1864

What is extraordinary about this election was that it took place at all in the midst of Civil War. But for Lincoln replacing bayonets by ballots was what the war was all about, even though in 1863 he thought he would not win it. The **Democrats** hoped to exploit schisms in the **Republican** ranks, the Northern backlash against African Americans, the unpopularity of the Northern draft, military setbacks, and with accusations that Lincoln was a military despot. Their candidate, **McClellan**, was popular and hoped to secure reunion by negotiation and without the emancipation of slaves. The Republican platform urged emancipation, the enlistment of black troops and an economic policy that encouraged immigration and the extension of homesteads in the West. The military turning point came on 4 July 1863 with the surrender of **Vicksburg** and Union victory at **Gettysburg** and, thereafter, **Sheridan**'s forays into the Shenandoah Valley and the capture of Atlanta and of Mobile all swelled the Republican ranks. Politically Lincoln's veto of the **Wade–Davis Bill** presented him as a moderate with regard to post-war **Reconstruction**. Eighteen states allowed absentee voting by soldiers and other states granted furloughs, which helped swing support behind the Republicans. Lincoln achieved a 15 per cent increase in the popular vote over 1860 and 78 per cent of soldiers' votes, and was the first president to be re-elected for a second term since **Jackson**. McClellan carried only New Jersey, Delaware and Kentucky (878 counties did not vote).

Year	Number of states	Candidate	Parties	Popular vote	Electoral vote	Percentage of popular vote
1864	36	ABRAHAM LINCOLN	Republican	2,206,938	212	55.0
		George B. McClellan	Democratic	1,803,787	21	45.0

Election, 1868

Johnson was broken by the failed impeachment and both parties wanted the new military hero, **Grant**, as their candidate. The **Republicans** got him and he was unanimously nominated on the first ballot at their Convention in Chicago with the plea 'Let us have peace'. The platform also pressed African American civil rights and enfranchisement – a highly contentious issue. The **Democrats** nominated Horatio Seymour, a former governor of New York, on a platform of restoration and amnesty to the South, the abolition of the **Freedmen's Bureau** and an end to 'military despotism and negro supremacy'. Grant's popular margin was assisted by 500,000 African American votes and six reconstructed Republican Southern states. Seymour carried eight states, predominantly in the South, but no voting took place in the unreconstructed states of Virginia, Mississippi and Texas.

Year	Number of states	Candidate	Parties	Popular vote	Electoral vote	Percentage of popular vote
1868	37	ULYSSES S. GRANT	Republican	3,013,421	214	52.7
		Horatio Seymour	Democratic	2,706,829	80	47.3

Election, 1872

Grant's attempts to acquire Santo Domingo and the perceived corruption of the administration led to a **Liberal Republican** breakaway which settled upon sectional conciliation, reduction in tariffs, civil service reform aimed against spoils and a one-term presidency only. Lyman Trumbull, Charles Francis Adams and Justice David Davis were the chief candidates but the newspaper editor, **Horace Greeley**, secured the nomination. The **Democrats**, reeling from the Tweed Ring scandal, threw their support behind this disastrous candidate, made worse by a speaking tour in the West where he urged an independent confederacy, if sustained by a referendum. Grant continued the policy of reconciliation with the South and the generous distribution of land and veterans' pension helped swell his support. He carried 31 states in all, while Greeley secured only 66 Electoral College votes, the lowest the Democrats recorded between 1864 and 1932.

Year	Number of states	Candidate	Parties	Popular vote	Electoral vote	Percentage of popular vote
1872	37	ULYSSES S. GRANT	Republican	3,596,745	286	55.6
		Horace Greeley	Democratic	2,843,446	*	43.9

Election, 1876

The continued corruption of the **Grant** administration, the panic of 1873 and the demonetisation of silver in the same year helped the **Democrats**, who regained control of the House of Representatives in the mid-term elections of 1874, and seven Southern states had returned to the Democratic fold. They also had a popular candidate in **Samuel Tilden**, the reformist governor of New York, who had helped to expose the Tweed Ring scandal. **Hayes** was nominated as **Republican** candidate in their Convention in Cincinnati and though the platform spoke of an enlightened approach to the South, no African American delegates were present. The resulting vote was a cliff-hanger, with Tilden one Electoral College vote short of victory. Disputed results in Florida (4), Louisiana (8), South Carolina (7) and one of Oregon's three votes led to an electoral commission of 15 being established, made up of 8 Republicans and 7 Democrats. The partisan decision resulted in their granting all 20 votes to Hayes on 29 January 1877. This deal struck in Congress formally ended **Reconstruction** in the South. A secret deal provided federal land grants to the South, loans for the Texas and Pacific Railroad and the removal of the last federal troops from the South in April 1877. *New York Nation* (5 April 1877): 'The negro will disappear from the field of national politics. Henceforth the nation, as a nation, will have nothing more to do with him.'

Year	Number of states	Candidate	Parties	Popular vote	Electoral vote	Percentage of popular vote
1876	38	RUTHERFORD B. HAYES	Republican	4,036,572	185	48.0
		Samuel J. Tilden	Democratic	4,284,020	184	51.0

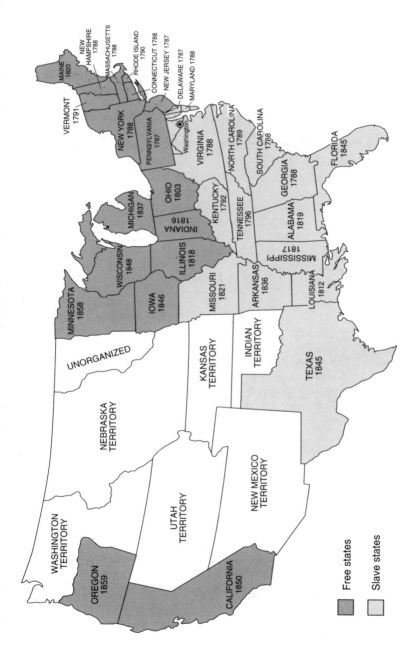

Map 1 The United States, 1860, with dates of states' admission to the Union

Map 2 The Kansas–Nebraska Act, 1854

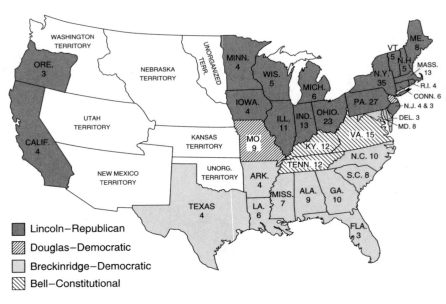

Lincoln–Republican
Douglas–Democratic
Breckinridge–Democratic
Bell–Constitutional

Map 3 Presidential election, 1860 (electoral vote by state)

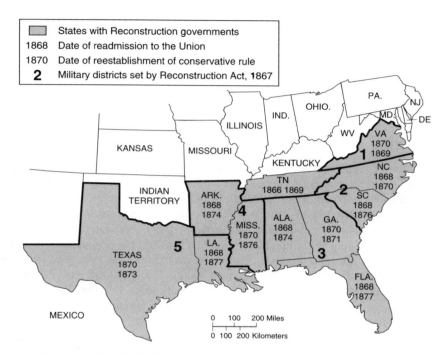

PA.

NJ

OHIO.

IND.

MD.

DE

ILLINOIS

WV

VA.
1870
1869

KANSAS

MISSOURI

KENTUCKY

1

INDIAN
TERRITORY

ARK.
1868
1874

TN
1866 1869

NC
1868
1870

2

SC
1868
1876

4

MISS.
1870
1876

ALA.
1868
1874

GA.
1870
1871

TEXAS
1870
1873

5

LA.
1868
1877

3

FLA.
1868
1877

MEXICO

0   100   200 Miles

0   100   200 Kilometers

Map 4   Reconstruction, 1865–77

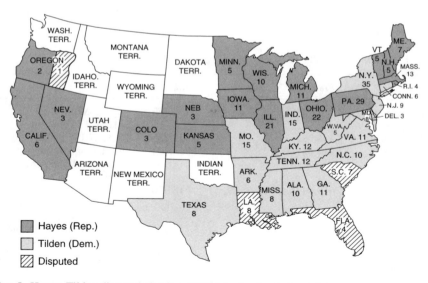

WASH.
TERR.

MONTANA
TERR.

VT
5

ME.
7

OREGON
2

IDAHO.
TERR.

DAKOTA
TERR.

MINN.
5

WIS.
10

N.H.
5

MASS.
13

WYOMING
TERR.

IOWA.
11

MICH.
11

N.Y.
35

R.I. 4

NEV.
3

NEB
3

PA. 29

CONN. 6

UTAH
TERR.

ILL.
21

IND.
15

OHIO.
22

N.J. 9

CALIF.
6

COLO
3

KANSAS
5

MO.
15

MD.
8

DEL. 3

W.VA.
5

VA. 11

ARIZONA
TERR.

NEW MEXICO
TERR.

INDIAN
TERR.

ARK.
6

KY. 12

TENN. 12

N.C. 10

S.C. 7

TEXAS
8

LA.
8

MISS.
8

ALA.
10

GA.
11

FLA.
4

Hayes (Rep.)

Tilden (Dem.)

Disputed

Map 5   Hayes–Tilden disputed election, 1876 (electoral vote by state)

SOCIAL AND ECONOMIC FACTORS

POPULATION

Table 1 shows population in 1860 by regions and states, and by status (free or slave). Map 6 illustrates the preponderance of the North. New Orleans was the only city in the South with a population over 100,000. In 1820 only 5 per cent of the population of the slave states lived in urban areas of 2,500 or more, as against 10 per cent in the free states. By 1840 the comparable figures were 10 per cent and 26 per cent. The ten largest cities in 1860 were New York (1,175,000), Philadelphia, Baltimore, Boston, St Louis, Chicago, Pittsburg, San Francisco (57,000 – an enormous increase since the Gold Rush of 1849), Detroit and Cleveland. In 1830 there were only 90 cities with a population of over 2,500. By 1860 there were 392, making up a total population of 6,216,000. This was also a highly literate population made up of the politically engaged. In 1860 there was a 94 per cent literacy rate in the free states and 58 per cent in the slave states, although this figure rises to 83 per cent if only the white population is counted. In 1800, 82 per cent of the slave states' labour force was in agriculture, as against 68 per cent in the free states. By 1860 that figure for the slave states had fallen only 1 per cent to 81 per cent, while only 40 per cent of the free state labour force was engaged in agriculture. The percentage of slaves in the total population in 1860 is shown in Map 7.

Table 1   Population, 1860

	Free	*Slave*	*Total*	
New England	3,135,283	–	3,135,283	[Conn., Maine, Mass., N.H., R.I., Vermont]
Middle States	7,458,985	–	7,458,985	[N.Y., N.J., Pa.]
Middle West	7,914,687	17	7,914,704	[Ill., Indiana, Iowa, Michigan, Minnesota, Ohio, Wisconsin]
Far West	618,947	29	618,976	[Cal., New Mexico, Oregon, Utah, Colorado, Nevada, Washington]
Border States	2,779,455	432,586	3,212,041	[Delaware, Ky, Maryland, Missouri, Washington, DC]
Upper South	2,925,433	1,208,758	4,134,191	[Arkansas, N. Ca, Tenn., Va]
Lower South	2,656,789	2,312,352	4,969,141	[Alabama, Florida, Georgia, La, Miss., S. Ca., Texas]
Totals	27,489,579	3,953,742	31,443,321	

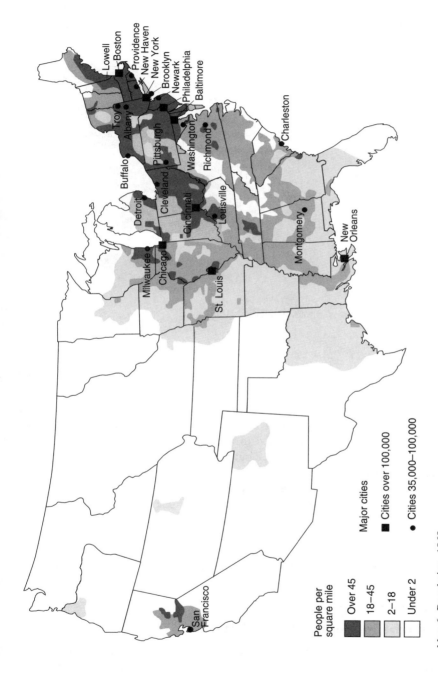

People per
square mile

■ Over 45

■ 18–45

■ 2–18

□ Under 2

Major cities

■ Cities over 100,000

● Cities 35,000–100,000

Map 6 Population, 1860

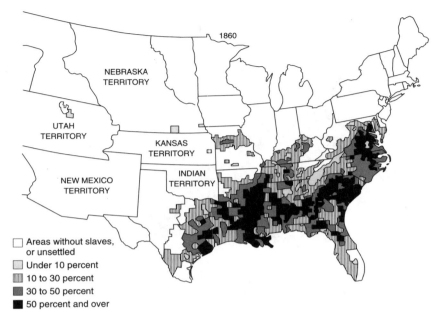

Map 7 Percentage of slaves in total population, 1860

Immigration

Population figures were boosted by mass immigration (see Figure 1), primarily from Ireland, England and Germany, where the potato famine and the failure of the 1848 revolutions in Europe respectively led to a large influx, especially from 1845 to 1855, with numbers falling off with the outbreak of war. Their arrival was to have a considerable impact on domestic politics, with xenophobic and nativist impulses influencing the **Know–Nothing** and **Republican** parties while many immigrants found a home among the **Democratic** ranks.

Occupation

Table 2 shows the principal occupations for free males aged 15 and over in 1850.

ECONOMIC DEVELOPMENT

US Territorial Expansion, 1790–1860 (Figure 2)

Although Jefferson's **Louisiana Purchase** of 1803 was substantial, an even greater acquisition of territory occurred in the Civil War period, particularly with the

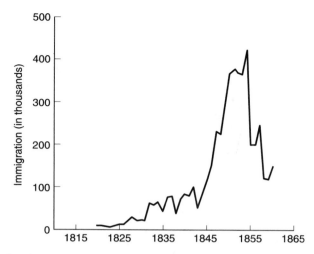

Figure 1 Immigration to the United States, 1815–60

Table 2 Principal occupations for free males 15 and over, 1850

	Number	*% of total*
Farmers	2,363,958	44.0
Labourers	909,786	16.9
Carpenters	184,671	3.4
Cordwainers	130,473	2.4
Mariners	103,473	2.0
Clerks	101,325	1.9
Merchants	100,752	1.9
Blacksmiths	99,703	1.9
Miners	77,410	1.4
Masons	63,342	1.2

implementation of '**Manifest Destiny**' during **Polk**'s presidency. Whether this huge, newly acquired territory was to be free or slave was the fundamental question of the period.

53

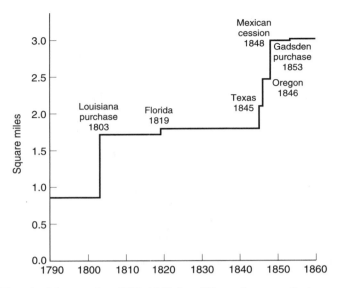

Figure 2 US territorial expansion, 1790–1860 (in millions of square miles)

US Railroads, 1860 (Map 8)

Railroad construction was a tangible symbol of the North's economic superiority when the war broke out. Railroads were also vital for troop mobility and the military strategy of both sides during the conflict.

Wheat (Map 9)

Rail, river and canal traffic aided the transport of wheat from the mid-West to the deficient East coast and, increasingly, to Europe from the 1850s onwards. The repeal of the English Corn Laws, the Irish potato famine and the Crimean War added to Britain's demand and was employed as a counter by the Union to the Confederate strategy of '**King Cotton**'. In 1830 wheat and flour exports were worth $6.1 million; by 1860 the figure had risen to $19.5 million.

Cotton (Figure 3)

The value of cotton, of cotton exports and slavery were inextricably linked. In 1830 cotton exports were worth $29.6 million; by 1860 that figure had risen to $191.8 million. The Civil War was fought, in part, by the **Confederacy** to perpetuate this valuable economic advantage and to use it as a formidable weapon by which to win their bid

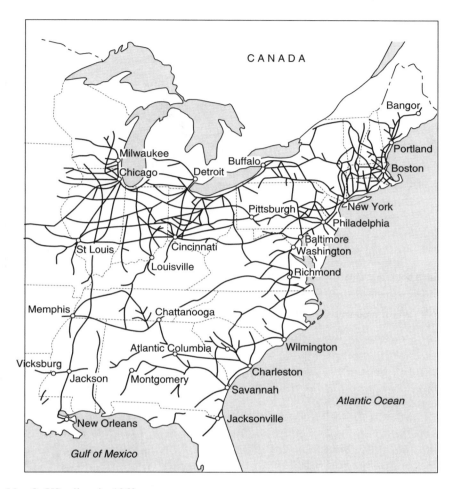

Map 8 US railroads, 1860

for independence. In Map 10 the Black Cotton Belt can be clearly discerned spreading westwards along the deep South, concentrated on the Lower Mississippi Valley and stretching into Texas. Other staple crops – sugar and rice – were cultivated in the coastal regions, tobacco and hemp in the upper South.

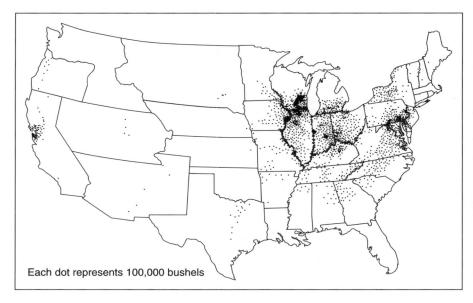

Each dot represents 100,000 bushels

Map 9 Wheat production, 1859

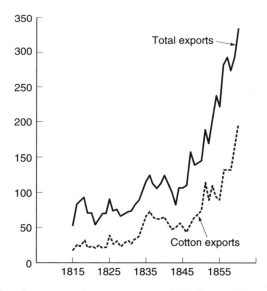

Total exports

Cotton exports

Figure 3 Value of total exports and cotton exports, 1815–60 (in millions of dollars)

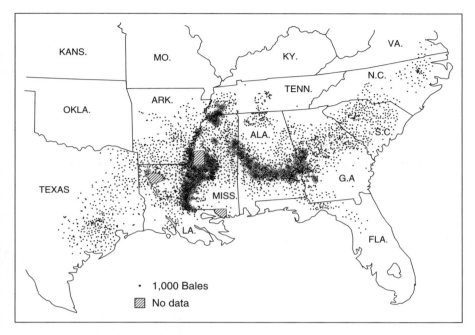

Map 10 Cotton production, 1859

MILITARY STRATEGY

CIVIL WAR STRATEGY (MAPS 11 AND 12)

The Constitutional doctrines of **states' rights**, **nullification** and **secession** had long been employed by the South to sustain the 'peculiar institution' of **slavery**, and when **Lincoln** was elected president in November 1860 on a **Republican** platform of the non-extension of slavery into the Western territories he triggered the secession of seven states, beginning with South Carolina on 20 December 1860. Following the surrender of the Unionist **Fort Sumter** on 13 April 1861, Lincoln issued a proclamation the following day summoning 75,000 militia to suppress the 'rebellion' and on 19 and 27 April ordered a **naval blockade** of Southern ports. Meanwhile four more Southern states, including the vital Virginia, seceded and joined the **Confederacy**. The Union possessed overwhelming material advantages: a population of 22 million as against 9 million in the Confederacy (of whom approximately 4 million were slaves), and an industrial capacity ten times greater than that of the South but, initially, the wresting of independence by arms seemed tenable for the Confederacy: it asked only to be let alone. If the North were to reforge union between the states it would have to penetrate enemy territory approximately the size of Europe and compel it by force of arms back into the Union. General **Winfield Scott** devised an **Anaconda Strategy** – a blockade of the Southern coast, capture of the Mississippi, splitting the Confederacy in two, and squeezing the Confederate capital, Richmond, from all directions – but this would take time and the North clamoured for decisive victories. The South, too, with its limited resources, hoped for a quick victory, but the longer the war continued, the greater the depletion of Southern manpower and the growing attrition by the Unionist juggernaut. Casualty figures were horrendous and all the more poignant because the strife was fracticidal between countrymen who shared the basic American tenets of religion, democracy and self-help. 'Both', as Lincoln said, 'read the same Bible and pray to the same God.' The rates of injury and mortality were awesomely high because the muzzle-loading and, later, breach-loading repeating rifle – fifteen times more rapid and with a much longer range – were perfected killing machines. The defensive saved lives, but decisive victory could only be achieved by taking the offensive and thus was hugely costly of lives. It has been persuasively argued that the Union won the war in the West: certainly the West was the training ground for future military leaders – **Grant**, **Sherman**, **Sheridan** – and **Davis**'s failure to hold out there was ultimately decisive. To secure the vital **border states** of Tennessee and Kentucky, regain control of the Mississippi and, finally, to liquidate the Western conflict in order to turn

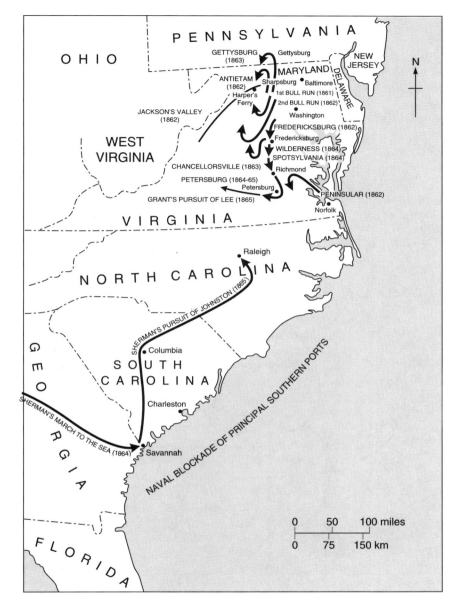

Map 11 Principal military campaign of the Civil War: Eastern theatre

their batteries on **Lee** in the East, were the major objectives. Grant's capture of **Forts Henry and Donelson** (6 and 16 February 1862) not only forced the surrender of 13,000 Confederate troops but their positions on the rivers Tennessee and

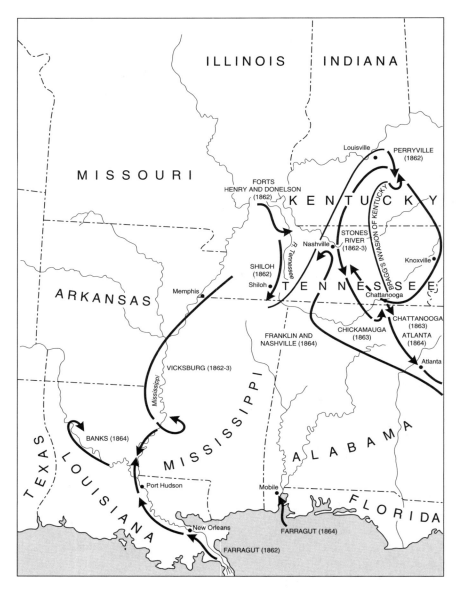

Map 12 Principal military campaign of the Civil War: Western theatre

Cumberland opened up the Southern heartland. On 25 February Confederate troops were forced to abandon Nashville and, following the bloody victory at **Shiloh**, 6–7 April, Grant entered Corinth, Mississippi, on 25 May. Davis launched a counter-attack led by his favourite general, **Braxton Bragg**, into Kentucky but was rebuffed at Perryville (8 October 1862) and Murfreesboro (31 December 1862–3 January 1863) and retreated to **Chattanooga**. Bragg temporarily regained the initiative against Rosecrans at **Chickamauga** (19–20 September 1863) but Grant's victory at Chattanooga (24–25 November 1863) opened the way for Sherman's march into Georgia. Meanwhile, on 7 April 1862, Pope had captured Island No. 10 on the Mississippi and **Farragut** captured New Orleans on 29 April 1862. **Vicksburg** fell to Grant, following a long and audacious siege, on 4 July 1863, giving the Union full control of the Mississippi. The Eastern theatre, especially the area of Virginia between the two capitals of Washington and Richmond which were only 100 miles apart, witnessed great devastation. The first major battle of the war at **First Bull Run** with the rout of Union troops encouraged the Confederacy and dismayed the Union but, paradoxically, the longer-term result was to render the South over-confident and force **McClellan** to reorganise thoroughly the 150,000 Army of the Potomac for a fresh onslaught. McDowell's replacement by McClellan was the beginning of Lincoln's search, as Commander in Chief, for a general who would actively engage the enemy head on on a number of fronts and achieve overwhelming victories. In turn McClellan, Burnside, **Hooker** and **Meade** failed to achieve the knock-out blow. Between July 1861 and April 1862 McClellan, instead of attacking the Confederate army directly, pursued his indirect **Peninsula Campaign**, finally retreating in July 1862 with no decisive accomplishment and Richmond untaken. In the following month the Union suffered a second defeat at Bull Run under General Pope. This was a low point in the Union's struggle. Lee, in contrast, made two bold and daring incursions into the North, taking war to the enemy and living off its land and provisions. The first invasion by the Army of Northern Virginia was repulsed by McClellan at **Antietam** (17 September 1862) but McClellan failed to follow through and Lee escaped in good order. Burnside, taking over command, pursued Lee but was defeated at **Fredericksburg** (13 December 1862). He was replaced by Hooker, but the Union suffered another defeat at **Chancellorsville** (2–4 March 1863). That summer Lee invaded Pennsylvania. Meade, just newly appointed, forced a second retreat after **Gettysburg** (1–3 July 1863) but again failed to demolish Lee's army. However, that victory and the simultaneous ending of the siege of Vicksburg was the turning point of the war. Thereafter the remorseless superior resources of the North began to assert themselves. Lincoln had, at last, found a winning combination: Grant, in overall charge, would wear down Confederate forces in the East; Sherman would move in from the West and advance on Richmond from the South; Sheridan would mop up opposition in the Shenandoah Valley; **Halleck** would co-ordinate strategy from Washington. Grant's long, grinding battle began in May 1864, suffering a reverse in the **Wilderness Campaign**, 5–6 May, but recouping at Spotsylvania (8–12 May) and Cold Harbor (1–3 June). On 15 June he lay siege to **Petersburg**, a vital rail junction 20 miles south of Richmond, which only ended on 2 April 1865.

Lee escaped west, hoping to join up with the remnants of **Johnston**'s army to the South, but failed and, harried ceaselessly, surrendered to Grant at **Appomattox** on 9 April. Sherman, meanwhile, in a daring strategy, swept south-east through Georgia, capturing Atlanta on 2 September 1864, and reaching the sea at Savannah before striking north through the Carolinas and forcing Johnston's surrender at Durham Station, 17 April 1865.

For more information on military strategy, see under the following entries: Beauregard; Butler; Hood; Jackson; Stewart; African American soldiers; Andersonville; Committee on the Conduct of War; Conscription; Contraband; Trent Incident.

PRIMARY DOCUMENTS

Judge Thomas Ruffin: Judgment in *N. Carolina v. Mann*, **1829**

This case is specifically concerned with whether the battery of a hired slave, Lydia, by the hirer, John Mann, constituted an indictable offence. More generally, although the judge noted greater humanitarianism in the treatment of slaves, he had logically to conclude that the master's power had, ultimately, to be absolute.

A Judge cannot but lament when such cases as the present are brought into judgment. It is impossible that the reasons on which they go can be appreciated, but where institutions similar to our own exist and are thoroughly understood. The struggle, too, in the Judge's own breast between the feelings of the man and the duty of the magistrate is a severe one, presenting strong temptation to put aside such questions, if it be possible. It is useless, however, to complain of things inherent in our political state. And it is criminal in a Court to avoid any responsibility which the laws impose. With whatever reluctance, therefore, it is done, the Court is compelled to express an opinion upon the extent of the dominion of the master over the slave in North Carolina ...

The difference is that which exists between freedom and slavery – and a greater cannot be imagined. In the one, the end in view is the happiness of the youth, born to equal rights with that governor, on whom the duty devolves of training the young to usefulness in a station which he is afterwards to assume among freemen. To such an end, and with such a subject, moral and intellectual instruction seem the natural means; and for the most part they are found to suffice. Moderate force is superadded only to make the others effectual. If that fail it is better to leave the party to his own headstrong passions and the ultimate correction of the law than to allow it to be immoderately inflicted by a private person. With slavery it is far otherwise. The end is the profit of the master, his security and the public safety; the subject, one doomed in his own person and his posterity, to live without knowledge and without the capacity to make anything his own, and to toil that another may reap the fruits. What moral considerations shall be addressed to such a being to convince him what it is impossible but that the most stupid must feel and know can never be true – that he is thus to labor upon a principle of natural duty, or for the sake of his own personal happiness, such services can only be expected from one who has no will of his own; who surrenders his will in implicit obedience to that of another. Such obedience is the consequence only of uncontrolled authority over the body. There is nothing else which can operate to produce the effect. The power of the master must be absolute to render the submission of the slave perfect. I most freely confess my sense of the harshness of this proposition; I feel it as deeply as any man can; and as a principle of moral right every person in his retirement must repudiate it. But in the actual condition of things it must be so. There is no remedy. This discipline belongs to the state of slavery. They cannot be disunited without abrogating at once the rights of the master and absolving the slave from his subjection. It constitutes the curse of slavery to both the bond and free portion of our population. But it is inherent in the relation of master and slave.

That there may be particular instances of cruelty and deliberate barbarity where, in conscience, the law might properly interfere, is most probable. The difficulty is to determine where a Court may properly begin. Merely in the abstract it may well be asked, which power of the master accords with right? The answer will probably sweep away all of them. But we cannot look at the matter in that light. The truth is that we are forbidden to enter upon a train of general reasoning on the subject. We cannot allow the right of the master to be brought into discussion in the courts of justice. The slave, to remain a slave, must be made sensible that there is no appeal from his master; that his power is in no instance usurped; but is conferred by the laws of man at least, if not by the law of God. The danger would be great, indeed, if the tribunals of justice should be called on to graduate the punishment appropriate to every temper and every dereliction of menial duty. No man can anticipate the many and aggravated provocations of the master which the slave would be constantly stimulated by his own passions or the instigation of others to give; or the consequent wrath of the master, prompting him to bloody vengeance upon the turbulent traitor – a vengeance generally practiced with impunity by reason of its privacy. The Court, therefore, disclaims the power of changing the relation in which these parts of our people stand to each other.

We are happy to see that there is daily less and less occasion for the interposition of the Courts. The protection already afforded by several statutes, that all-powerful motive, the private interest of the owner, the benevolences towards each other, seated in the hearts of those who have been born and bred together, the frowns and deep execrations of the community upon the barbarian who is guilty of excessive and brutal cruelty to his unprotected slave, all combined, have produced a mildness of treatment and attention to the comforts of the unfortunate class of slaves, greatly mitigating the rigors of servitude and ameliorating the condition of the slaves. The same causes are operating and will continue to operate with increased action until the disparity in numbers between the whites and blacks shall have rendered the latter in no degree dangerous to the former, when the police now existing may be further relaxed. This result, greatly to be desired, may be much more rationally expected from the events above alluded to, and now in progress, than from any rash expositions of abstract truths by a judiciary tainted with a false and fanatical philanthropy, seeking to redress an acknowledged evil by means still more wicked and appalling than even that evil.

I repeat that I would gladly have avoided this ungrateful question. But being brought to it the Court is compelled to declare that while slavery exists amongst us in its present state, or until it shall seem fit to the legislature to interpose express enactments to the contrary, it will be the imperative duty of the Judges to recognize the full dominion of the owner over the slave, except where the exercise of it is forbidden by statute. And this we do upon the ground that this dominion is essential to the value of slaves as property, to the security of the master, and the public tranquility, greatly dependent upon their subordination; and, in fine, as most effectually securing the general protection and comfort of the slaves themselves.

Thomas Dew: Review of the Debate in the Virginia Legislature, 1831–32

This defence of slavery followed the Nat Turner revolt in Virginia when the state legislature debated, and finally rejected, emancipation.

III. Injustice and Evils of Slavery – 1st. It is said slavery is wrong, in the *abstract* at least, and contrary to the spirit of Christianity … With regard to the assertion that slavery is against the spirit of Christianity, we are ready to admit the general assertion, but deny most positively, that there is any thing in the Old or New Testament, which would go to show that slavery, when once introduced, ought at all events to be abrogated, or that the master commits any offence in holding slaves. The children of Israel themselves were slaveholders, and were not condemned for it. All the patriarchs themselves were slaveholders; Abraham had more than three hundred; Isaac had a 'great store' of them, and even the patient and meek Job had '*a very great household*'. When the children of Israel conquered the land of Canaan, they made one whole tribe 'hewers of wood and drawers of water', and they were at that very time under the special guidance of Jehovah; they were permitted expressly to purchase slaves of the heathen, and keep them as an inheritance for their posterity; and even the children of Israel might be enslaved for six years. When we turn to the New Testament, we find not one single passage at all calculated to disturb the conscience of an honest slaveholder. No one can read it without seeing and admiring that the meek and humble Saviour of the world in no instance meddled with the established institutions of mankind; he came to save a fallen world, and not to excite the black passions of men, and array them in deadly hostility against each other. From no one did he turn away; his plan was offered alike to all – to the monarch and the subject, the rich and the poor, the master and the slave. He was born in the Roman world – a world in which the most galling slavery existed, a thousand times more cruel than the slavery in our own country; and yet he no where encourages insurrection, no where fosters discontent; but exhorts *always* to implicit obedience and fidelity. What a rebuke does the practice of the Redeemer of mankind imply upon the conduct of some of his nominal disciples of the day, who seek to destroy the contentment of the slaves, to rouse their most deadly passions, to break up the deep foundations of society, and to lead on to a night of darkness and confusion! 'Let every man (says Paul) abide in the same calling wherein he is called. Art thou called *being* a servant? care not for it; but if thou mayest be made free, use *it* rather' – (1 *Corinth*. vii. 20,21). Again: 'Let as many servants as are under the yoke, count their own masters worthy of all honor, that the name of God and his doctrines be not blasphemed; and they that have believing masters, let them not despise *them*, because they are brethren, but rather do them service, because they are faithful and beloved partakers of the benefit. These things teach and exhort' – (1 *Tim*. vi. 1,2). Servants are even commanded in Scripture to be faithful and obedient to unkind masters. 'Servants,' (says Peter) 'be subject to your masters with all fear; not only to the good and gentle, but to the froward. For what glory is it if when ye shall be buffeted for your faults ye take it patiently; but if when ye do well and suffer for it, ye take it patiently this is acceptable with God' – (1 *Peter*, ii. 18,20). These and many other passages in the New Testament, most convincingly prove that slavery in the Roman world was no where charged as fault or crime upon the holder, and every where is the most implicit obedience enjoined ...

2dly. But it *further said that the moral effects of slavery are of the most deleterious and hurtful kind;* and as Mr. Jefferson has given the sanction of his great name to this charge, we shall proceed to examine it with all that respectful deference to which every sentiment of so pure and philanthropic a heart is justly entitled.

'The whole commerce between master and slave,' says he, 'is a perpetual exercise of the most boisterous passions; the most unremitting despotism on the one part, and degrading submission on the other. Our children see this, and learn to imitate it, for man is an imitative animal – this quality is the germ of education in him. From his cradle to his grave, he is learning what he sees others do. If a parent had no other motive, either in his own philanthropy or self-love, for restraining the intemperance of passion towards his slave, it should always be a sufficient one that his child is present. But generally it is not sufficient. The parent storms, the child looks on, catches the lineaments of wrath, puts on the same airs in the circle of smaller slaves, gives a loose to his worst of passions, and thus nursed, educated, and daily exercised in the worst of tyranny cannot but be stamped by it with odious peculiarities.' Now we boldly assert that the fact does not bear Mr. Jefferson out in his conclusions. He has supposed the master in a continual passion – in the constant exercise of the most odious tyranny, and the child, a creature of imitation, looking on and learning. But is not this master sometimes kind and indulgent to his slaves? Does he not mete out to them, for faithful service, the reward of his cordial approbation? Is it not his interest to do it? and when thus acting humanely, and speaking kindly, where is the child, the creature of imitation, that he does not look on and learn? We may rest assured, in this intercourse between a good master and his servant, more good than evil *may* be taught the child; the exalted principles of morality and religion may thereby be sometimes indelibly inculcated upon his mind, and instead of being reared a selfish contracted being, with nought but self to look to – he acquires a more exalted benevolence, a greater generosity and elevation of soul, and embraces for the sphere of his generous actions a much wider field. Look to the slaveholding population of our country, and you every where find them characterized by noble and elevated sentiments, by humane and virtuous feelings. We do not find among them that cold, contracted, calculating *selfishness*, which withers and repels every thing around it, and lessens or destroys all the multiplied enjoyments of social intercourse. Go into our national councils, and ask for the most generous, the most disinterested, the most conscientious, and the least unjust and oppressive in their principles, and see whether the slave-holder will be past by in the selection ...

Is it not a fact, known to every man in the south, that the most cruel masters are those who have been unaccustomed to slavery. It is well known that northern gentlemen who marry southern heiresses are much severer masters than southern gentlemen. And yet, if Mr. Jefferson's reasoning were correct, they ought to be milder: in fact, it follows from his reasoning, that the authority which the father is called on to exercise over his children must be seriously detrimental; and yet we know that this is not the case; that, on the contrary, there is nothing which so much humanizes and softens the heart, as this *very authority*; and there are none, even among those who have no children themselves, so disposed to pardon the follies and indiscretion of youth, as those who have seen most of them, and suffered greatest annoyance. There may be many cruel masters, and there are unkind and cruel fathers too; but both the one and the other make all those around them shudder with horror. We are disposed to think that their example in society tends rather to strengthen than weaken the principle of benevolence and humanity.

Let us now look a moment to the slave, and contemplate his position. Mr. Jefferson has described him as hating, rather than loving his master, and as losing, too, all that *amor patriae* which characterizes the true patriot. We assert again, that Mr. Jefferson is not borne out by the fact. We are well convinced that there is nothing but mere relations of husband and wife, parent and child, brother and sister, which produce a closer tie, than the relation of master and servant. We have no hesitation in affirming that, throughout the whole slave-holding country, the slaves of a good master are his warmest, most constant, and most devoted friends; they have been accustomed to look up to him as their supporter, director and defender. Every one acquainted with southern slaves knows that the slave rejoices in the elevation and prosperity of his master; and the heart of no one is more gladdened at the successful debut of young master or miss on the great theatre of the world than that of either the young slave who has grown up with them, and shared in all their sports, and even partaken of all their delicacies – or the aged one who has looked on and watched them from birth to manhood, with the kindest and most affectionate solicitude, and has ever met from them all the kind treatment and generous sympathies of feeling, tender hearts. Judge Smith, in his able speech on Foote's Resolutions, in the Senate, said, in an emergency, he would rely upon his own slaves for his defence – he would put arms into their hands, and he had no doubt they would defend him faithfully. In the late Southampton insurrection, we know that many actually convened their slaves and armed them for defence, although slaves were here the cause of the evil which was to be repelled ...

In the debate in the Virginia Legislature, no speaker *insinuated even*, we believe, that the slaves in Virginia were not treated kindly; and all, too, agree that they were most abundantly fed; and we have no doubt but that they form the happiest portion of our society. A merrier being does not exist on the face of the globe, than the negro slave of the U. States. Even Captain Hall himself, with his thick 'crust of prejudice', is obliged to allow that they are happy and contented, and the master much less cruel than is generally imagined. Why, then, since the slave is happy, and happiness is the great object of all animated creation, should we endeavor to disturb his contentment by infusing into his mind a vain and indefinite desire for liberty – a something which he cannot comprehend, and which must inevitably dry up the very sources of his happiness.

The fact is that all of us, and the great author of the Declaration of Independence is like us in this respect, are prone to judge of the happiness of others by ourselves – we make self the standard, and endeavor to draw down every one to its dimensions – not recollecting that the benevolence of the Omnipotent has made the mind of man pliant and susceptible of happiness in almost every situation and employment. We might rather die than be the obscure slave that waits at our back – our education and our habits generate an ambition that makes us aspire at something loftier – and disposes us to look upon the slave as unsusceptible of happiness in his humble sphere, when he may indeed be much happier than we are, and have his ambition too; but his ambition is to excel all his other slaves in the performance of his servile duties – to please and to gratify his master – and to command the praise of all who witness his exertions. Let the wily philanthropist but come and whisper into the ears of such a slave that his situation is degrading and his lot a miserable one – let him but light up the dungeon in which he persuades the slave that he is caged – and that moment, like the serpent that entered the garden of Eden, he destroys his happiness and his usefulness. We cannot, therefore, agree with Mr. Jefferson, in the opinion that slavery makes the unfeeling tyrant and ungrateful dependent; and in regard to Virginia especially we are almost disposed, judging from the official returns of crimes and convictions, to assert, with a statesman who has descended to his tomb (Mr. Giles) 'that the whole population of Virginia, consisting of three *castes* – of free white, free colored, and slave colored population – is the soundest and most moral of any other, according to numbers, in the whole world, as far as is known to me.'

3dly. *It has been contended that slavery is unfavorable to a republican spirit*; but the whole history of the world proves that this is far from being the case. In the ancient republics of Greece and Rome, where the spirit of liberty glowed with most intensity, the slaves were more numerous than the freemen, Aristotle, and the great men of antiquity, believed slavery necessary to keep alive the spirit of freedom. In Sparta, the freemen were even forbidden to perform the offices of slaves, lest he might lose the spirit of independence. In modern times, too, liberty has always been more ardently desired by slaveholding communities. 'Such,' says Burke, 'were our Gothic ancestors; such, in our days, were the Poles; and such will be all masters of slaves who are not slaves themselves.' 'These people of the southern (American) colonies are much more strongly, and with a higher and more stubborn spirit, attached to liberty than those of the northward.' And from the time of Burke down to the present day, the Southern States have always borne the same honorable distinction. Burke says, 'it is because freedom is to them not only an enjoyment, but a kind of rank and privilege'. Another, and perhaps more efficient cause of this, is the perfect spirit of equality so prevalent among the whites of all the slaveholding States. Jack Cade, the English reformer, wished all mankind to he brought to one common level. We believe slavery in the U. States has accomplished this, in regard to the whites, as nearly as can be expected or even desired in this world. The menial and low offices being all performed by the blacks, there is at once taken away the greatest cause of distinction and separation of the ranks of society. The man to the north will not shake hands familiarly with his servant, and converse, and laugh and dine with him, no matter how honest and respectable he may be. But go to the south, and you will find that no white man feels such inferiority of rank as to be unworthy of association with those around him. Color alone is here the badge of distinction, the true mark of aristocracy, and all who are white are equal in spite of the variety of occupation ...

Frederick Law Olmsted: *A Journey in the Back Country*, 1860

Despite the growing paternalism observed by Ruffin, this horrifying and graphic description reveals the actual, physical consequences of the judges' legal reasoning.

The severest corporeal punishment of a negro that I witnessed at the South occurred while I was visiting this estate ... The manner of the overseer who inflicted the punishment, and his subsequent conversation with me about it, indicated that it was by no means an unusual occurrence with him. I had accidentally encountered him, and he was showing me his plantation. In going from one side of it to the other, we had twice crossed a deep gully, at the bottom of which was a thick covert of brushwood. We were crossing it a third time, and had nearly passed through the brush, when the overseer suddenly stopped his horse exclaiming, 'What's that? Hallo! who are you there?'

It was a girl lying at full length on the ground at the bottom of the gully, evidently intending to hide herself from us in the bushes. 'Who are you there?'

'Sam's Sall, sir.'

'What are you skulking there for?'

The girl half rose, but gave no answer. 'Have you been here all day?'

'No sir.'

'How did you get here?' The girl made no reply.

'Where have you been all day?' The answer was unintelligible.

After some further questioning, she said her father accidentally locked her in, when he went out in the morning.

'How did you manage to get out?'

'Pushed a plank off, sir, and crawled out.'

The overseer was silent for a moment, looking at the girl, and then said, 'That won't do – come out here.' The girl arose at once, and walked towards him; she was about eighteen years of age. A bunch of keys hung at her waist, which the overseer espied, and he said, 'Ah, your father locked you in; but you have got the keys.' After a little hesitation, the girl replied that these were the keys of some other locks; her father had the door key.

Whether her story were true or false could have been ascertained in two minutes by riding on to the gang with which her father was at work, but the overseer had made up his mind as to the facts of the case.

'That won't do,' said he, 'get down on your knees.' The girl knelt on the ground; he got off his horse and, holding her with his left hand, strick her thirty or forty blows across the shoulders with his tough, flexible, 'raw-hide' whip. They were well laid on, as a boatswain would thrash a skulking sailor, or as some people flog a baulking horse, but with no appearance of angry excitement on the part of the overseer. At every stroke the girl winced, and exclaimed, 'Yes, sir!' or 'Ah, sir!' or 'Please, sir!' not groaning or screaming. At length he stopped and said, 'Now tell me the truth.' The girl repeated the same story. 'You have not got enough yet,' said he. 'Pull up your clothes – lie down.' The girl without any hesitation, without a word or look of remonstrance or entreaty, drew closely all her garments under her shoulders, lay down upon the ground, with her face toward the overseer, who continued to flog her with the rawhide, across her naked loins and thigh, with as much strength as before. She now shrunk away from, not rising, but writhing, groveling, and screaming, 'Oh, don't, sir! oh, please stop, master! please, sir! please, sir! oh, that's enough, master! oh, Lord, oh, master, master! oh, God, master, do stop! oh, God, master! oh, God, master!'

A young gentleman of fifteen was with us; he had ridden in front, and now, turning on his horse looked back with an expression only of impatience at the delay. It was the first time I had ever seen a woman flogged. I had seen a man cudgeled and beaten, in the heat of passion before, but never flogged with a hundredth part of the severity used in this case. I glanced again at the perfectly passionless but rather grim business-like face of the overseer, and again at the young gentleman, who had turned away; if not indifferent he had evidently not the faintest sympathy with my emotion. Only my horse chafed with excitement. I gave him rein and spur and we plunged into the bushes and scrambled fiercely up the steep acclivity. The screaming yells and the whip strokes had ceased when I reached the top of the bank. Choking, sobbing spasmodic groans only were heard. I rode on to where the road coming diagonally up the ravine ran out upon the cotton field. My young companion met me there, and immediately afterward the overseer. He laughed as he joined us, and said, 'She meant to cheat me out of a day's work – and she has done it, too.'

'Did you succeed in getting another story from her?'

'No; she stuck to it.'

'Was it not perhaps true?'

'Oh no, sir, she slipped out of the gang when they were going to work, and she's been dodging about all day, going from one place to another as she saw me coming. She saw us crossing there a little while ago, and thought we had gone to the quarters, but we turned back so quick, we came into the gully before she knew it, and she could do nothing but lie down in the bushes.'

'I suppose they often slip off so.'

'No, sir; I never had one do so before – not like this; they often run away to the woods and are gone some time, but I never had a dodge-off like this before.'

'Was it necessary to punish her so severely?'

'Oh yes, sir,' (laughing again). 'If I hadn't punished her so hard she would have done the same thing again tomorrow, and half the people on the plantation would have followed her example. Oh, you've no idea how lazy these niggers are; you northern people don't know any thing about it. They'd never do any work at all if they were not afraid of being whipped.'

ABOLITIONISM

William Lloyd Garrison: *The Liberator*, 1 January 1831

In this stirring editorial Garrison contemptuously dismissed his earlier advocacy of gradualism and emphatically urged immediate emancipation.

In the month of August, I issued proposals for publishing *The Liberator* in Washington city; but the enterprise, though hailed in different sections of the country, was palsied by public indifference. Since that time, the removal of the *Genius of Universal Emancipation* to the Seat of Government has rendered less imperious the establishment of a similar periodical in that quarter. During my recent tour for the purpose of exciting the minds of the people by a series of discourses on the subject of slavery, every place that I visited gave fresh evidence of the fact that a greater revolution in public sentiment was to be effected in the free states – *and particularly in New England* – than at the south. I found contempt more bitter, opposition more active, detraction more relentless, prejudice more stubborn, and apathy more frozen, than among slave owners themselves. Of course, there were individual exceptions to the contrary. This state of things afflicted, but did not dishearten me. I determined, at every hazard, to lift up the standard of emancipation in the eyes of the nation, *within sight of Bunker Hill and in the birth place of liberty.* That standard is now unfurled; and long may it float, unhurt by the spoliations of time or the missiles of a desperate foe – yea, till every chain be broken, and every bondman set free! Let southern oppressors tremble – let their secret abettors tremble – let their Northern apologists tremble – let all the enemies of the persecuted blacks tremble.

I deem the publication of my original Prospectus unnecessary, as it has obtained a wide circulation. The principles therein inculcated will be steadily pursued in this paper, excepting that I shall not array myself as the political partisan of any man. In defending the great cause of human rights, I wish to derive the assistance of all religions and of all parties.

Assenting to the 'self-evident truth' maintained in the American Declaration of Independence, 'that all men are created equal, and endowed by their Creator with certain inalienable rights – among which are life, liberty and the pursuit of happiness', I shall strenuously contend for the immediate enfranchisement of our slave population. In Park-street Church, on the Fourth of July, 1829, in an address on slavery, I unreflectingly assented to the popular but pernicious doctrine of *gradual* abolition. I seize this opportunity to make a full and unequivocal recantation, and thus publicly to ask pardon of my God, of my country and of my brethren the poor slaves, for having uttered a sentiment so full of timidity, injustice and absurdity. A similar recantation, from my pen, was published in the *Genius of Universal Emancipation* at Baltimore, in September, 1829. My conscience is now satisfied.

I am aware that many object to the severity of my language; but is there not cause for severity? I *will be* as harsh as truth, and as uncompromising as justice. On this subject, I do not wish to think, or speak, or write, with moderation. No! no! Tell a man whose house is on fire to give a moderate alarm; tell him to moderately rescue his wife from the hands of the ravisher; tell the mother to gradually extricate her babe from the fire into which it has fallen; but urge me not to use moderation in a cause like the present. I am in earnest – I will not equivocate – I will not excuse – I will not retreat a single inch – AND I WILL BE HEARD. The apathy of the people is enough to make every statue leap from its pedestal, and to hasten the resurrection of the dead.

It is pretended that I am retarding the cause of emancipation, by the coarseness of my invective, and the precipitancy of my measures. *The charge is not true.* On this question my influence – humble as it is – is felt at this moment to a considerable extent, and shall be felt in coming years – not perniciously, but beneficially – not as a curse, but as a blessing; and posterity will bear testimony that I was right. I desire to thank God, that he enables me to disregard 'the fear of man which bringeth a snare' and to speak his truth in its simplicity and power ...

The Seneca Falls Declaration, 19 July 1848

Women's rights were intimately bound up with abolitionism, and this Declaration, the first of its kind ever, was modelled on Jefferson's Declaration of Independence.

1. DECLARATION OF SENTIMENTS

We hold these truths to be self-evident, that all men and women are created equal.

... The history of mankind is a history of repeated injuries and usurpations on the part of man toward woman, having in direct object the establishment of an absolute tyranny over her. To prove this, let facts be submitted to a candid world.

He has never permitted her to exercise her inalienable right to the elective franchise.

He has compelled her to submit to laws, in the formation of which she had no voice.

He has withheld from her rights which are given to the most ignorant and degraded men – both natives and foreigners.

Having deprived her of this first right of a citizen, the elective franchise, thereby leaving her without representation in the halls of legislation, he has oppressed her on all sides.

He has made her, if married, in the eye of the law, civilly dead.

He has taken from her all right in property, even to the wages she earns.

He has made her, morally, an irresponsible being, as she can commit many crimes with impunity, provided they be done in the presence of her husband. In the covenant of marriage, she is compelled to promise obedience to her husband, he becoming, to all intents and purposes, her master – the law giving him power to deprive her of her liberty, and to administer chastisement.

He has so framed the laws of divorce, as to what shall be the proper causes, and in case of separation, to whom the guardianship of the children shall be given, as to be wholly regardless of the happiness of women – the law, in all cases, going upon a false supposition of the supremacy of man, and giving all power into his hands.

After depriving her of all rights as a married woman, if single, and the owner of property, he has taxed her to support a government which recognizes her only when her property can be made profitable to it.

He has monopolized nearly all the profitable employments, and from those she is permitted to follow she receives but a scanty remuneration. He closes against her all the avenues to wealth and distinction which he considers most honorable to himself. As a teacher of theology, medicine, or law, she is not known.

He has denied her the facilities for obtaining a thorough education, all colleges being closed against her.

He allows her in Church, as well as State, but a subordinate position, claiming Apostolic authority for her exclusion from the ministry, and, with some exceptions, from any public participation in the affairs of the Church.

He has created a false public sentiment by giving to the world a different code of morals for men and women, by which moral delinquencies which exclude women from society, are not only tolerated, but deemed of little account in man.

He has usurped the prerogative of Jehovah himself, claiming it as his right to assign for her a sphere of action, when that belongs to her conscience and to her God.

He has endeavored, in every way that he could, to destroy her confidence in her own powers, to lessen her self-respect and to make her willing to lead a dependent and abject life.

Now, in view of this entire disfranchisement of one-half the people of this country, their social and religious degradation – in view of the unjust laws above mentioned, and because women do feel themselves aggrieved, oppressed, and fraudulently deprived of their most sacred rights, we insist that they have immediate admission to all the rights and privileges which belong to them as citizens of the United States.

In entering upon the great work before us, we anticipate no small amount of misconception, misrepresentation, and ridicule; but we shall use every instrumentality within our power to effect our object. We shall employ agents, circulate tracts, petition the State and National legislatures, and endeavor to enlist the pulpit and the press in our behalf. We hope this Convention will be followed by a series of Conventions embracing every part of the country.

Ralph Waldo Emerson: The Fugitive Slave Laws, 3 May 1851

This was Emerson's response to the arrest of a slave, Shadrack, in Boston. He was later rescued, but Emerson's damning indictment, delivered in his home town of Concord, implicates all Americans in the wrong of the Fugitive Slave Laws which Daniel Webster, Senator for Massachusetts, had supported.

Fellow citizens: I accepted your invitation to speak to you on the great question of these days, with very little consideration of what I might have to offer: for there seems to be no option. The last year has forced us all into politics, and made it a paramount duty to seek what it is often a duty to shun. We do not breathe well. There is infamy in the air. I have a new experience. I wake in the morning with a painful sensation, which I carry about all day, and which, when traced home, is the odious remembrance of that ignominy which has fallen on Massachusetts, which robs the landscape of beauty, and takes the sunshine out of every hour. I have lived all my life in this state, and never had any experience of personal inconvenience from the laws, until now. They never came near me to any discomfort before. I find the like sensibility in my neighbors; and in that class who take no interest in the ordinary questions of party politics. There are men who are as sure indexes of the equity of legislation and of the same state of public feeling, as the barometer is of the weight of the air, and it is a bad sign when these are discontented, for though they snuff oppression and dishonor at a distance, it is because they are more impressionable: the whole population will in a short time be as painfully affected.

Every hour brings us from distant quarters of the Union the expression of mortification at the late events in Massachusetts, and at the behavior of Boston. The tameness was indeed shocking. Boston, of whose fame for spirit and character we have all been so proud; Boston, whose citizens, intelligent people in England told me they could always distinguish by their culture among Americans; the Boston of the American Revolution, which figures so proudly in John Adams's Diary, which the whole country has been reading; Boston, spoiled by prosperity, must bow its ancient honor in the dust, and make us irretrievably ashamed. In Boston, we have said with such lofty confidence, no fugitive slave can be arrested, and now, we must transfer our vaunt to the country, and say, with a little less confidence, no fugitive man can be arrested here; at least we can brag thus until tomorrow, when the farmers also may be corrupted.

The tameness is indeed complete. The only haste in Boston, after the rescue of Shadrach, last February, was, who should first put his name on the list of volunteers in aid of the marshal. I met the smoothest of Episcopal Clergymen the other day, and allusion being made to Mr. Webster's treachery, he blandly replied, 'Why, do you know I think that the great action of his life.' It looked as if in the city and the suburbs all were involved in one hot haste of terror – presidents of colleges, and professors, saints, and brokers, insurers, lawyers, importers, manufacturers: not an unpleasing sentiment, not a liberal recollection, not so much as a snatch of an old song for freedom, dares intrude on their passive obedience.

The panic has paralyzed the journals, with the fewest exceptions, so that one cannot open a newspaper without being disgusted by new records of shame. I cannot read longer even the local good news. When I look down the columns at the titles of paragraphs, 'Education in Massachusetts', 'Board of Trade', 'Art Union', 'Revival of Religion', what bitter mockeries! The very convenience of property, the house and land we occupy, have lost their best value, and a man looks gloomily at his children, and thinks, 'What have I done that you should begin life in dishonor?' Every liberal study is discredited – literature and science appear effeminate, and the hiding of the head. The college, the churches, the schools, the very shops and factories are discredited; real estate, every kind of wealth, every branch of industry, every avenue to power, suffers injury, and the value of life is reduced. Just now a friend came into my house and said, 'if this law shall be repealed I shall be glad that I have lived; if not I shall be sorry that I was born'. What kind of law is that which extorts language like this from the heart of a free and civilized people?

One intellectual benefit we owe to late disgraces. The crisis had the illuminating power of a sheet of lightning at midnight. It showed truth. It ended a good deal of nonsense we had been wont to hear and to repeat, on the 19 April, the 17 June, the 4 July. It showed the slightness and unreliableness of our social fabric, it showed what stuff reputations are made of, what straws we dignify by office and title, and how competent we are to give counsel and help in a day of trial. It showed the shallowness of leaders; the divergence of parties from their alleged grounds; showed that men would not stick to what they had said, that the resolutions of public bodies, or the pledges never so often given and put on record of public men, will not bind them. The fact comes out more plainly that you cannot rely on any man for the defence of truth, who is not constitutionally or by blood and temperament on that side. A man of a greedy and unscrupulous selfishness may maintain morals when they are in fashion: but he will not stick ... The popular assumption that all men loved freedom, and believed in the Christian religion, was fundamentally hollow American brag; only persons who were known and tried benefactors are found standing for freedom: the sentimentalists went downstream. I question the value of our civilization, when I see that the public mind had never less hold of the strongest of all truths. The sense of injustice is blunted; a sure sign of the shallowness of our intellect. I cannot accept the railroad and telegraph in exchange for reason and charity. It is not skill in iron locomotives that makes so fine civility, as the jealousy of liberty. I cannot think the most judicious tubing a compensation for metaphysical debility. What is the use of admirable law-forms, and political forms, if a hurricane of party feeling and a combination of monied interests can beat them to the ground? What is the use of courts, if judges only quote authorities, and no judge exerts original jurisdiction, or recurs to first principles? What is the use of a Federal Bench, if its opinions are the political breath of the hour? And what is the use of constitutions, if all the guaranties provided by the jealousy of ages for the protection of liberty are made of no effect, when a bad act of Congress finds a wilting commissioner? The levity of the public mind has been shown in the past year by the most extravagant actions. Who could have believed it, if foretold that a hundred guns would be fired in Boston on the passage of the Fugitive Slave Bill? Nothing proves the want of all thought, the absence of standard in men's minds, more than the dominion of party. Here are humane people who have tears for misery, an open purse for want; who should have been the defenders of the poor man, are found his embittered enemies, rejoicing in his rendition, merely from party ties. I thought none, that was not ready to go on all fours, would back this law. And yet here are upright men, *compotes mentis*, husbands, fathers, trustees, friends, open, generous, brave, who can see nothing in this claim for bare humanity, and the health and honor of their native State, but canting fanaticism, sedition and 'one idea'. Because of this preoccupied mind, the whole wealth and power of Boston – two hundred thousand souls, and one hundred and eighty millions of money – are thrown into the scale of crime: and the poor black boy, whom the fame of Boston had reached in the recesses of a vile swamp, or in the alleys of Savannah, on arriving here finds all this force employed to catch him. The famous town of Boston is his master's hound. The learning of the universities, the culture of elegant society, the acumen of lawyers, the majesty of the Bench, the eloquence of the Christian pulpit, the stoutness of Democracy, the respectability of the Whig party are all combined to kidnap him.

The crisis is interesting as it shows the self-protecting nature of the world and of the Divine laws. It is the law of the world – as much immorality as there is, so much misery. The greatest prosperity will in vain resist the greatest calamity. You borrow the succour of the devil and he must have his fee. He was never known to abate a penny of his rents. In every nation all the immorality that exists breeds plagues. But of the corrupt society that exists we have never been able to combine any pure prosperity. There is always something in the very advantages of a condition which hurts it. Africa has its malformation; England has its Ireland; Germany its hatred of classes; France its love of gunpowder; Italy its Pope; and America, the most prosperous country in the Universe, has the greatest calamity in the Universe, negro slavery.

Frederick Douglass: Fourth of July Address, 1852

Douglass, the ex-slave, addressed the Rochester Ladies Antislavery Society, exposing the hypocrisy of Americans and the wide disparity between the idealism of the Declaration of Independence and American practice.

... This Fourth of July is *yours*, not *mine* ...

I shall see this day and its popular characteristics from the slave's point of view. Standing there, identified with the American bondman, making his wrongs mine, I do not hesitate to declare, with all my soul, that the character and conduct of this nation never looked blacker to me than on this Fourth of July! Whether we turn to the declarations of the past, or to the professions of the present, the conduct of the nation seems equally hideous and revolting. America is false to the past, false to the present, and solemnly binds herself to be false to the future ...

What to the American slave is your Fourth of July? I answer, a day that reveals to him, more than all other days in the year, the gross injustice and cruelty to which he is the constant victim. To him, your celebration is a sham; your boasted liberty, an unholy license; your national greatness, swelling vanity; your sounds of rejoicing are empty and heartless; your denunciations of tyrants, brass-fronted impudence; your shouts of liberty and equality, hollow mockery; your prayers and hymns, your sermons and thanksgivings, with all your religious parade and solemnity, are to him mere bombast, fraud, deception, impiety, and hypocrisy – a thin veil to cover up crimes which would disgrace a nation of savages. There is not a nation on the earth guilty of practices more shocking and bloody than are the people of these United States, at this very hour.

Go where you may, search where you will, roam through all the monarchies and despotisms of the old world, travel through South America, search out every abuse, and when you have found the last lay your facts by the side of the every-day practices of this nation, and you will say with me, that, for revolting barbarity and shameless hypocrisy, America reigns without a rival ...

Fellow-citizens, I will not enlarge further on your national inconsistencies. The existence of slavery in this country brands your republicanism as a sham, your humanity as a base pretense, and your Christianity as a lie. It destroys your moral power abroad; it corrupts your politicians at home. It saps the foundation of religion; it makes your name a hissing and a byword to a mocking earth. It is the antagonistic force in your government, the only thing that seriously disturbs and endangers your union. It fetters your progress; it is the enemy of improvement; the deadly foe of education; it fosters pride; it breeds insolence; it promotes vice ...

CAUSES OF THE CIVIL WAR

Andrew Jackson: Proclamation to the People of South Carolina, 10 December 1832

President Jackson's response to the South Carolina Ordinance of Nullification concerning federal tariffs is a stirring affirmation of unionism which was to serve as a model for Lincoln's Inaugural Address of 1861.

The ordinance is founded, not on the indefeasible right of resisting acts which are plainly unconstitutional and too oppressive to be endured, but on the strange position that any one state may not only declare an act of Congress void, but prohibit its execution; that they may do this consistently with the Constitution; that the true construction of that instrument permits a State to retain its place in the Union and yet be bound by no other of its laws than those it may choose to consider as constitutional.

... The Constitution of the United States, then, forms a government, not a league; and, whether it be formed by compact between the States or in any other manner, its character is the same. It is a Government in which all the people are represented, which operates directly on the people individually, not upon the States; they retained all the power they did not grant. But each State, having expressly parted with so many powers as to constitute, jointly with the other States, a single nation, can not, from that period, possess any right to secede, because such secession does not break a league, but destroys the unity of a nation; and any injury to that unity is not only a breach which would result from the contravention of a compact, but it is an offense against the whole Union. To say that any State may at pleasure secede from the Union is to say that the United States are not a nation, because it would be a solecism to contend that any part of a nation might dissolve its connection with the other parts, to their injury or ruin, without committing any offense. Secession, like any other revolutionary act, may be morally justified by the extremity of oppression; but to call it a constitutional right is confounding the meaning of terms, and can only be done through gross error or to deceive those who are willing to assert a right, but would pause before they made a revolution or incur the penalties consequent on a failure.

Because the Union was formed by a compact, it is said the parties to that compact may, when they feel themselves aggrieved, depart from it; but it is precisely because it is a compact that they can not. A compact is an agreement or binding obligation ... An attempt; by force of arms, to destroy a government is an offense, by whatever means the constitutional compact may have been formed: and such government has the right by the law of self-defense to pass acts for punishing the offender, unless that right is modified, restrained, or resumed by the constitutional act. In our system, although it is modified in the case of treason, yet authority is expressly given to pass all laws necessary to carry its powers into effect, and under this grant provision has been made for punishing acts which obstruct the due administration of the laws ...

This, then, is the position in which we stand: A small majority of the citizens of one State in the Union have elected delegates to a State convention; that convention has ordained that all the revenue laws of the United States must be repealed, or that they are no longer a member of the Union. The governor of that State has recommended to the legislature the raising of an army to carry the secession into effect, and that he may be empowered to give clearances to vessels in the name of the State. No act of violent opposition to the laws has yet been committed, but such a state of things is hourly apprehended. And it is the intent of this instrument to *proclaim*, not only that the duty imposed on me by the Constitution 'to take care that the laws be faithfully executed' shall be performed to the extent of the powers already vested in me by law, or of such others as the wisdom of Congress shall devise and intrust to me for that purpose, but to warn the citizens of South Carolina who have been deluded into an opposition to the laws of the danger they will incur by obedience to the illegal and disorganizing ordinance of the convention; to exhort those who have refused to support it to persevere in their determination to uphold the Constitution and laws of their country; and to point out to all the perilous situation into which the good people of that State have been led, and that the course they are urged to pursue is one of ruin and disgrace to the very State whose rights they affect to support ...

If your leaders could succeed in establishing a separation, what would be your situation? Are you united at home? Are you free from the apprehension of civil discord, with all its fearful consequences? Do our neighboring republics, every day suffering some new revolution or contending with some new insurrection, do they excite your envy? But the dictates of a high duty oblige me solemnly to announce that you can not succeed. The laws of the United States must be executed. I have no discretionary power on the subject; my duty is emphatically pronounced in the Constitution. Those who told you that you might peaceably prevent their execution deceived you; they could not have been deceived themselves. They know that a forcible opposition could alone prevent the execution of the laws, and they know that such opposition must be repelled. Their object is disunion. But be not deceived by names. Disunion by armed force is *treason*. Are you really ready to incur its guilt? If you are, on the heads of instigators of the act be the dreadful consequences; on their heads be the dishonor, but on yours may fall the punishment. On your unhappy State will inevitably fall all the evils of the conflict you force upon the Government of your country ...

Having the fullest confidence in the justness of legal and constitutional opinion of my duties which has been expressed, I rely with equal confidence on your undivided support in my determination to execute the laws, to preserve the Union by all constitutional means, to arrest, if possible, by moderate and firm measures the necessity of a recourse to force; and, if it be the will of Heaven that the recurrence of its primeval curse on man for the shedding of a brother's blood should fall upon our land, that it be not called down by any offensive act on the part of the United States.

Fellow-citizens, the momentous case is before you. On your undivided support of your Government depends the decision of the great question it involves – whether your sacred Union will be preserved and the blessing it secures to us as one people shall be perpetuated ...

May the Great Ruler of Nations grant that the signal blessings with which He has favored ours may not, by the madness of party or personal ambition, be disregarded and lost; and may His wise providence bring those who have produced this crisis to see the folly before they feel the misery of civil strife, and inspire a returning veneration for Union which, if we may dare to penetrate His designs, He has chosen as the only means of attaining the high destinies to which we may reasonably aspire.

Roger Taney, *Dred Scott v. Sandford*, 6 March 1857

In this critical Supreme Court decision Dred Scott, a slave, was denied freedom and citizenship and the Missouri Compromise of 1820 declared unconstitutional.

The question then arises, whether the provisions of the Constitution, in relation to the personal rights and privileges to which the citizen of a State should be entitled, embraced the negro African race, at that time in this country, or who might afterwards be imported, who had then or should afterwards be made free in any State; and to put it in the power of a single State to make him a citizen of the United States, and endue him with the full rights of citizenship in every other State without their consent. Does the Constitution of the United States act upon him whenever he shall be made free under the laws of a State, and raised there to the rank of a citizen, and immediately clothe him with all the privileges of a citizen in every other State, and in its own courts?

... It is difficult at this day to realize the state of public opinion in relation to that unfortunate race, which prevailed in the civilized and enlightened portions of the world at the time of the Declaration of Independence, and when the Constitution of the United States was framed and adopted ...

They had for more than a century before been regarded as beings of an inferior order; and altogether unfit to associate with the white race, either in social or political relations; and so far inferior that they had no rights which the white man was bound to respect; and that the negro might justly and lawfully be reduced to slavery for his benefit ... This opinion was at that time fixed and universal in the civilized portion of the white race. It was regarded as an axiom in morals as well as in politics, which no one thought of disputing, or supposed to be open to dispute; and men in every grade and position in society daily and habitually acted upon it in their private pursuits, as well as in matters of public concern, without doubting for a moment the correctness of this opinion ...

... But there are two clauses in the Constitution which point directly and specifically to the negro race as a separate class of persons, and show clearly that they were not regarded as a portion of the people or citizens of the Government then formed.

One of these clauses reserves to each of the thirteen States the right to import slaves until the year 1808, if he thinks it proper. And the importation which it thus sanctions was unquestionably of persons of the race of which we are speaking, as the traffic in slaves in the United States had always been confined to them. And by the other provision the States pledge themselves to each other to maintain the right of property of the master, by delivering up to him any slave who may have escaped from his service, and be found within their respective territories ... And these two provisions show, conclusively, that neither the description of persons therein referred to, nor their descendants, were embraced in any of the other provisions of the Constitution; for certainly these two clauses were not intended to confer on them or their posterity the blessings of liberty, or any of the personal rights so carefully provided for the citizen ...

... And upon a full and careful consideration of the subject, the court is of opinion that, upon the facts stated in the plea in abatement, Dred Scott was not a citizen of Missouri within the meaning of the Constitution of the United States, and not entitled as such to sue in its courts; and, consequently, that the Circuit Court had no jurisdiction of the case, and that the judgment on the plea in abatement is erroneous ...

We proceed, therefore, to inquire whether the facts relied on by the plaintiff entitled him to his freedom ...

... It seems, however, to be supposed that there is a difference between property in a slave and other property, and that different rules may be applied to it in expounding the Constitution of the United States. And the laws and usages of nations, and the writings of eminent jurists upon the relation of master and slave and their mutual rights and duties, and the powers which governments may exercise over it, have been dwelt upon in the argument.

But ... if the Constitution recognizes the right of property of the master in a slave, and makes no distinction between that description of property and other property owned by a citizen, no tribunal, acting under the authority of the United States, whether it be legislative, executive, or judicial, has a right to draw such a distinction, or deny to it the benefit of the provisions and guarantees which have been provided for the protection of private property against the encroachments of the Government.

Now ... the right of property in a slave is distinctly and expressly affirmed in the Constitution. The right to traffic in it, like an ordinary article of merchandise and property, was guaranteed to the citizens of the United States, in every State that might desire it, for twenty years. And the Government in express terms is pledged to protect it in all future time, if the slave escapes from his owner ... And no word can be found in the Constitution which gives Congress a greater power over slave property, or which entitles property of that kind to less protection than property of any other description. The only power conferred is the power coupled with the duty of guarding and protecting the owner in his rights.

'Upon these considerations, it is the opinion of the court that the Act of Congress which prohibited a citizen from holding and owning property of this kind in the territory of the United States north of the line therein mentioned is not warranted by the Constitution, and is therefore void; and that neither Dred Scott himself, nor any of his family, were made free by being carried into this territory; even if they had been carried there by the owner, with the intention of becoming a permanent resident ...'

Abraham Lincoln: The 'House Divided' Speech, 17 June 1858

This speech, delivered at the Illinois Republican Convention in Springfield, constructs a conspiracy theory to extend the Slave Power by Stephen (Douglas), Franklin (Pierce), Roger (Taney) and James (Buchanan).

MR. PRESIDENT AND GENTLEMEN OF THE CONVENTION: If we could first know where we are, and whither we are tending, we could better judge what to do, and how to do it. We are now far into the fifth year since a policy was initiated with the avowed object and confident promise of putting an end to slavery agitation. Under the operation of that policy, that agitation has not only not ceased, but has constantly augmented. In my opinion, it will not cease until a crisis shall have been reached and passed. 'A house divided against itself cannot stand.' I believe this government cannot endure permanently half slave and half free. I do not expect the Union to be dissolved; I do not expect the house to fall; but I do expect it will cease to be divided. It will become all one thing, or all the other. Either the opponents of slavery will arrest the further spread of it, and place it where the public mind shall rest in the belief that it is in the course of ultimate extinction, or its advocates will push it forward till it shall become alike lawful in all the States, old as well as new, North as well as South.

Have we no tendency to the latter condition?

Let any one who doubts carefully contemplate that now almost complete legal combination – piece of machinery, so to speak – compounded of the Nebraska doctrine and the Dred Scott decision. Let him consider, not only what work the machinery is adapted to do, and how well adapted, but also let him study the history of its construction, and trace, if he can, or rather fail, if he can, to trace the evidences of design, and concert of action, among its chief architects, from the beginning.

... At length a squabble springs up between the President and the author of the Nebraska Bill, on the mere question of *fact*, whether the Lecompton Constitution was or was not in any just sense made by the people of Kansas; and in that quarrel the latter declares that all he wants is a fair vote for the people, and that he cares not whether slavery be voted *down* or voted *up*. I do not understand his declaration. That he cares not whether slavery be voted down or voted up, to be intended by him other than as an apt definition of the policy he would impress upon the public mind ... That principle is the only shred left of his original Nebraska doctrine. Under the Dred Scott decision 'squatter sovereignty' squatted out of existence, tumbled down like temporary scaffolding; like the mould at the foundry, served through one blast, and fell back into loose sand; helped to carry an election, and then was kicked to the winds.

... The several points of the Dred Scott decision, in connection with Senator Douglas's 'care not' policy, constitute the piece of machinery, in its present state of advancement. This was the third point gained. The working points of that machinery are:

Firstly, That no negro slave, imported as such from Africa, and no descendant of such slave, can ever be a citizen of any State, in the sense of that term as used in the Constitution of the United States. This point is made in order to deprive the negro, in every possible event, of the benefit of that provision of the United States Constitution which declares that 'The citizens of each State shall be entitled to all privileges and immunities of citizens in the several States'.

Secondly, That, 'subject to the Constitution of the United States', neither Congress nor a Territorial Legislature can exclude slavery from any United States Territory. This point is made in order that individual men may fill up the Territories with slaves, without danger of losing them as property, and thus to enhance the chances of permanency to the institution through all the future.

Thirdly, That whether the holding a negro in actual slavery in a free State makes him free, as against the holder, the United States courts will not decide, but will leave to be decided by the courts of any slave State the negro may be forced into by the master. This point is made, not to be pressed immediately; but, if acquiesced in for a while, and apparently indorsed by the people at an election, then to sustain the logical conclusion that what Dred Scott's master might lawfully do with Dred Scott, in the free State of Illinois, every other master may lawfully do with any other one, or one thousand slaves, in Illinois, or in any other free State.

We cannot absolutely know that all these exact adaptations are the result of preconcert. But when we see a lot of framed timbers, different portions of which we know have been gotten out at different times and places and by different workmen – Stephen, Franklin, Roger, and James, for instance – and when we see these timbers joined together, and see they exactly make the frame of a house or a mill, all the tenons and mortises exactly fitting, and all the lengths and proportions of the different pieces exactly adapted to their respective places, and not a piece too many or too few – not omitting even scaffolding – or, if a single piece be lacking, we see the place in the frame exactly fitted and prepared yet to bring such piece in, in such a case, we find it impossible not to believe that Stephen and Franklin and Roger and James all understood one another from the beginning, and all worked upon a common plan or draft drawn up before the first blow was struck ...

South Carolina Declaration of Causes of Secession, 24 December 1860

This justification for secession from the Founding State of the Confederacy captures well the rationale and underlying mood of the South in the secession winter of 1860–61.

In 1787, Deputies were appointed by the States to revise the articles of Confederation; and on 17th September 1787, these Deputies recommended, for the adoption of the States, the Articles of Union, known as the Constitution of the United States.

... Thus was established by compact between the States a Government with defined objects and powers, limited to the express words of the grant ... We hold that the Government thus established is subject to the two great principles asserted in the Declaration of Independence; and we hold further that the mode of its formation subjects it to a third fundamental principle, namely, the law of Compact. We maintain that in every compact between two or more parties the obligation is mutual; that the failure of one of the contracting parties to perform a material part of the agreement entirely releases the obligation of the other; and that, where no arbiter is provided, each party is remitted to his own judgment to determine the fact of failure, with all its consequences.

In the present case, that fact is established with certainty. We assert that fourteen of the States have deliberately refused for years past to fulfil their constitutional obligations, and we refer to their own statutes for the proof.

The Constitution of the United States, in its fourth Article, provides as follows:

'No person held to service or labor in one State under the laws thereof, escaping into another, shall, in consequence of any law or regulation therein, be discharged from such service or labor, but shall be delivered up, on claim of the party to whom such service or labor may be due.'

This stipulation was so material to the compact that without it that compact would not have been made. The greater number of the contracting parties held slaves, and they had previously evinced their estimate of the value of such a stipulation by making it a condition in the Ordinance for the government of the territory ceded by Virginia, which obligations, and the laws of the General Government, have ceased to effect the objects of the Constitution. The States of Maine, New Hampshire, Vermont, Massachusetts, Connecticut, Rhode Island, New York, Pennsylvania, Illinois, Indiana, Michigan, Wisconsin and Iowa, have enacted laws which either nullify the acts of Congress, or render useless any attempt to execute them ...

Thus the constitutional compact has been deliberately broken and disregarded by the non-slaveholding States; and the consequence follows that South Carolina is released from her obligation ...

We affirm that these ends for which this Government was instituted have been defeated, and the Government itself has been destructive of them by the action of the non-slaveholding States. Those States have assumed the right of deciding upon the propriety of our domestic institutions; and have denied the rights of property established in fifteen of the States and recognized by the Constitution; they have denounced as sinful the institution of Slavery; they have permitted the open establishment among them of societies, whose avowed object is to disturb the peace of and eloin the property of the citizens of other States. They have encouraged and assisted thousands of our slaves to leave their homes; and those who remain have been incited by emissaries, books, and pictures, to servile insurrection.

For twenty-five years this agitation has been steadily increasing, until it has now secured to its aid the power of the common Government. Observing the *forms* of the Constitution, a sectional party has found within that article establishing the Executive Department the means of subverting the Constitution itself. A geographical line has been drawn across the Union, and all the States north of that line have united in the election of a man to the high office of President of the United States whose opinions and purposes are hostile to Slavery. He is to be intrusted with the administration of the common Government, because he has declared that 'Government cannot endure permanently half slave, half free', and that the public mind must rest in the belief that Slavery is in the course of ultimate extinction.

This sectional combination for the subversion of the Constitution has been aided, in some of the States, by elevating to citizenship persons who, by the supreme law of the land, are incapable of becoming citizens; and their votes have been used to inaugurate a new policy, hostile to the South, and destructive of its peace and safety.

On the 4th of March next this party will take possession of the Government. It has announced that the South shall be excluded from the common territory, that the judicial tribunal shall be made sectional, and that a war must be waged against Slavery until it shall cease throughout the United States.

The guarantees of the Constitution will then no longer exist; the equal rights of the States will be lost. The Slaveholding States will no longer have the power of self-government, or self-protection, and the Federal Government will have become their enemy.

Sectional interest and animosity will deepen the irritation; and all hope of remedy is rendered vain by the fact that the public opinion at the North has invested a great political error with the sanctions of a more erroneous religious belief.

We, therefore, the people of South Carolina, by our delegates in Convention assembled, appealing to the Supreme judge of the world for the rectitude of our intentions, have solemnly declared that the Union heretofore existing between this State and the other States of North America is dissolved, and that the State of South Carolina has resumed her position among the nations of the world, as a separate and independent state, with full power to levy war, conclude peace, contract alliances, establish commerce, and to do all other acts and things which independent States may of right do.

Abraham Lincoln: First Inaugural Address, 4 March 1861

This address was a skilful and moving appeal against disunion after seven Southern States had already seceded. Seward, Secretary of State, urged Lincoln to end on a conciliatory note.

It is seventy-two years since the first inauguration of a President under our national Constitution. During that period fifteen different and greatly distinguished citizens have in succession administered the executive branch of the government. They have conducted it through many perils, and generally with great success. Yet, with all this scope for precedent, I now enter upon the same task for the brief constitutional term of four years under great and peculiar difficulty. A disruption of the federal Union, heretofore only menaced, is now formidably attempted.

I hold that in contemplation of universal law and of the Constitution the union of these states is perpetual. Perpetuity is implied, if not expressed, in the fundamental law of all national governments. It is safe to assert that no government proper ever had a provision in its organic law for its own termination. Continue to execute all the express provisions of our national Constitution, and the Union will endure forever, it being impossible to destroy it except by some action not provided for in the instrument itself.

Again: If the United States be not a government proper, but an association of states in the nature of contract merely, can it, as a contract, be peaceably unmade by less than all the parties who made it? One party to a contract may violate it – break it, so to speak – but does it not require all to lawfully rescind it?

It follows from these views that no state upon its own mere motion can lawfully get out of the Union; that *resolves* and *ordinances* to that effect are legally void, and that acts of violence within any state or states against the authority of the United States are insurrectionary or revolutionary, according to circumstances.

I therefore consider that in view of the Constitution and the laws the Union is unbroken, and to the extent of my ability I shall take care, as the Constitution itself expressly enjoins upon me, that the laws of the Union be faithfully executed in all the states. Doing this I deem to be only a simple duty on my part; and I shall perform it so far as practicable unless my rightful masters, the

American people, shall withhold the requisite means or in some authoritative manner direct the contrary. I trust this will not be regarded as a menace, but only as the declared purpose of the Union that it *will* constitutionally defend and maintain itself.

In doing this, there needs to be no bloodshed or violence, and there shall be none unless it be forced upon the national authority. The power confided to me will be used to hold, occupy, and possess the property and places belonging to the government and to collect the duties and imposts; but, beyond what may be necessary for these objects, there will be no invasion, no using of force against or among the people anywhere. Where hostility to the United States in any interior locality shall be so great and so universal as to prevent competent resident citizens from holding the federal offices, there will be no attempt to force obnoxious strangers among the people for that object. While the strict legal right may exist in the government to enforce the exercise of these offices, the attempt to do so would be so irritating and so nearly impracticable withal that I deem it better to forego for the time the uses of such offices.

The mails, unless repelled, will continue to be furnished in all parts of the Union. So far as possible the people everywhere shall have that sense of perfect security which is most favorable to calm thought and reflection. The course here indicated will be followed unless current events and experience shall show a modification or change to be proper, and in every case and exigency my best discretion will be exercised, according to circumstances actually existing and with a view and a hope of a peaceful solution of the national troubles and the restoration of fraternal sympathies and affections.

That there are persons in one section or another who seek to destroy the Union at all events and are glad of any pretext to do it I will neither affirm nor deny; but if there be such I need address no word to them. To those, however, who really love the Union may I not speak?

Before entering upon so grave a matter as the destruction of our national fabric, with all its benefits, its memories, and its hopes, would it not be wise to ascertain precisely why we do it? Will you hazard so desperate a step while there is any possibility that any portion of the ills you fly from have no real existence? Will you, while the certain ills you fly to are greater than all the real ones you fly from, will you risk the commission of so fearful a mistake?

All profess to be content in the Union if all constitutional rights can be maintained. Is it true, then, that any right plainly written in the Constitution has been denied? I think not. Happily, the human mind is so constituted that no party can reach to the audacity of doing this. Think, if you can, of a single instance in which a plainly written provision of the Constitution has ever been denied. If by the mere force of numbers a majority should deprive a minority of any clearly written constitutional right, it might to a moral point of view justify revolution; certainly would if such right were a vital one. But such is not our case. All the vital rights of minorities and of individuals are so plainly assured to them by affirmations and negations, guaranties and prohibitions in the Constitution that controversies never arise concerning them. But no organic law can ever be framed with a provision specifically applicable to every question which may occur in practical administration. No foresight can anticipate nor any document of reasonable length contain express provisions for all possible questions. Shall fugitives from labor be surrendered by national or by state authority? The Constitution does not expressly say. *May* Congress prohibit slavery in the territories? The Constitution does not expressly say. *Must* Congress protect slavery in the territories? The Constitution does not expressly say.

From questions of this class spring all our constitutional controversies, and we divide upon them into majorities and minorities. If the minority will not acquiesce, the majority must, or the government must cease. There is no other alternative, for continuing the government is acquiescence on one side or the other. If a minority in such case will secede rather than acquiesce, they make a precedent which in turn will divide and ruin them, for a minority of their own will secede from them whenever a majority refuses to be controlled by such minority. For instance, why may not any portion of a new confederacy a year or two hence arbitrarily secede again, precisely as portions of the present Union now claim to secede from it? All who cherish disunion sentiments are now being educated to the exact temper of doing this.

Is there such perfect identity of interests among the states to compose a new union as to produce harmony only and prevent renewed secession?

Plainly the central idea of secession is the essence of anarchy. A majority held in restraint by constitutional checks and limitations, and always changing easily with deliberate changes of popular opinions and sentiments, is the only true sovereign of a free people. Whoever rejects it does of necessity fly to anarchy or to despotism. Unanimity is impossible. The rule of a minority, as a permanent arrangement, is wholly inadmissible; so that, rejecting the majority principle, anarchy, or despotism in some form is all that is left.

I do not forget the position assumed by some that constitutional questions are to be decided by the Supreme Court, nor do I deny that such decisions must be binding in any case upon the parties to a suit as to the object of that suit, while they are also entitled to very high respect and consideration in all parallel cases by all other departments of the government. And, while it is obviously possible that such decision may be erroneous in any given case, still the evil effect following it, being limited to that particular case, with the chance that it may be overruled and never become a precedent for other cases, can better be borne than could the evils of a different practice. At the same time, the candid citizen must confess that, if the policy of the government upon vital questions affecting the whole people is to be irrevocably fixed by decisions of the Supreme Court, the instant they are made in ordinary litigation between parties in personal actions the people will have ceased to be their own rulers, having to that extent practically resigned their government into the hands of that eminent tribunal. Nor is there in this view any assault upon the Court or the judges. It is a duty from which they may not shrink to decide cases properly brought before them, and it is no fault of theirs if others seek to turn their decisions to political purposes.

One section of our country believes slavery is *right* and ought to be extended, while the other believes it is *wrong* and ought not to be extended. This is the only substantial dispute. The fugitive-slave clause of the Constitution and the law for the suppression of the foreign slave trade are each as well enforced, perhaps, as any law can ever be in a community where the moral sense of the people imperfectly supports the law itself. The great body of the people abide by the dry legal obligation in both cases, and a few break over in each. This, I think, cannot be perfectly cured, and it would be worse in both cases *after* the separation of the sections than before. The foreign slave trade, now imperfectly suppressed, would be ultimately revived without restriction in one section, while fugitive slaves, now only partially surrendered, would not be surrendered at all by the other.

Physically speaking, we cannot separate. We cannot remove our respective sections from each other nor build an impassable wall between them. A husband and wife may be divorced and go out of the presence and beyond the reach of each other, but the different parts of our country cannot do this. They cannot but remain face to face, and intercourse, either amicable or hostile, must continue between them. Is it possible, then, to make that intercourse more advantageous or more satisfactory after separation than before? Can aliens make treaties easier than friends can make laws? Can treaties be more faithfully enforced between aliens than laws can among friends? Suppose you go to war, you cannot fight always; and when, after much loss on both sides and no gain on either, you cease fighting, the identical old questions, as to terms of intercourse, are again upon you.

This country, with its institutions, belongs to the people who inhabit it. Whenever they shall grow weary of the existing government, they can exercise their *constitutional* right of amending it or their *revolutionary* right to dismember or overthrow it. I cannot be ignorant of the fact that many worthy and patriotic citizens are desirous of having the national Constitution amended. While I make no recommendation of amendments, I fully recognize the rightful authority of the people over the whole subject, to be exercised in either of the modes prescribed in the instrument itself; and I should, under existing circumstances, favor rather than oppose a fair opportunity being afforded the people to act upon it. I will venture to add that to me the convention mode seems preferable, in that it allows amendments to originate with the people themselves, instead of only permitting them to take or reject propositions originated by others, not especially chosen for the purpose, and which might not be precisely such as they would wish to either accept or refuse. I understand a proposed amendment to the Constitution – which amendment, however, I have not seen – has passed Congress, to the effect that the federal government shall never interfere with the domestic institutions of the states, including that of persons held to service. To avoid misconstruction of what I have said, I depart from my purpose not to speak of particular amendments so far as to say that, holding such a provision to now be implied constitutional law, I have no objection to its being made express and irrevocable.

The Chief Magistrate derives all his authority from the people, and they have conferred none upon him to fix terms for the separation of the states. The people themselves can do this also if they choose, but the Executive as such has nothing to do with it. His duty is to administer the present government as it came to his hands and to transmit it unimpaired by him to his successor.

Why should there not be a patient confidence in the ultimate justice of the people? Is there any better or equal hope in the world? In our present differences, is either party without faith of being in the right? If the Almighty Ruler of Nations, with His eternal truth and justice, be on your side of the North, or on yours of the South, that truth and that justice will surely prevail by the judgment of this great tribunal of the American people.

By the frame of the government under which we live this same people have wisely given their public servants but little power for mischief and have with equal wisdom provided for the return of that little to their own hands at very short intervals. While the people retain their virtue and vigilance no administration by any extreme of wickedness or folly can very seriously injure the government in the short space of four years.

My countrymen, one and all, think calmly and *well* upon this whole subject. Nothing valuable can be lost by taking time. If there be an object to *hurry* any of you in hot haste to a step which you would never take *deliberately,* that object will be frustrated by taking time; but no good object can be frustrated by it. Such of you as are now dissatisfied still have the old Constitution unimpaired, and, on the sensitive point, the laws of your own framing under it; while the new administration will have no immediate power, if it would, to change either. If it were admitted that you who are dissatisfied hold the right side in the dispute, there still is no single good reason for precipitate action. Intelligence, patriotism, Christianity, and a firm reliance on Him who has never yet forsaken this favored land are still competent to adjust in the best way all our present difficulty.

In *your* hands, my dissatisfied fellow-countrymen, and not in *mine,* is the momentous issue of civil war. The government will not assail *you.* You can have no conflict without being yourselves the aggressors. *You* have no oath registered in heaven to destroy the government, while *I* shall have the most solemn one to 'preserve, protect, and defend it'.

I am loath to close. We are not enemies, but friends. We must not be enemies. Though passion may have strained, it must not break our bonds of affection. The mystic chords of memory, stretching from every battlefield and patriot grave to every living heart and hearthstone all over this broad land, will yet swell the chorus of the Union, when again touched, as surely they will be, by the better angels of our nature.

CIVIL WAR

Jefferson Davis: Inaugural Address, 18 February 1861

Davis's Inauguration, delivered in Montgomery, Alabama, is an eloquent justification of Confederate secession, but his hopes for a peaceful separation were not to be realised.

Called to the difficult and responsible station of Chief Executive of the Provisional Government which you have instituted, I approach the discharge of the duties assigned me with an humble distrust of my abilities, but with a sustaining confidence in the wisdom of those who are to guide and aid me in the administration of public affairs, and an abiding faith in the virtue and patriotism of the people. Looking forward to the speedy establishment of a permanent government to take the place of this, and which by its greater moral and physical power will be better able to combat with the many difficulties which arise from the conflicting interests of separate nations, I enter upon the duties of the office to which I have been chosen, with the hope that the beginning of our career as a confederacy may not be obstructed by hostile opposition to our enjoyment of the separate existence and independence which we have asserted, and which, with the blessing of Providence, we intend to maintain.

Our present condition, achieved in a manner unprecedented in the history of nations, illustrates the American idea that governments rest upon the consent of the governed, and that it is the right of the people to alter and abolish governments whenever they become destructive to the ends for which they were established. The declared compact of the Union from which we have withdrawn was to establish justice, ensure domestic tranquillity, provide for the common defence, promote the general welfare, and secure the blessings of liberty to ourselves and our posterity; and when in the judgment of the sovereign States now composing this confederacy it has been perverted from the purposes for which it was ordained, and ceased to answer the ends for which it was established, a peaceful appeal to the ballot-box declared that, so far as they were concerned, the government created by that compact should cease to exist. In this they merely asserted the right which the Declaration of Independence of 1776 defined to be inalienable. Of the time and occasion of its exercise they as sovereigns were the final judges, each for itself. The impartial enlightened verdict of mankind will vindicate the rectitude of our conduct; and He who knows the hearts of men will judge the sincerity with which we labored to preserve the government of our fathers in its spirit.

The right solemnly proclaimed at the birth of the States, and which has been affirmed and reaffirmed in the bills of rights of the States subsequently admitted into the Union of 1789, undeniably recognizes in the people the power to resume the authority delegated for the purposes of government. Thus the sovereign States here represented, proceeded to form this confederacy; and it is by the abuse of language that their act has been denominated revolution. They formed a new alliance, but within each State its government has remained. The rights of person and property have not been disturbed. The agent through whom they communicated with foreign nations is changed, but this does not necessarily interrupt their international relations. Sustained by the consciousness that the transition from the former Union to the present confederacy has not proceeded from a disregard on our part of our just obligations or any failure to perform every constitutional duty, moved by no interest or passion to invade the rights of others, anxious to cultivate peace and commerce with all nations, if we may not hope to avoid war, we may at least expect that posterity will acquit us of having needlessly engaged in it. Doubly justified by the absence of wrong on our part, and by wanton aggression on the part of others, there can be no cause to doubt the courage and patriotism of the people of the Confederate States will be found equal to any measures of defence which soon their security may require.

An agricultural people, whose chief interest is the export of a commodity required in every manufacturing country, our true policy is peace, and the freest trade which our necessities will permit. It is alike our interest and that of all those to whom we would sell and from whom we would buy that there should be the fewest practicable restrictions upon the interchange of commodities. There can be but little rivalry between ours and any manufacturing or navigating community, such as the northeastern States of the American Union. It must follow, therefore, that mutual interest would invite good will and kind offices. If, however, passion or lust of dominion should cloud the judgment or inflame the ambition of those States, we must prepare to meet the emergency and maintain by the final arbitrament of the sword the position which we have assumed among the nations of the earth.

We have entered upon a career of independence, and it must be inflexibly pursued through many years of controversy with our late associates of the Northern States. We have vainly endeavored to secure tranquillity and obtain respect for the rights to which we were entitled. As a necessity, not a choice, we have resorted to the remedy of separation, and henceforth our energies must be directed to the conduct of our own affairs, and the perpetuity of the confederacy which we have formed. If a just perception of mutual interest shall permit us peaceably to pursue our separate political career, my most earnest desire will have been fulfilled. But if this be denied us, and the integrity of our territory and jurisdiction be assailed, it will but remain for us with firm resolve to appeal to arms and invoke the blessing of Providence on a just cause.

Alexander Stephens: Address on the Confederate Constitution, 21 March 1861

The Confederate Vice President delivered this address in Savannah, Georgia, making it abundantly clear that slavery 'was the immediate cause of the late rupture and present revolution'.

… The new Constitution has put at rest forever all the agitating questions relating to our peculiar institutions – African slavery as it exists among us – the proper status of the negro in our form of civilization. This was the immediate cause of the late rupture and present revolution. JEFFERSON, in his forecast, had anticipated this, as the 'rock upon which the old Union would split'. He was right. What was conjecture with him is now a realized fact. But whether he fully comprehended the great truth upon which that rock stood and stands may be doubted. The prevailing ideas entertained by him and most of the leading statesmen at the time of the formation of the old Constitution were that the enslavement of the African was in violation of the laws of nature; that it was wrong in principle, socially, morally and politically. It was an evil they knew not well how to deal with; but the general opinion of the men of that day was that, somehow or other, in the order of Providence, the institution would be evanescent and pass away. This idea, though not incorporated in the Constitution, was the prevailing idea at the time. The Constitution, it is true, secured every essential guarantee to the institution while it should last, and hence no argument can be justly used against the constitutional guarantees thus secured, because of the common sentiment of the day. Those ideas, however, were fundamentally wrong. They rested upon the assumption of the equality of races. This was an error. It was a sandy foundation, and the idea of a Government built upon it – when the 'storm came and the wind blew, it fell'.

Our new Government is founded upon exactly the opposite ideas; its foundations are laid, its cornerstone rests upon the great truth that the negro is not equal to the white man; that slavery, subordination to the superior race, is his natural and moral condition. This, our new Government, is the first, in the history of the world, based upon this great physical, philosophical and moral truth. This truth has been slow in the process of its development, like all other truths in the various departments of science. It is so even amongst us. Many who hear me, perhaps, can recollect well that this truth was not generally admitted, even within their day. The errors of the past generation still clung to many as late as twenty years ago. Those at the North who still cling to these errors with a zeal above knowledge, we justly denominate fanatics. All fanaticism springs from an aberration of the mind; from a defeat in reasoning. It is a species of insanity. One of the most striking characteristics of insanity, in many instances, is forming correct conclusions from fancied or erroneous premises; so with the antislavery fanatics: their conclusions are right if their premises are. They assume that the negro is equal, and hence conclude that he is entitled to equal privileges and rights with the white man. If their premises were correct, their conclusions would be logical and just; but their premises being wrong their whole argument fails. I recollect once of having heard a gentleman from one of the Northern States, of great power and ability, announce in the House of Representatives, with imposing effect, that we of the South would be compelled, ultimately, to yield upon this subject of slavery; that it was as impossible to war successfully against a principle in politics as it was in physics or mechanics. That the principle would ultimately prevail. That we, in maintaining slavery as it exists with us, were warring against a principle – a principle founded in nature, the principle of the equality of man. The reply I made to him was that upon his own grounds we should succeed, and that he and his associates in their crusade against our institutions would ultimately fail. The truth announced, that it was as impossible to war successfully against a principle in politics as well as in physics and mechanics, I admitted, but told him it was he and those acting with him who were warring against a principle. They were attempting to make things equal which the Creator had made unequal.

Abraham Lincoln: Message to Congress, 4 July 1861

This message to a specially convened session of Congress was a succinct summary of the issues separating North from South.

At the beginning of the present Presidential term, four months ago, the functions of the Federal Government were found to be generally suspended within the several States of South Carolina, Georgia, Alabama, Mississippi, Louisiana and Florida, excepting only those of the Post-office Department ...

The purpose to sever the Federal Union was openly avowed. In accordance with this purpose, an ordinance had been adopted in each of these States, declaring the States respectively to be separated from the national Union. A formula for instituting a combined government of these States had been promulgated; and this illegal organization, in the character of confederate States, was already invoking recognition, aid and intervention from foreign powers ...

And this issue embraces more than the fate of these United States. It presents to the whole family of man the question whether a constitutional republic or democracy – a government of the people by the same people – can or cannot maintain its territorial integrity against its own domestic foes. It presents the question whether discontented individuals, too few in number to control administration according to organic law in any case, can always, upon the pretenses made in this case, or on any other pretenses, or arbitrarily without any pretense, break up their government, and thus practically put an end to free government upon the earth. It forces us to ask: Is there in all republics this inherent and fatal weakness? Must a government, of necessity, be too strong for the liberties of its own people, or too weak to maintain its own existence?

So viewing the issue, no choice was left but to call out the war power of the government, and so to resist force employed for its destruction by force for its preservation ...

The forbearance of this government had been so extraordinary and so long continued as to lead some foreign nations to shape their action as if they supposed the early destruction of our national Union was probable. While this, on discovery, gave the executive some concern, he is now happy to say that the sovereignty and rights of the United States are now everywhere practically respected by foreign powers; and a general sympathy with the country is manifested throughout the world ...

It might seem, at first thought, to be of little difference whether the present movement at the South be called 'secession' or 'rebellion'. The movers, however, well understand the difference. At the beginning they knew they could never raise their treason to any respectable magnitude by any name which implies *violation* of law. They knew their people possessed as much of moral sense, as much of devotion to law and order, and as much pride in and reverence for the history and government of their common country as any other civilized and patriotic people. They knew they could make no advancement directly in the teeth of these strong and noble sentiments. Accordingly, they commenced by an insidious debauching of the public mind. They invented an ingenious sophism which, if conceeded, was followed by perfectly logical steps, through all the incidents, to the complete destruction of the Union. The sophism itself is that any State of the Union may *consistently* with the national Constitution, and therefore lawfully and peacefully, withdraw from the Union without the consent of the Union or of any other State ...

This sophism derives much, perhaps the whole, of its currency from the assumption that there is some omnipotent and sacred supremacy pertaining to a State – to each State of our Federal Union.

This is essentially a people's contest. On the side of the Union it is a struggle for maintaining in the world that form and substance of government whose leading object is to elevate the condition of men – to lift artificial weights from all shoulders; to clear the paths of laudable pursuit for all; to afford all an unfettered start, and a fair chance in the race of life. Yielding to partial and temporary departures, from necessity, this is the leading object of the government for whose existence we contend ...

Our popular government has often been called an experiment. Two points in it our people have already settled – the successful establishing and the successful administering of it. One still remains – its successful maintenance against a formidable internal attempt to overthrow it. It is now for them to demonstrate to the world that those who can fairly carry an election can also suppress a rebellion; that ballots are the rightful and peaceful successors of bullets; and that when ballots have fairly and constitutionally decided there can be no successful appeal back to bullets; that there can be no successful appeal, except to ballots themselves, at succeeding elections. Such will be a great lesson of peace: teaching men that what they cannot take by an election neither can they take it by war; teaching all the folly of being the beginners of a war ...

Abraham Lincoln: Gettysburg Address, 19 November 1863

This brief address at the dedication of the Gettysburg National Cemetery is a noble vision of 'a new birth of freedom' in America.

Fourscore and seven years ago our fathers brought forth on this continent a new nation, conceived in liberty, and dedicated to the proposition that all men are created equal. Now we are engaged in a great civil war, testing whether that nation, or any nation so conceived and so dedicated, can long endure. We are met on a great battlefield of that war. We have come to dedicate a portion of that field as a final resting-place for those who here gave their lives that that nation might live. It is altogether fitting and proper that we should do this.

But, in a larger sense, we cannot dedicate – we cannot consecrate – we cannot hallow – this ground. The brave men, living and dead, who struggled here, have consecrated it far above our poor power to add or detract. The world will little note nor long remember what we say here, but it can never forget what they did here. It is for us, the living, rather, to be dedicated here to the unfinished work which they who fought here have thus far so nobly advanced. It is rather for us to be dedicated here to the great task remaining before us – that from these honored dead we take increased devotion to that cause for which they gave the last full measure of devotion; that we here highly resolve that these dead shall not have died in vain; that this nation, under God, shall have a new birth of freedom; and that government of the people, by the people, for the people, shall not perish from the earth.

Abraham Lincoln: Second Inaugural Address, 4 March 1865

This address interprets the war in providential terms and looks forward to a peaceful Reconstruction.

FELLOW-COUNTRYMEN: – At this second appearing to take the oath of the presidential office there is less occasion for an extended address than there was at the first. Then a statement somewhat in detail of a course to be pursued seemed fitting and proper. Now, at the expiration of four years, during which public declarations have been constantly called forth on every point and phase of the great contest which still absorbs the attention and engrosses the energies of the nation, little that is new could be presented. The progress of our arms, upon which all else chiefly depends, is as well known to the public as to myself, and it is, I trust, reasonably satisfactory and encouraging to all. With high hope for the future, no prediction in regard to it is ventured.

On the occasion corresponding to this four years ago all thoughts were anxiously directed to an impending civil war. All dreaded it, all sought to avert it. While the inaugural address was being delivered from this place, devoted altogether to saving the Union without war, insurgent agents were in the city seeking to destroy it without war – seeking to dissolve the Union and divide effects by negotiation. Both parties deprecated war, but one of them would make war rather than let the nation survive, and the other would accept war rather than let it perish, and the war came.

One eighth of the whole population was colored slaves, not distributed generally over the Union, but localized in the southern part of it. These slaves constituted a peculiar and powerful interest. All knew that this interest was somehow the cause of the war. To strengthen, perpetuate, and extend this interest was the object for which the insurgents would rend the Union even by war, while the Government claimed no right to do more than to restrict the territorial enlargement of it. Neither party expected for the war the magnitude or the duration which it has already attained. Neither anticipated that the cause of the conflict might cease with or even before the conflict itself should cease. Each looked for an easier triumph, and a result less fundamental and astounding. Both read the same Bible and pray to the same God, and each invokes His aid against the other. It may seem strange that any men should dare to ask a just God's assistance in wringing their bread from the sweat of other men's faces, but let us judge not, that we be not judged. The prayers of both could not be answered. That of neither has been answered fully. The Almighty has His own purposes. 'Woe unto the world because of offenses; for it must needs be that offenses come, but woe to that man by whom the offense cometh.' If we shall suppose that American slavery is one of those offenses which, in the providence of God, must needs come, but which, having continued through His appointed time, He now wills to remove, and that He gives to both North and South this terrible war as the woe due to those by whom the offense came, shall we discern therein any departure from those divine attributes which the believers in a living God always ascribe to Him? Fondly do we hope, fervently do we pray, that this mighty scourge of war may speedily pass away. Yet, if God wills that it continue until all the wealth piled by the bondman's two hundred and fifty years of unrequited toil shall be sunk, and until every drop of blood drawn with the lash shall be paid by another drawn with the sword, as was said three thousand years ago, so still it must be said, 'The judgments of the Lord are true and righteous altogether'.

With malice toward none, with charity for all, with firmness in the right as God gives us to see the right, let us strive on to finish the work we are in, to bind up the nation's wounds, to care for him who shall have borne the battle and for his widow and his orphan, to do all which may achieve and cherish a just and a lasting peace among ourselves and with all nations.

RECONSTRUCTION

Thaddeus Stevens: Speech on Reconstruction, 18 December 1865

Stevens puts the case for radical, congressional Reconstruction.

A candid examination of the power and proper principles of reconstruction can be offensive to no one, and may possibly be profitable by exciting inquiry. One of the suggestions of the message which we are now considering has special reference to this. Perhaps it is the principle most interesting to the people at this time. The President assumes, what no one doubts, that the late rebel States have lost their constitutional relations to the Union, and are incapable of representation in Congress, except by permission of the Government. It matters but little, with this admission, whether you call them States out of the Union, and now conquered territories, or assert that, because the Constitution forbids them to do what they did do, that they are therefore only dead as to all national and political action, and will remain so until the Government shall breathe into them the breath of life anew and permit them to occupy their former position. In other words, that they are not out of the Union, but are only dead carcasses lying within the Union. In either case, it is very plain that it requires the action of Congress to enable them to form a State government and send representatives to Congress. Nobody, I believe, pretends that with their old constitutions and frames of government they can be permitted to claim their old rights under the Constitution. They have torn their constitutional States into atoms, and built on their foundations fabrics of a totally different character. Dead men cannot raise themselves. Dead States cannot restore their own existence 'as it was'. Whose especial duty is it to do it? In whom does the Constitution place the power? Not in the judicial branch of Government, for it only adjudicates and does not prescribe laws. Not in the Executive, for he only executes and cannot make laws. Not in the Commander-in-Chief of the armies, for he can only hold them under military rule until the sovereign legislative power of the conqueror shall give them law.

There is fortunately no difficulty in solving the question. There are two provisions in the Constitution, under one of which the case must fall. The fourth article says:

'New States may be admitted by the Congress into this Union.'

In my judgment this is the controlling provision in this case. Unless the law of nations is a dead letter, the late war between two acknowledged belligerents severed their original compacts, and broke all the ties that bound them together. The future condition of the conquered power depends on the will of the conqueror. They must come in as new States or remain as conquered provinces. Congress – the Senate and House of Representatives with the concurrence of the President – is the only power that can act in the matter. But suppose, as some dreaming theorists imagine, that these States have never been out of the Union, but have only destroyed their State governments so as to be incapable of political action; then the fourth section of the fourth article applies, which says:

'The United States shall guaranty to every State in this Union a republican form of government.'

Who is the United States? Not the judiciary; not the President; but the sovereign power of the people, exercised through their representatives in Congress, with the concurrence of the Executive. It means the political Government – the concurrent action of both branches of Congress and the Executive. The separate action of each amounts to nothing either in admitting new States or guarantying republican governments to lapsed or outlawed States. Whence springs the preposterous idea that either the President, or the Senate, or the House of Representatives, acting separately, can determine the right of States to send members or Senators to the Congress of the Union?

... It is obvious from all this that the first duty of Congress is to pass a law declaring the condition of these outside or defunct States, and providing proper civil governments for them. Since the conquest they have been governed by martial law. Military rule is necessarily despotic, and ought not to exist longer than is absolutely necessary. As there are no symptoms that the people of these provinces will be prepared to participate in constitutional government for some years, I know of no arrangement so proper for them as territorial governments. There they can learn the principles of freedom and eat the fruit of foul rebellion. Under such governments, while electing members to the Territorial Legislatures, they will necessarily mingle with those to whom Congress shall extend the right of suffrage. In Territories Congress fixes the qualifications of electors; and I know of no better place nor better occasion for the conquered rebels and the conqueror to practice justice to all men, and accustom themselves to make and to obey equal laws.

... But this is not all that we ought to do before these inveterate rebels are invited to participate in our legislation. We have turned, or are about to turn, loose four million slaves without a hut to shelter them or a cent in their pockets. The infernal laws of slavery have prevented them from acquiring an education, understanding the commonest laws of contract, or of managing the ordinary business of life. This Congress is bound to provide for them until they can take care of themselves. If we do not furnish them with homesteads, and hedge them around with protective laws; if we leave them to the legislation of their late masters, we had better have left them in bondage. Their condition would be worse than that of our prisoners at Andersonville. If we fail in this great duty now, when we have the power, we shall deserve and receive the execration of history and of all future ages.

... This Congress owes it to its own character to set the seal of reprobation upon a doctrine which is becoming too fashionable, and unless rebuked will be the recognized principle of our Government. Governor Perry and other provisional governors and orators proclaim that 'this is the white man's Government'. The whole copperhead party, pandering to the lowest prejudices of the ignorant, repeat the cuckoo cry, 'This is the white man's Government.' Demagogues of all parties, even some high in authority, gravely shout, 'This is the white man's Government.' What is implied by this? That one race of men are to have the exclusive right forever to rule this nation, and exercise all acts of sovereignty, while all other races and nations and colors are to be their subjects, and have no voice in making the laws and choosing the rulers by whom they are to be governed. Where does this differ from slavery except in degree? Does not this contradict all the distinctive principles of the Declaration of Independence? When the great and good men promulgated that instrument, and pledged their lives and sacred honors to defend it, it was supposed to form an epoch in civil government. Before that time it was held that the right to rule was vested in families, dynasties, or races, not because of superior intelligence or virtue, but because of a divine right to enjoy exclusive privileges.

Our fathers repudiated the whole doctrine of the legal superiority of families or races, and proclaimed the equality of men before the law. Upon that they created a revolution and built the Republic. They were prevented by slavery from perfecting the superstructure whose foundation they had thus broadly laid. For the sake of the Union they consented to wait, but never relinquished the idea of its final completion. The time to which they looked forward with anxiety has come. It is our duty to complete their work. If this Republic is not now made to stand on their great principles, it has no honest foundation, and the Father of all men will still shake it to its center. If we have not yet been sufficiently scourged for our national sin to teach us to do justice to all God's creatures, without distinction of race or color, we must expect the still more heavy vengeance of an offended Father, still increasing his inflictions as he increased the severity of the plagues of Egypt until the tyrant consented to do justice.

And when that tyrant repented of his reluctant consent, and attempted to reënslave the people, as our southern tyrants are attempting to do now, he filled the Red sea with broken chariots and drowned horses, and strewed the shores with dead carcasses.

Andrew Johnson: Second Annual Message to Congress, 3 December 1866

President Johnson puts the case for moderate, presidential Reconstruction.

All of the States in which the insurrection had existed promptly amended their constitutions so as to make them conform to the great change thus effected in the organic law of the land; declared null and void all ordinances and laws of secession; repudiated all pretended debts and obligations created for the revolutionary purposes of the insurrection, and proceeded in good faith to the enactment of measures for the protection and amelioration of the condition of the colored race. Congress, however, yet hesitated to admit any of these States to representation, and it was not until toward the close of the eighth month of the session that an exception was made in favor of Tennessee by the admission of her Senators and Representatives.

I deem it a subject of profound regret that Congress has thus far failed to admit to seats loyal Senators and Representatives from the other States whose inhabitants, with those of Tennessee, had engaged in the rebellion. Ten States – more than one-fourth of the whole number – remain without representation; the seats of fifty members in the House of Representatives and of twenty members in the Senate are yet vacant, not by their own consent, not by a failure of election, but by the refusal of Congress to accept their credentials. Their admission, it is believed, would have accomplished much toward the renewal and strengthening of our relations as one people and removed serious cause for discontent on the part of the inhabitants of those States. It would have accorded with the great principle enunciated in the Declaration of American Independence that no people ought to bear the burden of taxation and yet be denied the right of representation. It would have been in consonance with the express provisions of the

Constitution that 'each State have at least one Representative' and 'that no State, without its consent, shall be deprived of its equal suffrage in the Senate'. These provisions were intended to secure to every State and to the people of every State the right of representation in each House of Congress; and so important was it deemed by the framers of the Constitution that the equality of the States in the Senate should be preserved that not even by an amendment of the Constitution can any State, without its consent, be denied a voice in that branch of the National Legislature.

It is true it has been assumed that the existence of the States was terminated by the rebellious acts of their inhabitants, and that, the insurrection having been suppressed, they were thenceforward to be considered merely as conquered territories. The legislative, executive, and judicial departments of the Government have, however, with great distinctness and uniform consistency, refused to sanction an assumption so incompatible with the nature of our republican system and with the professed objects of the war. Throughout the recent legislation of Congress the undeniable fact makes itself apparent that these ten political communities are nothing less than States of this Union. At the very commencement of the rebellion each House declared, with a unanimity as remarkable as it was significant, that the war was not 'waged upon our part in any spirit of oppression, nor for any purpose of conquest or subjugation, nor purpose of overthrowing or interfering with the rights or established institutions of those States, but to defend and maintain the supremacy of the Constitution and all laws made in pursuance thereof, and to preserve the Union, with all the dignity, equality, and rights of the several States unimpaired; and that as soon as these objects' were 'accomplished the war ought to cease' ...

The action of the executive department of the Government upon this subject has been equally definite and uniform, and the purpose of the war was specifically stated in the proclamation issued by my predecessor on the 2nd day of September 1862. It was then solemnly proclaimed and declared 'that hereafter, as heretofore, the war will be prosecuted for the object of practically restoring the constitutional relation between the United States and each of the States and the people thereof in which States that relation is or may be suspended or disturbed'.

The recognition of the States by the judicial department of the Government has also been clear and conclusive in all proceedings affecting them as States had in the Supreme, circuit, and district courts.

In the admission of Senators and Representatives from any and all of the States there can be no just ground of apprehension that persons who are disloyal will be clothed with the powers of legislation, for this could not happen when the Constitution and the laws are enforced by a vigilant and faithful Congress. Each House is made the 'judge of the elections, returns, and qualifications of its own members', and may, 'with the concurrence of two-thirds, expel a member' ...

The Constitution of the United States makes it the duty of the President to recommend to the consideration of Congress 'such measures as he shall judge necessary and expedient'. I know of no measure more imperatively demanded by every consideration of national interest, sound policy, and equal justice than the admission of loyal members from the now unrepresented States. This would consummate the work of restoration and exert a most salutary influence in the re-establishment of peace, harmony, and fraternal feeling. It would tend greatly to renew the confidence of the American people in the vigor and stability of their institutions. It would bind us more closely together as a nation and enable us to show to the world the inherent and recuperative power of a government founded upon the will of the people and established upon the principles of liberty, justice, and intelligence ...

In our efforts to preserve 'the unity of government which constitutes us one people' by restoring the States to the condition which they held prior to the rebellion, we should be cautious, lest, having rescued our nation from perils of threatened disintegration, we resort to consolidation, and in the end absolute despotism, as a remedy for the recurrence of similar troubles. The war having terminated, and with it all occasion for the exercise of powers of doubtful constitutionality, we should hasten to bring legislation within the boundaries prescribed by the Constitution and to return to the ancient landmarks established by our fathers for the guidance of succeeding generations.

Frederick Douglass: Speech to Republican National Convention, 1876

In Cincinnati, Ohio, Douglass urges the continued struggle for racial justice.

Mr. Chairman and Gentlemen of the National Convention: Allow me to express my deep, my heartfelt gratitude to you for the warm, cordial invitation you have extended to me to make my appearance on this platform at this time. The work to which you have called me is somewhat new; it is the first time in my life that I have ever had the pleasure of looking the Republican Party squarely in the face, and I must say, and I hope you will acquit me of everything like a disposition to flatter, that you are pretty good looking men. But I will not detain you here by any attempt at a speech. You have had speeches, eloquent speeches, glorious speeches, wise speeches, patriotic speeches, speeches in respect of the importance of managing correctly your currency, speeches in defense of purity of administration, and speeches in respect of the great principles for which you struggled, and for which the race to which I belong struggled on the battlefield and poured out their blood.

The thing, however, in which I feel the deepest interest, and the thing in which I believe this country feels the deepest interest, is that the principles involved in the contest which carried your sons and brothers to the battlefield, which draped our Northern churches with the weeds of mourning and filled our towns and our cities with mere stumps of men, armless, legless, maimed, and mutilated – the thing for which you poured out your blood and piled a debt for after-coming generations higher than a mountain of gold to weigh down the necks of your children and your children's children – I say those principles involved in that tremendous contest are to be dearer to the American people in the great political struggle now upon them than any other principles we have.

LITERATURE

Ralph Waldo Emerson: Concord Hymn

CONCORD HYMN
SUNG AT THE COMPLETION OF THE BATTLE
MONUMENT, JULY 4, 1837

By the rude bridge that arched the flood,
   Their flag to April's breeze unfurled,
Here once the embattled farmers stood
   And fired the shot heard round the world.

The foe long since in silence slept;
   Alike the conqueror silent sleeps;
And Time the ruined bridge has swept
   Down the dark stream which seaward creeps.

On this green bank, by this soft stream,
   We set today a votive stone;
That memory may their deed redeem,
   When, like our sires, our sons are gone.

Spirit, that made those heroes dare
   To die, and leave their children free,
Bid Time and Nature gently spare
   The shaft we raise to them and thee.

Herman Melville: Shiloh: A Requiem

SHILOH
A REQUIEM (APRIL 1862)

Skimming lightly, wheeling still,
   The swallows fly low
Over the field in clouded days,
   The forest-field of Shiloh –
Over the field where April rain
Solaced the parched ones stretched in pain

Through the pause of night
That followed the Sunday fight
   Around the church of Shiloh –
The church so lone, the log-built one,
That echoed to many a parting groan
   And natural prayer
   Of dying foemen mingled there –
Foeman at morn, but friends at eve –
   Fame or country least their care:
(What like a bullet can undeceive!)
   But now they lie low,
While over them the swallows skim,
   And all is hushed at Shiloh.

Walt Whitman: O Captain! my Captain!

This poem was dedicated to the martyred President Lincoln.

O Captain! my Captain! our fearful trip is done,
The ship has weathered every rack, the prize we sought is won,
The port is near, the bells I hear, the people all exulting,
While follow eyes the steady keel, the vessel grim and daring;
   But O heart! heart! heart!
     O the bleeding drops of red,
       Where on the deck my Captain lies,
       Fallen cold and dead.

O Captain! my Captain! rise up and hear the bells;
Rise up – for you the flag is flung – for you the bugle trills,
For you bouquets and ribbon'd wreaths – for you the shores a-crowding,
For you they call, the swaying mass, their eager faces turning;
   Here Captain! dear father!
     The arm beneath your head!
       It is some dream that on the deck,
       You've fallen cold and dead.

My Captain does not answer, his lips are pale and still,
My father does not feel my arm, he has no pulse nor will,
The ship is anchor'd safe and sound, its voyage closed and done,
From fearful trip the victor ship comes in with object won;
   Exult O shores, and ring O bells!
     But I with mournful tread,
       Walk the deck my Captain lies,
       Fallen cold and dead.

Emily Dickinson: Much Madness is Divinest Sense

Much Madness is divinest Sense –
To a discerning Eye –
Much Sense – the starkest Madness –
'Tis the Majority
In this, as All, prevail –
Assent – and you are sane –
Demur – you're straightway dangerous –
And handled with a Chain –

Emily Dickinson: Success is Counted Sweetest

Success is counted sweetest
By those who ne'er succeed.
To comprehend a nectar
Requires sorest need.

Not one of all the purple Host
Who took the Flag today
Can tell the definition
So clear of Victory

As he defeated – dying –
On whose forbidden ear
The distant strains of triumph
Burst agonized and clear!

Emily Dickinson: Ample Make this Bed

Ample make this Bed –
Make this Bed with Awe –
In it wait till judgement break
Excellent and Fair.

Be it's Mattress straight –
Be it's Pillow round –
Let no sunrise' yellow noise
Interrupt this Ground –

Emily Dickinson: Safe in their
Alabaster Chambers (1861 version)

Safe in their Alabaster Chambers –
Untouched by Morning –

And untouched by Noon –
Lie the meek members of the Resurrection –
Rafter of Satin – and Roof of Stone!

Grand go the Years – in the Crescent – above them –
Worlds scoop their Arcs –
And Firmaments – row –
Diadems – drop – and Doges – surrender –
Soundless as dots – on a Disc of Snow –

Julia Ward Howe:
The Battle Hymn of the Republic

Mine eyes have seen the glory of the coming of the Lord
He is trampling out the vintage where the grapes of wrath are stored
He has loosed the fateful lightning of His terrible swift sword
His truth is marching on.

Glory, Glory, Hallelujah!
Glory, Glory, Hallelujah!
Glory, Glory, Hallelujah!
His truth is marching on.

I have seen Him in the watch-fires of a hundred circling camps
They have builded Him an altar in the evening dews and damps
I can read His righteous sentence by the dim and flaring lamps
His day is marching on.

I have read a fiery gospel writ in burnish'd rows of steel
'As ye deal with my contemners, So with you my grace shall deal.'
Let the Hero, born of woman, crush the serpent with His heel
Since God is marching on.

He has sounded forth the trumpet that shall never call retreat
He is sifting out the hearts of men before His judgment-seat,
Oh, be swift my soul, to answer Him! Be jubilant, my feet!
Our God is marching on.

In the beauty of the lilies Christ was born across the sea,
With a glory in His bosom that transfigures you and me:
As He died to make men holy, let us die to make men free,
While God is marching on.

Spiritual: Nobody Knows the Trouble I Seen

Nobody knows the trouble I seen
Nobody knows but Jesus
Nobody knows the trouble I seen
Glory Hallelujah!

Sometimes I'm up, sometimes I'm down,
Oh, yes, Lord.
Sometimes I'm almost to the ground,
Oh, yes, Lord.

Nobody knows the trouble I seen
Nobody knows my sorrow,
Nobody knows the trouble I seen
Glory Hallelujah!

Nobody knows the trouble I seen
Nobody knows but Jesus,
Nobody knows the trouble I seen
Glory Hallelujah!

I never shall forget that day
Oh, yes, Lord,
When Jesus washed my sins away,
Oh, yes, Lord.

Nobody knows the trouble I seen
Nobody knows but Jesus
Nobody knows the trouble I seen
Glory Hallelujah!

PART III
BIOGRAPHIES, GLOSSARY
AND REFERENCES

BIOGRAPHIES

A

CHARLES FRANCIS ADAMS (1807–86) (Massachusetts), politician and diplomat Son of President **John Quincy Adams** and grandson of President John Adams. A 'conscience' **Whig**, he stood as vice president of the **Free Soil Party** with **Van Buren** as presidential candidate, 1848. From 1860 to 1868 US ambassador to Great Britain, where he played crucial and complex role in keeping Britain neutral during American Civil War. This required delicate defusing of the **Trent Incident**, countering pro-Southern sympathies among some members of the cabinet, and culminated in the crisis of the Laird Rams warships constructed in Liverpool to serve the **Confederacy** in breaking the Union blockade. In September 1863 rams were near completion. On 5 September Adams informed cabinet that if they were released 'it would be superfluous in me to point out … that this is war'. Three days later delivery of the rams was halted. In 1870–71 helped effect Anglo-American conciliation by sitting on Arbitration Tribunal at Geneva, which settled **Alabama Claims**. In 1872 he was **Greeley**'s running mate as **Liberal Republican** candidate opposed to **Grant**'s corrupt administration and mishandling of **Reconstruction**.

JOHN QUINCY ADAMS (1767–1848) (Massachusetts), 6th President of the United States Son of John and Abigail Adams. At 14 served as Secretary to US mission in Russia, then held other diplomatic posts in England,

Holland and Prussia. In 1814 negotiated treaty of Ghent, which concluded the Anglo-American war of 1812. He was President Monroe's Secretary of State and prime author of the 1823 Monroe Doctrine, unilateral declaration against further European intervention in western hemisphere. In the disputed election of 1824 was accused of 'corrupt bargain' with **Clay** (whom he made Secretary of State), which gave him presidency and deprived **Jackson** of the post despite his popular majority. As a **Whig** he pursued policies on internal, federal improvement. Lost presidential election of 1828 to Jackson. Elected to House of Representatives from Plymouth district of Massachusetts in 1830. Increasingly **Free Soil** and anti-slavery. In 1841 successfully argued for freeing of African American mutineers of slave ship *Amistad*. Opposed annexation of Texas and **Mexican War**. In 1836–44 fought heroic battle in House against '**gag rule**'. 'Old Man Eloquence' died on the floor of the House.

AMOS BRONSON ALCOTT (1799–1888) (Connecticut), utopian reformer From 1834 to 1839, he was an unorthodox teacher in Boston. School had to close because parents disapproved of mixed-race classes. In 1840 to Concord, mixing in **Emerson**'s circle and contributing 'Orphic Sayings' to **Transcendentalist** journal, *The Dial*. Trip to England, 1842. Met Carlyle, who commented that Alcott was 'all bent on saving the world by a return to acorns and the golden age'. In 1844 made brief utopian experiment in communal living at Fruitlands in Cambridge, Massachusetts. **Garrisonian** abolitionist and vegetarian. Rescued from insolvency by publication of his daughter's – Louisa May Alcott – hugely popular *Little Women* (1868).

SUSAN BROWNELL ANTHONY (1820–1906) (Massachusetts), feminist and reformer Advocate of temperance, abolitionism and franchise for all freedpersons – female as well as male. In 1869 she was Chairperson of Executive Committee of National Women's Suffrage Association with **Elizabeth Cady Stanton**. Close lifetime collaboration between these two. In 1872 she defied the Constitution by voting in Rochester, New York State. Arrested, tried and fined, but refused to pay. Her motto: 'The true republic – man, their rights and nothing more; women – their rights and nothing less.' Women did not achieve the vote until the 19th Amendment, ratified 1920.

B

GEORGE BANCROFT (1800–1891) (Massachusetts), historian and diplomat Studied in Germany and attended Hegel's Berlin lectures. Met Goethe and Byron. In 1834 embarked on ten-volume *History of the United States*, completed in 1874, espousing **Manifest Destiny** and the inexorable advance of the American empire. From 1846 to 1849, ambassador to Britain. In 1867 appointed minister to Prussia by President **Johnson**.

CLARA BARTON (1821–1912) (Massachusetts), female reformer Grew up a shy tomboy. Spent two years nursing invalid brother following serious accident. In 1861 worked in Patent Office in Washington. Procured medical supplies following battle of **First Bull Run**. With support from Senator **Henry Wilson** of Massachusetts, granted pass to travel with army ambulances 'for the purpose

of distributing comfort for the sick and wounded, and nursing them'. Three years following army in Virginia and South Carolina, working in Fredericksburg hospital and on ground succouring Union and Confederate wounded as 'the angel of the battlefield'. After war worked to locate names of men missing in action, including 13,000 who died in **Andersonville Prison**. Trip to Europe, 1870. Observed Franco-Prussian War and work of International Red Cross founded in 1864. On return, joined American branch of Red Cross 1881, remaining as head until 1904.

PIERRE BEAUREGARD (1818–93) (Louisiana), Confederate soldier In 1838 graduated from West Point. Appointed superintendent there when war intervened. Ordered firing on **Fort Sumter**. Second in command to **Joseph Johnston** at battle of **First Bull Run**. Spring 1862 second in command to Albert Johnston in Tennessee whom he succeeded when Johnston was mortally wounded at **Shiloh**. Arrival of Buell's Union army forced him to retreat to, and finally evacuate, Corinth, Mississippi, 30 May 1862. Sickness, and President **Davis**, relieved him of his command. After recovery served again under Joseph Johnston. Defeated **Ben Butler** at Drewry's Bluff and held the fort until **Lee** arrived to protect Richmond and Petersburg. Urged execution of all Union prisoners – African Americans and whites – following **Emancipation Proclamation**.

JUDAH BENJAMIN (1811–84) (British West Indies), Confederate politician British subject but went to US in 1813. In 1832 called to New Orleans bar. In 1852 elected Senator from Louisiana. Strong advocate of **secession** and resigned from Senate in 1861. First Confederate Attorney General, then Secretary of War (1861–62) and finally Secretary of State 1862–65. In 1864 urged emancipation of slaves in return for European diplomatic recognition. In last days of war advocated freeing and arming of slaves to fight Confederate cause. Escape from Richmond to England, where he became highly successful QC.

BRAXTON BRAGG (1817–76) (N. Carolina), Confederate soldier   In 1837 graduated from West Point. Participated in Seminole and **Mexican Wars**. In 1861, following **Shiloh**, took command of army of Tennessee from **Beauregard**. A favourite of President **Davis**, but testy and quarrelsome and very unpopular with subordinates. On 8 October 1862 engaged Buell at Perryville. Indecisive outcome, but withdrew, failing to get Kentucky to join Confederacy. September 1863 victory at **Chickamauga**, but decisively defeated by **Grant** at **Chattanooga**, November 1863. Relieved of command, but continued as military adviser to Davis, and escaped with him from Richmond before capture, 9 May 1865.

JOHN BRECKINRIDGE (1821–75) (Kentucky), politician   From great Kentucky political dynasty. In 1856 **Buchanan**'s vice-presidential running mate. In **Democratic Party** split of 1860 was nominated to run for Southern pro-slavery wing against **Douglas**. Won 72 **Electoral College** votes, but lost Kentucky and defeated by **Lincoln**. Worked at first to maintain Union but when this failed tried to keep Kentucky in Confederacy – but again failed. Resigned as presiding officer of Senate and fled to avoid arrest. Declared traitor 2 December 1861. Patchy war record serving under Albert Johnston in West and Jubal Early in Shenandoah Valley. On 4 September 1865 appointed President **Davis**'s sixth and last Secretary of War. In 1865 fled to Cuba, then Britain. In 1869 allowed to return to Kentucky.

ALBERT BRISBANE (1809–90) (New York), utopian reformer   From 1827 to 1834 in Europe, where he fell under influence of French visionary, Charles Fourier, dedicated to 'the dignifying and rendering attractive the manual labours of mankind' and 'a just and wise organisation of human society'. In 1840 published *Social Destiny of Man,* urging community and cooperation instead of *laissez-faire* competition, 'phalanxes' consisting of optimal 1,600 members (800 males matching 800 females), self-support, varying tasks and distribution of surpluses equally among labour, talent and capital. Reached wider audience through **Greeley** and *New York Tribune*. Thirty phalanxes at high tide of popularity during period of economic downturn as alternative to wage and slave labour. But endemic impracticality and economic upturn led to collapse of experiment.

JOHN BROWN (1800–1859) (Connecticut), abolitionist   Erratic early career, a restless drifter and failed businessman. Had 20 children and sued business associates 21 times. A dedicated abolitionist and genuine believer in racial equality, he joined an African American community at North Elba, New York State, established by Gerrit Smith, and worked as agent for **Underground Railroad**. Carrying out guerrilla war in **Bleeding Kansas**, he and his sons hacked five suspected pro-slavery settlers to death at Pottawatomie Creek, 24 May 1856. On 16 October 1859, with five African Americans and 17 whites (including three of his own sons), he occupied the federal arsenal at Harpers Ferry, Virginia, intending to trigger a slave insurrection. Raid was a complete fiasco. Slaves received no news of the raid and Brown was quickly arrested. Accused of treason, Brown refused to plead insanity and, on day of execution, 2 December 1859, declared 'I, John Brown, am now quite certain that the crimes of this guilty land will never be purged away but with blood.' Consequences of the raid were immense, crystallising Southern fears of abolitionists inciting slaves to revolt, but transformed Brown into a holy martyr in North which, in turn, served to reinforce Southern fear and hatred of the North. But not all Northerners supported raid. **Emerson** on 'the new saint who will make the gallows glorious like the cross' was answered by **Lincoln**: 'It was so absurd that the slaves, with all their ignorance, saw plainly enough it could not succeed.' But Union soldiers marched throughout the war to the words of *John Brown's Body*.

JAMES BUCHANAN (1791–1868) (Pennsylvania), 15th President of the United States **Democratic Party** politician. From 1844 to 1849 **Polk**'s Secretary of State engaged in negotiations over Oregon question, annexation of Texas and **Mexican War**. From 1853 to 1856 President **Pierce**'s ambassador to Britain avoiding political involvement in **Kansas–Nebraska Act** imbroglio. His pro-Southern stand on expansionism, opposition to the **Wilmot Proviso**, the inviolable rights of slaveowners and advocacy of the acquisition of Cuba (**Ostend Manifesto**, 1854) made him available candidate in 1856 when he carried every slave state except Maryland, but only five Northern out of 16, where he was outpolled by **Frémont** (**Republican**) and **Fillmore** (**American party**). Four in his cabinet were Southerners. Once in office he proved vacillating and irresolute when faced with the growing sectional crisis and unable to halt drift to war. Hoped **1850 Compromise** would remain final, but acceptance of the Lecompton Constitution and his pressure on the Supreme Court to settle the slave question in **Dred Scott** backfired disastrously. Stated in his annual message, 3 December 1860, that states had no constitutional right to secede, but that federal government had no power to prevent it. Also indecisive as to what to do about **Fort Sumter**. In 1866 published *Mr Buchanan's Administration on the Eve of the Rebellion*, which attempted to justify his presidency, and lay blame principally on Northern politicians and abolitionist fanatics for exacerbating slave question – an institution which he believed was dying out anyway.

ANTHONY BURNS (1834–62) (Virginia), African American abolitionist A slave who learned to read and write. Moved to

Richmond, 'but soon after I began to learn that there is a Christ who came to make us free; I began to hear about a North, and to feel the necessity for freedom of soul and body'. Took ship to Boston; arrived March 1854. Arrested under tightened Fugitive Slave law, 24 May, and held in federal court house while master, Charles Suttle, arrived to claim property. Abolitionist feeling running high. Two groups – mainly white meeting at Fauneil Hall and African Americans in basement of Tremont Temple – combined to march on prison. **Thomas Wentworth Higginson** and others charged building with battering ram, but beaten back by federal marshals. One marshal killed and 13 arrested. President Pierce reinforced prison, sent 2,000 troops to maintain order and provisioned ship to return Burns to Virginia. Convicted 2 June. Total of 50,000 Bostonians witnessed his departure in chains. Black church purchased his freedom 27 February 1855. Studied at Oberlin for ministry. Moved to Canada and church on shores of Lake Ontario. Died aged 28.

BENJAMIN BUTLER (1818–93) (New Hampshire), soldier and politician In 1853 entered politics as **Democrat**. Political appointment to army. On 13 May 1861 occupied Baltimore and placed in command of Fort Monroe, where he declared escaped slaves as 'contraband of war' and put them to work. As commander of New Orleans, executed citizen for lowering Union flag and, in infamous Order No. 28, 15 May 1862, ordered that any female insulting Union soldiers 'shall be regarded and held liable to be treated as a woman of the town plying her avocation'. Hence nickname 'Beast' Butler. Recalled December 1862. An incompetent soldier though highest-ranking officer in Eastern theatre after **Grant**. **Radical Republican** during **Reconstruction** and fought strenuously for impeachment of President **Johnson**. Ended political career as advocate of populism and 'greenbacks'.

C

JOHN CALHOUN (1782–1850) (S. Carolina), politician and political theorist Began political career as nationalist. From 1811 to 1817 House of Representatives. From 1817 to 1825 Monroe's Secretary of War, and vice president under **John Quincy Adams** and **Jackson**'s first administration. Growing struggle between Calhoun and President Jackson over 'tariff of abominations' 1828. On 28 December 1832 resigned from Jackson's cabinet and entered Senate to fight tariff, and Jackson's coercion of South Carolina. Matter resolved by **Clay**'s compromise, but Calhoun's theoretical writings thereafter, to maintain power of South and slavery in increasingly alien American environment. Argued for right of state interposition and nullification of federal laws 'in case of a deliberate, palpable and dangerous exercise of power not delegated'; a 'concurrent majority' whereby each section had veto power over legislation passed by a majority; a dual executive reflecting the interests of North and South; and the ultimate right of **secession** to protect **slavery** which was 'a positive good … the most safe and stable basis for free institutions in the world'. Opposed **Wilmot Proviso**, distribution of abolitionist literature in South, and supported **gag rule** in Congress. Died during Congressional debates on **Compromise of 1850**, which he opposed.

LEWIS CASS (1782–1866) (New Hampshire), politician Served in 1812 War. From 1813 to 1831 governor of territory of Michigan. From 1831 to 1836 Secretary of War under **Jackson**. Favoured annexation of Texas and **Mexican War** but opposed **Wilmot Proviso**. Lost **Democratic** nomination to **Polk** in 1844 and to **Pierce** in 1852. As Democratic candidate in 1848 lost to **Zachary Taylor**

(**Whig**). December 1847, in Nicholson Letter, alighted upon '**popular sovereignty**' to avoid further sectional conflict: 'Leave to the people who will be affected by this question to adjust it upon their own responsibility and in their own manner.' From 1857 to 1860 **Buchanan**'s Secretary of State but resigned, 12 December 1860, over President's failure to reinforce **Fort Sumter**.

SALMON P. CHASE (1808–73) (New Hampshire), politician and jurist Settled in Cincinnati in 1829 as lawyer and involved in antislavery politics in Ohio. Supported James Birney's **Liberty Party** and **Van Buren**'s candidacy for **Free Soil Party** in 1848. Crucial role, along with Joshua Giddings, in establishing **Republican Party** in Ohio and opposing **1850 Compromise**. 1849–55 Senate. 1855 Republican Governor of Ohio. 1861–64, **Lincoln**'s Secretary of the Treasury. Deeply ambitious and very fractious in ongoing struggle with **Seward** in cabinet. As Secretary his responsibility was to finance the North's massive war effort. On 25 February 1863 instituted **National Banking Act** (a uniform national banking system with paper money – 'greenbacks' – as legal tender), domestic taxes including federal income tax, and the issuing of war bonds by public subscription. Resigned from cabinet June 1864. From 1864 to 1873 Chief Justice of the Supreme Court. In *Ex parte Milligan* held that military trials for civilians unconstitutional except where invasion or war made civil courts impracticable.

MARY BOYKIN CHESNUT (1823–86) (S. Carolina), writer Born into Southern aristocracy. Father first Governor then Senator for North Carolina. Husband – married in 1840 – became Senator for South Carolina 1858 and then they resided in Washington. Close friends of Jefferson and Varina **Davis**, and husband served as Aide to President through most of the war in Richmond. Kept a diary during war which she wrote up between 1881 and 1884 and first published in 1905 as

A Diary from Dixie, a graphic description of Southern life in the ante-bellum, Civil War and **Reconstruction** period. Lively and well educated, she resented the subordination of women – 'There is no slave, after all, like a wife' – and expressed doubts about the 'peculiar institution': 'I wonder if it is a sin to think slavery a curse to any land.'

LYDIA MARIA CHILD (1802–80) (Massachusetts), reformer From **abolitionist** family, began as schoolteacher. In 1828 married David Lee Child, Boston lawyer. Dedicated to abolitionism and cause of racial equality. First novel, *Hobomok* (1824), wrote of interracial marriage and an ancient black civilisation derived from Homer and 'the blameless Ethiopian'. In *Appeal for that Class of Americans Called Africans* (1833), advocated education of African Americans and, 1840–44, edited highly influential *Weekly National Antislavery Standard* with husband. *The Freedmen's Book* included positive biographies of Toussaint L'Ouverture and **Frederick Douglass** and she edited Harriet Jacobs's *Incidents in the Life of a Slave Girl* (1861) for publication. Edited first monthly magazine for children, opposed capital punishment and the expulsion of the Cherokee Indians from Georgia in 1830s, and condemned urban poverty. In *The Progress of Religious Ideas* argued for an ecumenical and undogmatic religion.

HENRY CLAY (1777–1852) (Virginia) politician Westerner and Unionist. In 1797 went to Lexington, Kentucky. Slaveowner. In 1810 entered House of Representatives, of which he became Speaker, and leading advocate of compromise between North and South over **Missouri** (1820) tariffs (1833) and issue of slavery's extension (Great **Compromise of 1850**). Hoped to encourage economic unity by '**American System**' which combined national Bank of the United States, tariffs, and federal funding of internal improvement. Politically tarnished by 'corrupt bargain' when **John Quincy Adams** appointed

him Secretary of State in 1824. Became **Whig** focus of anti-Jacksonian forces. Four failed attempts to gain presidency against **Jackson** (1832), **Harrison** (1840), **Polk** (1844) – when he equivocated over the question of the annexation of Texas – and **Taylor** in 1848. 'If anyone desires to know the leading and paramount object of my public life, the preservation of the union will furnish him the key.'

JOHN CRITTENDEN (1787–1863) (Kentucky), politician **Whig** and fervent unionist from border state. 'The dissolution of the Union can never be regarded – ought never to be regarded – as a remedy, but as a consummation of the greatest evil that can befall us.' In 1841 Attorney General to President **Harrison** and, in 1849, to **Fillmore**. In 1848 Governor of Kentucky. In 1860 supported Bell's **Unionist** party and helped stop Kentucky from seceding. Introduced **Crittenden Amendment**, 18 December 1860, to hold Union together by reimposing **Missouri Compromise** and extending dividing line of 36°30′ between free and slave territory to Pacific. Rejected by **Lincoln** and **Republican** party. Opposed **Emancipation Proclamation** and enlistment of African Americans into Union army.

D

JEFFERSON DAVIS (1808–89) (Kentucky), Confederate president Moved in childhood to plantation in Mississippi. Married daughter of **Zachary Taylor**, but she died three months later. Spent a number of isolated years on plantation. In 1845 married Varina Howell. Won brilliant military reputation at Buena Vista during **Mexican War**, 1846. In 1853 President **Pierce** appointed him Secretary of War, and Davis urged **Gadsden**

Purchase, 1854, as Southern route for transcontinental railroad. Senator for Mississippi 1847–51 and 1857–61. A reluctant secessionist, and would have preferred to be Commander in Chief, but unanimously elected President of the new Confederation, 9 February 1861, and delivered his Inaugural Address at Montgomery, Alabama, 18 February 1861. Reputation declined as Confederate's military strategy faltered: enmities and animosities grew both within cabinet and between the States and the Confederate government. Rancorous conflicts developed between Davis and General **Joseph Johnston**, for example, while President accused of favouritism towards incompetent generals such as **Braxton Bragg**, and dogmatic armchair strategy far from the field of battle. Poor at handling subordinates and plagued throughout war by debilitating psychosomatic illnesses. Davis fled Richmond but captured 10 May 1865, and imprisoned for two years in Fort Monroe. In 1881 published two-volume *apologia*, *The Rise and the Fall of the Confederate Government*, but never regained citizenship. Argued that **slavery** both necessary and benign, but war fought fundamentally for **states' rights**. 'To preserve a sectional equilibrium and maintain the equality of the States was the effort of one side, to acquire empire was a manifest purpose on the other.' A vast historiographical debate surrounds Davis's presidential performance. One contemporary, **Grant**, wrote that 'on several occasions he came to the relief of the Union army by means of his superior military genius'. Current historians tend to be more favourable, arguing that joint offensive/defensive strategy of Davis and **Lee** was an excellent combination which, however, faced insuperable long-term odds.

EMILY DICKINSON (1830–86) (Massachusetts), poet   Virtually unknown in her lifetime and now considered perhaps the outstanding American poet of the nineteenth century. From 1847 to 1848 at Mount Holyoke Female Seminary, but only few and brief excursions from her Amherst home thereafter, and later became a virtual recluse. Nearly 2,000 poems – brief, intense, elliptical – written: 'My letter to the world/That never wrote to me', though only a few published, heavily rewritten, during her lifetime. Loss of family, friends and neighbours in the Civil War captured in many poignant letters and verses. Described herself to **T.W. Higginson** as 'small, like the wren; and my hair is gold like the chestnut burr; and my eyes like the sherry in the glass that the guest leaves'.

DOROTHEA DIX (1802–87) (Maine), reformer Unhappy childhood. Moved to live with grandmother in Boston. In 1841, taught Sunday School Class in East Cambridge House of Correction and horrified by treatment of inmates: mentally disturbed, of both sexes, mingled with criminals, often unclothed and in the dark; unheated rooms without sanitary facilities, chained and frequently flogged. Travelled for two years to collect evidence for Report to Massachusetts legislature in 1843, arguing for compassionate warders and state taxes to improve material conditions in asylums. Helped to establish 32 new asylums in 15 separate states. Superintendent of nurses during civil war. 'I have no particular love for my species, but own to an exhaustless fund of compassion.'

STEPHEN DOUGLAS (1813–61) (Vermont), politician   In 1833 moved West to Jacksonville, Illinois, as lawyer. Jacksonian Democrat. Railroad interest and substantial real estate in Chicago. 'The Little Giant's' (he was only 5 feet tall) aim was to keep Northern and Southern wings of the **Democratic** party together. In 1850 played vital role in **Great Compromise**. In 1854 urged '**popular sovereignty**' in **Kansas–Nebraska** bill, whereby voters themselves could choose between becoming free or slave states. Northern opposition to this was vital catalyst in establishing

Republican party. In 1856 supported **Buchanan** for president, but split Democratic party by rejecting Kansas's fraudulent Lecompton Constitution which Buchanan supported. In 1858 **Lincoln–Douglas Debates** in Illinois for Senate brought unknown Lincoln to national prominence where he exposed Douglas's moral indifference to slavery. At 1860 Democratic Convention at Charleston, Douglas failed to gain two-thirds majority vote as presidential candidate. Southern wing defected and elected **Breckinridge** at Baltimore. Elected official, mainstream Democratic candidate. In 1860 election Lincoln polled 1.8 million popular votes against 1.4 million for Douglas. Loyal supporter of Lincoln with outbreak of war.

FREDERICK DOUGLASS (1817?–95) (Maryland), abolitionist and reformer   Born into slavery of white father and black slave mother. Taught to read and write. Various attempts at escape finally successful in 1838. From 1845 to 1847 in Britain on behalf of abolitionist cause. Freedom bought on his return to US and launched *North Star* – African American abolitionist paper – which continued for 17 years. In 1848 a delegate at **Seneca Falls Convention**. **Republican Party** attacked for not being abolitionist: 'The cry of the free man was raised, not for the extension of liberty to the black man, but for the protection for the liberty of the white.' Supported **John Brown**'s raid on Harper's Ferry, and urged racial equality and black franchise. Pressed for emancipation and recruitment of African Americans into Union army with outbreak of war. 'Fire must be met by water … War for the destruction of liberty must be met with war for the destruction of slavery', and two sons served in 54th and 55th Massachusetts regiments. March 1865 attended **Lincoln**'s second inaugural reception. In 1884 second marriage to white woman, Helen Pitts. From 1889 to 1891 Minister to Haiti. Wrote three autobiographies, including *Narrative of the Life of Frederick Douglass: An American Slave* (1845).

E

RALPH WALDO EMERSON (1803–82) (Massachusetts), writer 'The Sage of Concord' and eminent **Transcendentalist**. In 1826 preacher in Boston, but growing doubts about strict Unitarianism led him to resign 1832. In that year to Europe, where he met Wordsworth and Coleridge and initiated lifelong friendship with Carlyle. Influence of German Idealism. In 1834 settled in Concord. Freelance writing and lecturing. First meeting of the Transcendental Club, 1836, and, 1840–44, edited *Dial* with **Margaret Fuller**. In 1837, Harvard Address, 'The American Scholar', declared cultural independence from Europe. 'A man contains all that is needful to his government within himself … The highest revelation is that God is in every man.' Growing involvement in anti-slavery cause: opposition to **Fugitive Slave Laws** and eulogy to martyred **John Brown**. 'I think we must get rid of slavery or we must get rid of freedom.'

F

DAVID GLASGOW FARRAGUT (1801–70) (Tennessee), naval commander   In 1801 family moved to New Orleans and David, aged nine, entered navy as midshipman. December 1861 appointed Commander of Western Gulf Blockading Squadron and New Orleans captured 24 April 1862. Assisted **Grant** at siege of **Vicksburg**. Destroyed Confederate ironclad *Tennessee*, but lost his own *Tecumseh*, which was torpedoed during assault on Mobile, 5 August 1864. Mobile finally occupied April 1865. In 1866 created Admiral, first in history of US navy.

WILLIAM PITT FESSENDEN (1806–69) (New Hampshire), politician In 1827 admitted to bar. Helped organise new **Republican Party**. In 1854 elected Senator for Maine. July 1861 Chairman of Senate Finance Committee. Supported Secretary of Treasury **Chase** in urging income tax and sale of war bonds to finance war, but opposed to inflationary 'greenbacks' as legal tender. In June 1864 replaced Chase as Secretary of Treasury. In December 1865, Chairman of important Joint Committee on Reconstruction. Stressed Congressional over Presidential Reconstruction. Disliked President **Johnson** but moderate and voted against his impeachment.

MILLARD FILLMORE (1800–74) (New York), 13th President of the United States Possibly the obscurest of all American presidents. In 1823 admitted to bar. From 1833 to 1843 anti-Jacksonian **Whig** in Congress. In 1848 appointed vice president to **Taylor** in Whig convention at Buffalo. Assumed presidency on Taylor's death, 9 July 1850. Supported Great **Compromise of 1850**. In 1851 halted filibuster for invasion of Cuba. In 1856 nominated as presidential candidate for **American ('Know-Nothing') Party**, gaining 21 per cent of popular vote.

CHARLES GRANDISON FINNEY (1792–1875) (Connecticut), evangelical and abolitionist In 1821 experienced violent religious conversion. Ordination in 1824. The year 1825 marked beginning of seven-year revivalist agitation and Second Great Awakening in upstate New York, preaching the necessity of sanctification and the possibility of perfectionism. From 1835 to 1837, preacher in Broadway Tabernacle. In 1835 Professor of Theology at strongly abolitionist Oberlin College, Ohio, and its President, 1851–66. Stressed evils of slavery and insisted upon immediate emancipation.

HAMILTON FISH (1808–93) (New York) politician From 1849 to 1851 Governor of New York. Senate from 1851 to 1857. Supervised treatment of prisoners of war and exchanges during Civil War. From 1869 to 1877 President **Grant**'s Secretary of State. Settled **Alabama Claims** in 1871 in Treaty of Washington and curbed Grant's expansionism in Cuba and Dominican Republic.

GEORGE FITZHUGH (1806–81) (Virginia), writer Pro-slavery advocate. In 1856 travelled north and met abolitionists, Gerrit Smith and **Harriet Beecher Stowe**. Wrote *Sociology for the South or The Failure of Free Society* (1854) and *Cannibals All! Or Slaves Without Masters* (1857). Borrowed from **Marx** to expose ruthless capitalist exploitation of Northern wage labour in contrast to benign, hierarchic communitarianism of South; hence **Richard Hofstadter**'s reference to him as 'the Marx of the Master Class'. 'Capitalism exercises a more perfect compulsion over free laborers than human masters over slaves; for free laborers must at all times work or starve and slaves are supported whether they work or not.'

STEPHEN FOSTER (1826–64) (Pennsylvania), songwriter and musician Helped create romantic myth of happy, harmonious antebellum South, though only visited it once, briefly, in 1852. Wrote songs for Christy Minstrels and 'My Old Kentucky Home' (1853) incorporated into stage productions of *Uncle Tom's Cabin*. Also wrote 'Oh! Susannah' (1847), 'Swannee River' (1851) and 'Old Black Joe' (1860). Died in extreme poverty in Bowery lodging rooms.

JOHN FRÉMONT (1813–90) (Georgia), explorer and politician In 1838 joined Army Topographical Corp; spent 1841 exploring upper Mississippi and Missouri rivers, and 1842 the Rockies and opening up of Oregon trail with Kit Carson as guide. Eloped with and married Jessie, daughter of Senator **Thomas Hart Benton** of Missouri 1841, a useful political alliance. Further Western exploration in what became California, Nevada, Arizona and Utah in 1843, and in 1847 involved in Bear Flag Revolt and helped secure California from Mexico. Arrested and court-martialled for disobedience and conduct prejudicial to order. Resigned from army. Presidential candidate for new **Republican Party** in 1856, gaining a third of popular vote. Led army of West in early days of war and ordered confiscation of '**contra-band**' slaves held in rebel hands. Counter-manded by **Lincoln**. In 1862 resigned his commission. From 1878 to 1883, he was Governor of Arizona.

MARGARET FULLER (1801–50) (Massa-chusetts), writer and feminist A precocious child who could read Latin at six. Translated Goethe and – daringly for the time – praised the scandalous Lord Byron. From 1840 to 1842, edited the **Transcendentalist** *Dial*; in 1844 literary critic for *New York Tribune*. Wrote feminist *Woman in the Nineteenth Century* (1845), which questioned the insti-tution of marriage and denied that intellect was a wholly male characteristic. Went to Europe in 1846. Embroiled in Italian Revolution in Rome where she served as nurse. In 1847 married Count Giovanni Ossoli, by whom she had a daughter. On 19 July 1850 shipwrecked with daughter off Fire Island on way home to America. *Memoirs* (1851) edited by **Emerson** and Channing.

G

WILLIAM LLOYD GARRISON (1805–79) (Massachusetts), abolitionist Humble ori-gins and unstable childhood. In 1818 appren-ticed to printer. Meeting with Benjamin Lundy, 1828, led him to co-edit *The Genius of Universal Emancipation* in Baltimore. On 1 January 1831 produced famous first issue of *The Liberator*, which ran for thirty-five years. Total rejection of compromise of colonisation of African Americans, compensation for slaveowners and grad-ualism. Demanded, instead, immediatism through the force of moral suasion in its appeal to the conscience and full recogni-tion of sin in the holding of human property. Rejected an established clergy which accepted slavery, the expediency of party politics, the Union ('Let the erring sister [the South] depart in peace') and the Constitu-tion – 'A covenant of death and an agreement with hell' – a copy of which he burned in public, for a form of radical Christian anar-chy. 'I have need to be all on fire, for I have mountains of ice about me to melt.' In 1833 went to England, where he met Wilberforce and Clarkson. In October 1835 he was set upon by Boston mob and placed in jail for his own safety. Georgia offered a reward of $5,000 for his arrest and conviction. In 1841 elected President of American Antislavery Society, serving for twenty-two years. In 1840 he boycotted World Antislavery Convention in London because it refused to seat women. December 1865 ceased publication of *Libera-tor* with ratification of 13th Amendment.

WILLIAM EWART GLADSTONE (1809–98) (Great Britain), Liberal statesman and prime minister As Chancellor of Exchequer in Palmerston's Administration, delivered speech at Newcastle banquet, 7 October 1862, that **Jefferson Davis** had made an army, had made a navy 'and, what was more, had made a nation'. Convinced, like many others at the time, that Union could not win war and that reunion was impossible. Recanted in 1867 and much embarrassed when he later tried to nurture good Anglo-American rela-tions. In May 1871, Treaty of Washington submitted **Alabama Claims** to arbitration, and in Geneva the following year, US was awarded compensation. Gladstone had atoned for his rashness.

ULYSSES S. GRANT (1822–85) (Ohio), Union General and 18th President of the United States Graduated from West Point 1839 and fought in Mexico. In 1854 had to resign commission temporarily because of binge drinking. Outbreak of war found him working in family leathergoods store in Galena, Illinois. In 1861 entered Colonel of Illinois regiment. In 1862 captured **Forts Henry and Donelson** (cutting Joseph Johnston's army in two) and bloody battle of **Shiloh** taught him necessity of total war. On 4 July 1863 **Vicksburg** surrendered to him under siege. Had emerged as leading commander of Union forces, coordinating war strategy and decisive military victories which finally compelled Confederacy to surrender. His abilities quickly recognised by **Lincoln**: 'I can't spare this man: he fights.' Costly but ultimately effective seven-week campaign in the **Wilderness**, Cold Harbor, Spotsylvania and **Petersburg** slowly eroded **Lee**'s forces and pinned them down to defence of Richmond and Petersburg. 'I propose to fight it out on this line if it takes all summer.' On 9 April 1865, accepted Lee's surrender at **Appomattox Court House**. Strained relations with President **Johnson**, though served briefly as Secretary of War following dismissal of **Edwin Stanton** 1867. Both political parties wanted him as presidential candidate, though Grant was not a political animal and only voted once in his life – for **Buchanan** in 1856. Received 100 per cent of votes on first ballot in **Republican** nominating convention 1868, but his two terms proved gravely disappointing. 'The progress of evolution from President Washington to President Grant was alone evidence enough to upset Darwin' (Henry Adams's *Education*). His **Reconstruction** policy – 'Let us have peace' – was conservative and never wholly successful despite the Force and Klan Acts, and his administration was rocked by corruption and scandal. Failed attempt to annex the Dominican Republic led to bitter breach with **Sumner**. Entering into a friend's crooked investment, he became bankrupt but, with full knowledge that he was dying of throat cancer, pressed ahead with two volumes of *Memoirs* which he heroically completed days before his death.

HORACE GREELEY (1811–72) (New Hampshire), newspaper editor   In 1831 went to New York City as journeyman printer. By 1841 editor of highly influential *New York Tribune* filling gap between Gordon Bennett's sensationalist *Herald* and William Cullen Bryant's staid *Evening Post*. By 1860 had reached circulation of over 2,000 and the status, in the words of **James Ford Rhodes**, of 'a political bible', though proscribed in the South for its anti-slavery views. Advocated **free soil**, Western homesteads for urban poor and tariffs to protect industry. Sought peaceful separation from South, but when war came urged in his 'Prayer of Twenty Millions' (19 August 1862) for emancipation of slaves. **Lincoln**, in reply (22 August), insisted on putting unionism above issue of slavery. In 1864, convinced Lincoln would lose election, urged peace with South. Nominated presidential candidate for **Liberal Republican** breakaway at Cincinnati against **Grant**'s corruption and mishandling of **Reconstruction**. Disastrous and exhausting campaign led to his death.

SARAH (1792–1873) AND ANGELINA GRIMKÉ (1805–79) (South Carolina), feminists and abolitionists Daughters of wealthy slaveowner. Brother, Henry, fathered two sons by household slave. In 1821 Sarah left home and joined Quakers in Philadelphia. Joined by Angelina 1829. Horrified genteel society by delivering public lectures against slavery. In 1836 Sarah published *Epistle to Clergy of the Southern States* and in 1838 *Letters on the Equality of the Sexes and the Condition of Women*. Angelina's *Appeal to the Christian Women of the South* linked the subjection of women to that of slavery. This book was publicly burned in her home state and she was threatened with imprisonment if she returned. In 1838 Angelina married prominent abolitionist **Theodore Weld**, and they taught together in biracial school in New Jersey.

H

HENRY HALLECK (1815–72) (New York), Unionist soldier and administrator   Professor of Engineering at West Point. In 1846 published *Elements of Military Art and Science* and translated Jomini's *Life of Napoleon* from the French; hence the title 'Old Brains'. In 1861 replaced **Frémont** as Commander of Department of Missouri and briefly became supreme commander in West. But sluggish and undistinguished in the field and, after capture of Corinth, criticised for allowing **Beauregard** to escape. On 11 July 1862 returned to Washington as military adviser to **Lincoln** and became chief coordinator between Lincoln and **Grant**. Lincoln spoke of him as 'little more than a first-rate clerk', but he grasped the overall long-run strategy of the war, writing to Grant in March 1863: 'There is now no possible hope of reconciliation with the rebels. The Union party in the South is virtually destroyed. There can be no peace but that which is forced by the sword. We must conquer the rebels or be conquered by them.'

WILLIAM HENRY HARRISON (1773–1841) (Virginia), 9th President of the United States   In 1791 he was in army in North West Territory. In 1798 appointed Secretary of North West Territory and Governor of Indiana, 1800–12. On 7 October 1811 decisive victory against native Indian rising under Tecumseh at Tippecanoe Creek. From 1825 to 1828 Senator. In 1840 employed by **Whigs** as popular military hero to combat **Van Buren**'s Democratic bid for re-election. Popular, earthy carnival atmosphere of campaign gave rise to slogans 'log cabin and hard cider' and 'Tippecanoe and **Tyler** too'. Died 4 April 1841, one month after inaugural. Succeeded by Vice President John Tyler.

NATHANIEL HAWTHORNE (1804–64) (Massachusetts), novelist   Friend of Longfellow and **Franklin Pierce** at Bowdoin College, where he graduated in 1825. In 1840 briefly joined Brook Farm utopian community and wrote up experiences in *The Blithedale Romance*. Wrote *The Scarlet Letter* (1850), a subtle analysis of the Puritan conscience and *The House of the Seven Gables* (1851). Campaign biography of Pierce led to his appointment as US Consul in Liverpool, 1853–57, written up as *Our Old Home* (1863).

JOHN HAY (1838–1905) (Indiana), writer and diplomat   In 1858 graduated from Brown University, and in 1859 studied law under uncle in Springfield, Illinois, in office next to **Lincoln**. In 1861 admitted to bar and appointed private secretary to Lincoln along with John Nicolay. Referred to Lincoln as 'the ancient' and 'tycoon'. In 1871 published *Pike County Ballads* and, from 1890 onwards, with Nicolay, published a ten-volume *Life of Abraham Lincoln* and, in 1894, *Lincoln: The Complete Works* in two volumes. Later a distinguished ambassador to Britain and Secretary of State under McKinley and Theodore Roosevelt.

RUTHERFORD B. HAYES (1822–93) (Ohio), 19th President of the United States   Educated at Kenyon College and Harvard Law School, where he graduated in 1845. Supported first anti-slavery **Whigs**, then **Republican Party**. In 1861 joined 23rd Ohio regiment under Rosecrans and wounded at battle of South Mountain 1862. Served in Congress 1865–67 and 1868–72. In 1876–77 Governor of Ohio where he failed to get biracial state manhood suffrage passed. Rose to prominence through 'sound money' campaign. In disputed presidential election of 1876 Congressional Electoral Commission voted 8 to 7 in his favour against the **Democratic** candidate, **Samuel Tilden**. The deal gave 'Home rule' to the South, formally ended **Reconstruction** and ushered in the Gilded Age when the Republican Party emphasis shifted from civil rights to economic expansion.

HINTON ROWAN HELPER (1829–1909) (North Carolina), writer Vociferous representative of non-slaveholding Southern whites. *The Impending Crisis of the South* (1857) argued that slavery had gravely retarded Southern economic development and urged poorer whites to rise up and destroy 'oligarchical despotism' of slaveowners. Book was banned in the South and Helper had to flee North to New York City. Retained hatred of African Americans and urged their deportation.

THOMAS WENTWORTH HIGGINSON (1823–1911) (Massachusetts), soldier, reformer and writer Urged antislavery measures and female suffrage in Boston. In 1850 stood as **Free Soil** candidate for Congress and in 1851 joined Boston Vigilante Commission against Fugitive Slave laws; in 1854, helped batter down door in Boston Court House to rescue fugitive Anthony Burns. Friend of **John Brown** and one of the 'Secret Six' who financially supported him. From November 1862 to May 1864 Colonel of First South Carolina volunteers, the first African American regiment. Wounded and retired, and thereafter Gilded Age man of letters. Wrote *Army Life in a Black Regiment* (1870). Corresponded with **Emily Dickinson** and in 1890 brought out first edition of her poems.

JOHN BELL HOOD (1831–79) (Kentucky), Confederate soldier Graduated from West Point in 1853 and later appointed instructor there. Fought initially with Army of Tennessee. Left arm crippled at **Gettysburg** and his right leg amputated at **Chickamauga**. Opposed **Joseph Johnston**'s cautious strategy but was himself reckless – 'All lion, none of the fox', as **Lee** put it. Tried to draw **Sherman** away from Atlanta on towards Tennessee but failed and, on 1 September, evacuated Atlanta. On 15–16 December his army almost annihilated by Thomas at Nashville; resigned 13 January 1865.

JOSEPH HOOKER (1814–79) (Massachusetts), Unionist soldier 'Fighting Joe' educated at West Point and served in **Mexican War**.

In 1862 engaged in **Peninsula Campaign** under **McClellan**. Badly wounded at **Antietam**. Spoke of the need for a military dictator, to which **Lincoln** replied: 'Only those generals who gain successes can set up a dictatorship. What I now ask of you is military success, and I will risk the dictatorship.' In December 1862 replaced Burnside as Commander of the Army of the Potomac following Union failure at **Fredericksburg**, but he himself partially lost his nerve at **Chancellorsville** when he was defeated by **Lee**. June 1863 Hooker replaced by **Meade** and sent West. Later engaged in Atlanta campaign.

OLIVER O. HOWARD (1830–1909) (Maine), soldier and administrator Assistant Professor of Mathematics at West Point. Engaged in most battles of Civil War and wounded twice, losing right arm at Fair Oaks. With death of McPherson was appointed Commander of Army of Tennessee. Appointed 12 May 1865 and served until 1874 as Commissioner of **Freedmen's Bureau**, advising freedpersons: 'You must begin at the bottom of the ladder and climb up.' Clashed with President **Johnson** and charges levelled against him, but exonerated. In 1869 helped establish and became first President of Howard University, the first African American college of higher education.

JULIA WARD HOWE (1819–1910) (New York), author and reformer Daughter of wealthy banker. In 1843 married Samuel Gridley Howe and, together, published abolitionist *Commonwealth*. In 1861, in army camp near Washington, heard tune of *John Brown's Body* and set new words to this *Battle Hymn of the American Republic* printed in *Atlantic Monthly*, February 1862. 'Mine eyes have seen the glory of the coming of the Lord:/ He is trampling out the vintage where the grapes of wrath are stored:/ He has loosed the fateful lightning of His terrible swift sword/ His truth is marching on.' Later engaged in reform for female emancipation and world peace.

J

ANDREW JACKSON (1767–1845) (Carolinas), 7th President of the United States Born on frontier in Carolinas. In 1795 settled near Nashville, Tennessee. Slaveowner. In 1796 Tennessee's first representative in Congress. Joined state militia in 1802. In 1815 defeated British at battle of New Orleans and helped acquire Florida for US. Great military hero and 'Old Hickory' became personification of West and of the common man against the Eastern élitist **Whigs**. This was reinforced by the 'corrupt bargain' between **John Quincy Adams** and **Clay** in the presidential election of 1824. Gained presidency four years later, gaining 92 per cent of the **Electoral College** vote in the South and 49 per cent in the free states. A rebarbative and activist president, he destroyed the Bank of the United States, threatened force against treason when South Carolina attempted to nullify the tariff of 1828 and vetoed more congressional bills than all the presidents before him put together (12). South Carolina's defiance in 1832 seen as a rehearsal for civil war.

THOMAS 'STONEWALL' JACKSON (1824–63) (Virginia), Confederate soldier Distinguished himself at Vera Cruz during **Mexican War**. Earned soubriquet 'Stonewall' at battle of **First Bull Run** when General Bee exclaimed: 'There is Jackson standing like a stone wall. Rally behind the Virginians.' Brilliant skirmishing operations in Shenandoah Valley where he managed to pin down Union forces, who invariably outnumbered him, who might otherwise have sustained **McClellan** in his assault on Richmond. With famous foot cavalry managed to outflank the enemy by approaching from rear. Fought at Second Bull Run, **Antietam**, **Fredericksburg** and **Chancellorsville**, 1863, where he was shot by Confederate sniper. An aggressive fighter, strict disciplinarian but adored by his soldiers. **Lee** acknowledged: 'I know not how to replace him.'

ANDREW JOHNSON (1808–75) (North Carolina), 17th President of the United States Humble origins. In 1826 moved to Greenville, Tennessee, and took up trade as tailor. Rose through politics as champion of common yeoman farmer. From 1853 to 1857 Governor of Tennessee. Thought South mistreated but a strong Unionist and the only Southern congressman to oppose secession: 'Treason is a crime and must be made odious.' In 1862 **Lincoln** appointed him Military Governor of Tennessee, where he reimposed law and order, and in 1864 Lincoln's Vice President to retain support of **War Democrats** and secure **border states**. Became President with Lincoln's assassination, 15 April 1865. Intended to continue Lincoln's moderate **Reconstruction** policy but intense personal battle ensued between moderates and radicals in an unparalleled constitutional crisis between President and Congress. Johnson offered pardon and amnesty to most ex-confederates, restitution of property (except slaves) supported new Southern **Black Codes** and insisted only that South renounce secession, swear allegiance to Union, repudiate war debt and accept **13th Amendment**. Encouraged South in rejection of **14th Amendment**. On 19 February 1866, vetoed **Freedmen**'s Bill and, later, **Civil Rights Act**. **Radical Republicans**, emboldened by 1866 mid-term elections, and disgusted by Johnson's polemical campaign of vindication – 'The Swing Around the Circle' – led to Army Appropriation Bill (which undercut President's military powers) and Tenure of Office Act (1867), which required Senatorial advice and consent in dismissal of presidential officers. Johnson tested this by dismissing **Edwin Stanton**, Secretary of War, who refused to budge. On 24 February 1868 impeachment proceedings began and, after trial lasting seven weeks, a two-thirds Senate majority failed by only one vote. Johnson thereafter rendered impotent, but, in 1875, Tennessee elected him as Senator. Justice David Davis referred to him as 'obstinate, self-willed, combative'.

JOSEPH EGGLESTON JOHNSTON (1807–91) (Virginia), Confederate soldier Graduated from West Point in 1829 along with **Lee**. Served in **Mexican War**. Evaded Union forces at Harper's Ferry and helped secure **Beauregard**'s victory at **First Bull Run**. Countered **McClellan**'s drive on **Peninsula Campaign**, but badly wounded at Seven Pines. In charge of Confederate forces along Mississippi but failed to relieve Pemberton besieged by **Grant** at **Vicksburg**, and Pemberton forced to surrender July 1863. Command of Army of Tennessee, but great hostility between President **Davis** and Johnston, who complained that President failed to supply him adequately with forces and resources. Sent to repel **Sherman** but driven back to Atlanta and replaced by **Hood**. On 26 April 1865 surrendered to Sherman at Durham Station, North Carolina. Never achieved major military victory, but Grant insisted that he admired and feared Johnston more than he did Lee.

L

ROBERT E. LEE (1807–70) (Virginia), Confederate soldier Scion of aristocratic Virginia family and son of 'Lightfoot' Lee who fought in Revolutionary War. Served in **Mexican War** and participated in capture of **John Brown** at Harper's Ferry, October 1859. Uniquely, offered command of Union and Confederate forces, but put Virginia before the Union: 'I cannot raise my hand against my birthplace, my home, my children.' June 1862, with wounding of **Joseph Johnston**, took command of the Army of North Virginia, and executed a

dazzling series of spectacular successes of Seven Days' Battle, Second Bull Run (29–30 August 1862), **Chancellorsville** (1–4 May 1863), along with two daring invasions of the North which led, however, to the defeats at **Antietam** (September 1862) and **Gettysburg** (July 1863), with over 40,000 casualties at Gettysburg alone. Thereafter on the defensive and retreating before **Grant** at Spotsylvania and Cold Harbor until, following fall of **Petersburg**, surrendered to Grant at **Appomattox Court House**, 9 April 1865. Having won most battles he had lost the war, partly by concentrating troops on the Eastern front at the expense of the West, but did manage to keep Union forces out of Richmond, the Confederate capital, for three years. Personally reserved, enigmatic and inscrutable (rather like Grant) but energised by battle and daring offensives: 'It is well that war is so terrible else men would learn to love it too much.' After war became President of Washington University in Lexington, Virginia (later Washington and Lee), and became central symbol of 'the lost cause' of the South. T. Harry Williams recalls a Sunday School girl who could never remember whether Lee figured in the Old or New Testament.

ABRAHAM LINCOLN (1809–65) (Kentucky), 16th President of the United States Pivotal figure of the age. Born in log cabin. Family travelled via Indiana to Illinois, and settled first in New Salem and then, 1836, Springfield, the state capital, to practise law. In 1847–49 in House of Representatives as **Whig**, but opposition to **Mexican War** made him unpopular. Engagement in **Lincoln–Douglas Debates** for Senate made him national figure. Opposed both **'popular sovereignty'** ('A house divided against itself cannot stand. I believe this government cannot endure permanently half slave and half free') and the **Dred Scott Decision** of 1857, insisting upon **'free soil'** and the non-extension of slavery. Elected as party candidate at **Republican** convention in Chicago,

1860, only to face, following his election as President, the greatest crisis of the Union and the secession of eleven Southern states to form the new Confederacy. Following his inaugural he assumed broad executive powers and, after the firing on **Fort Sumter**, overall command of Union forces: 'The tug has to come, and better now, than any time hereafter.' Called for extensive recruitment, blockaded Southern ports, raised unappropriated expenditures and suspended *habeas corpus* in certain areas. Moved only cautiously to African American emancipation, and then on grounds of military necessity. The initial **Emancipation Proclamation** came in September 1862, and formally proclaimed 1 January 1863, in wake of Unionist victory at **Antietam**. As Commander in Chief spent the first, discouraging years of the war seeking a general who would comply with his insistence on engaging and destroying the enemy head on. **Grant**'s capture of **Vicksburg** and **Meade**'s victory at **Gettysburg**, July 1863, marked a military turning point in the war. His Gettysburg Address extended the providential nature of the war beyond Unionism to the very survival of popular government itself. In 1864, aided by **Sheridan**'s successes in the Shenandoah Valley and **Sherman**'s 'Christmas present' of the capture of Savannah, assured Lincoln of re-election against the **Democrat** candidate **McClellan**, with 78 per cent of Union soldiers voting for him. His Second Inaugural looked towards a magnanimous peace – 'with malice towards none' – and a mild, presidential **Reconstruction** with 10 per cent of state citizens taking 'ironclad' oath of allegiance to reorganise state governments and re-enter Union. A harsher Congressional **Wade–Davis Bill** on Reconstruction hinted at future constitutional struggles, but Lincoln imposed a pocket veto on the bill. On 14 April 1865 shot by John Wilkes Booth at Ford's Theatre, Washington, and died the following day. Succeeded by Vice President, **Andrew Johnson**.

JAMES RUSSELL LOWELL (1819–91) (Massachusetts), author Graduated from Harvard in 1838. Wife's influence turned him to **abolitionism** and, 1848–52, edited *National Antislavery Standard* and contributed to *Pennsylvania Freeman*. In 1848 his highly popular, vernacular *Biglow Papers* were sharp satires on the extension of **slavery** and the **Mexican War**. In 1855 succeeded Longfellow as Smith Professor of Modern Languages, a post held for twenty years. From 1857 to 1861 helped establish and edit *Atlantic Monthly* and, 1862–72, edited *North American Review* along with Charles Eliot Norton. In 1876 a presidential elector who voted for **Hayes** and awarded with Madrid embassy, 1877–80, and London embassy, 1880–85.

M

GEORGE MCCLELLAN (1826–85) (Pennsylvania), Union soldier Known as 'Little Napoleon' or 'Little Mac' to his troops who adored him (not least because he protected their lives). Graduated from West Point in 1846 and observer in Crimean War in 1855. In early days of war secured West Virginia for Union and, in July 1861, following demoralisation of Union army after **First Bull Run** and at age of only 34, put in command of Army of the Potomac. Brilliant at reorganising army ('If he can't fight himself, he excels in making others ready to fight': **Lincoln**) but substituted direct assault on Richmond, by indirect approach of **Peninsula Campaign** via Fort Monroe. Got to within four miles of Richmond, but the absence of McDowell's forces – left to protect Washington – and **Jackson**'s pinning down of Union troops in Shenandoah Valley led to inconclusive engagement of the Seven

Days' Battle (26 June–1 July) and retreat to the James River. Defeat at Gaine's Mill and inconclusive Battle of Malvern Hill led to order, 3 August 1862, recalling army to Washington. Yet again, in pursuing **Lee** in his invasion of Maryland, McClellan achieved a victory at **Antietam** but failed to follow through and destroy Lee's army. November 1862 relieved of command and replaced by Burnside. McClellan was immensely able and talented and checked the Confederacy in its early and strongest period, but fatally paralysed by fears of failure, of action and of taking risks. Lincoln despaired: spoke of McClellan having 'the slows' and dictated an ironic, but unsent, letter to his Commander: 'If you don't want to use the army, I should like to borrow it for a while.' Failed to grasp the total nature of the war. 'It should not be at all a war upon a population, but against armed forces and political organisations. Neither confiscation of property, political execution of persons, territorial organisation of states, or forcible abolition of slavery, should be contemplated for a moment' (to Lincoln, July 1862). Such sentiments led him to run against Lincoln as a **Democrat** in 1864 and lose. In 1878–81 Governor of New Jersey.

GEORGE MEADE (1815–72) (Spain), Union soldier   Graduated from West Point in 1835 and served in Seminole and **Mexican Wars**. Seriously wounded at Glendale during 1862 **Peninsula Campaign** but recovered to fight at Second Bull Run and, when **Hooker** was wounded, took temporary command at **Antietam**. On 28 June 1863 **Lincoln** appointed him Commander of Army of the Potomac, replacing Hooker and, two days later, achieved victory at **Gettysburg**. But failed to counter-attack and allowed **Lee** to retreat southwards in good order. From 1868 to 1869 Commander of 3rd Military District – covering Alabama, Georgia and Florida – during **Reconstruction**.

HERMAN MELVILLE (1819–91) (New York), novelist   Bankrupt father died when he was only 12, and family lapsed into genteel poverty. In 1839 cabin boy on trip to Liverpool. From 1841 to 1844 sailed on whaler *Acushnet* to South Seas, jumped ship and encountered many adventures retold in *Typee* (1846), *Omoo* (1847) and *Mardi* (1849). Epic masterpiece, *Moby Dick* (1851), dedicated to **Hawthorne**, but achieved little critical success and from 1866 served as custom's official in New York harbour. *Billy Budd*, a powerful short story which pitched absolute goodness and innocence against evil, completed just before death. Literary revival began in 1920s and *Moby Dick* regarded by many as the supreme work of American fiction.

N

NAPOLEON III, LOUIS NAPOLEON BONAPARTE (1808–73) (France), emperor   Assumed title of emperor a year after *coup d'état* of 2 December 1851. An adventurous foreign policy. Toyed with possibility of formally recognising **Confederacy** but would not act without Britain, which remained unwilling. Using pretext of outstanding debts, French troops invaded Mexico in summer of 1862, toppling Republican President, Benito Juarez, and installing Habsburg Archduke Maximilian as Emperor of Mexico. **Lincoln** recalled Mexican minister, Banks, and refused to recognise new regime. The 1864 Prusso-Danish war diverted Napoleon's attention back to Europe and in 1867, deserted, Maximilian was executed. Napoleon was himself toppled in 1870, following his resounding defeat at Sedan in the Franco-Prussian War. Referred to by Lewis Namier as 'a mountebank dictator'.

JOHN HUMPHREY NOYES (1811–86) (Vermont) utopian reformer, Graduated from Dartmouth College in 1830. In 1831 converted by **Charles Finney** and continued at Andover Theological Seminary and Yale. In 1833 he was preaching the possibility of sinless perfectionism, which he himself attained in 1837. Advocated free love, complex marriages, male continence through 'coitus reservatus', the holding of property in common, and 'stirpiculture', a form of eugenics intended to breed a perfect, sinless race. Escaping arrest for adultery, 1848 established 'Bible Communism' at Oneida in upstate New York and by 1875 had 300 members; tobacco, alcohol, swearing and obscenities forbidden. In 1879 crossed border to Canada to escape legal proceedings, though the community continued to flourish for some time manufacturing animal traps.

O

FREDERICK LAW OLMSTED (1822–1903) (Connecticut), writer, landscaper In 1844 studied agriculture. Commissioned by *New York Times* in 1852 to travel through and write impressions of South. Three graphic books emerged: *A Journey in the Seaboard Slave States* (1856), *A Journey through Texas* (1857) and *A Journey through the Back Country* (1860), combined in *Journeys and Explorations in the Cotton Kingdom* (1861), giving a vivid and graphic description of the last days of the ante-bellum South. From 1867 onwards designed New York's Central Park with aid of Calvert Vaux, and 1861–63 secretary of US Sanitary Commission inspecting and distributing relief for the Union army. Secured Yosemite as national park.

THEODORE PARKER (1810–60) (Massachusetts), clergyman Graduated from Harvard Divinity School in 1836 and began to deviate from Unitarian orthodoxy, questioning the Bible's infallibility, miracles and exclusive claims of Christianity. Increasingly engaged in secular concerns – education, prison reform, temperance and **abolitionism**. Aided fugitive Anthony Burns escape and, as friend of **John Brown**, became one of the 'Secret Six' who financed raid on Harper's Ferry. 'Democracy is direct self-government, over all the people, by all the people, for all the people.'

FRANCIS PARKMAN (1823–93) (Massachusetts), historian Graduated from Harvard in 1844 then made extensive tour of Europe. In 1846 followed Oregon trail to Fort Laramie, Wyoming, and studied culture of plains Indians. Wrote *The Oregon Trail: Sketches of Prairie and Rocky Mountain life* (1849). In 1851 embarked on 8-volume *History of America to 1763*, charting providential struggle between despotic France and self-governing British on North American continent. Wrote of 'the history of the American forest'.

WENDELL PHILLIPS (1811–84) (Massachusetts), abolitionist and reformer Graduated from Harvard in 1831. The mobbing of **Garrison** in 1835 and the murder of **abolitionist** publisher Elijah Lovejoy in Alton, Illinois, in 1837 turned him into a dedicated abolitionist. 'The conviction that slavery is a sin is the Gibraltar of our cause.' Succeeded Garrison as president of American Anti-slavery Society when Garrison wished to disband it (1867–70). Thereafter extended his reforming zeal to prohibition, female suffrage, penal reform and the rights of native

Indians. As champion of labour and regulation of business corporations, encouraged trade unionism.

FRANKLIN PIERCE (1804–69) (New Hampshire), 14th President of the United States Graduated from Bowdoin College in 1827. In 1827 admitted to bar. In 1833 entered Congress and then served under **Scott** in **Mexican War**. Democratic convention in Baltimore (1852): deadlock among leading candidates – **Cass, Buchanan, Douglas** – led to emergence of Pierce as 'dark horse', who was endorsed on the 49th ballot, and roundly defeated **Whig**, Winfield Scott, in presidential election. Widely regarded in North as pro-Southern **'doughface'**. Enforced Fugitive Slave laws, endorsed **Kansas–Nebraska Act** of 1854, attempted to acquire Cuba, approved of William Walker's filibustering acquisition of Nicaragua, and acquired **Gadsden Purchase** to build Southern railroad route from Mississippi to Pacific.

JAMES POLK (1795–1849) (North Carolina), 11th President of the United States Graduated from University of North Carolina, in 1818; in 1820 admitted to bar. Represented Tennessee in House of Representatives, 1825–39 Speaker of House, 1835–39 and Governor of Tennessee, 1839–41. In 1844 stood as **Democratic** candidate running against **Clay (Whig)** and Birney (**Free Soil**) on platform of expansionism. Called for 54°40′ or fight in Oregon dispute with Britain but settled on the 49th Parallel in 1846. In contrast declared war against Mexico in May 1846 and sent General Zachary **Taylor** to Rio Grande. **Scott**'s capture of Mexico City resulted in Treaty of Guadaloupe Hidalgo, 2nd February 1848, which acquired California, large areas of the south-west and Mexican territory north of 31st Parallel. 'Mr. Polk's war' was the apotheosis of **'Manifest Destiny'** and during his one term the US acquired more territory – enlarged by two-thirds – than under any other president.

R

EDMUND RUFFIN (1794–1865) (Virginia), agriculturalist and fire-eater Strong advocate of agricultural improvement in South. Veteran of 1812 war. From 1833 to 1842 edited *Farmers' Register*. Increasingly pro-slavery and pro-secession for Southern independence. Wrote *The Political Economy of Slavery* and *African Colonisation Unveiled* (1858). Fired first shot on **Fort Sumter** and, though 67, fought at the battle of **First Bull Run**. His country house, Marlbourne, destroyed by Union troops. On 17 June 1865, and with fall of Confederacy, took own life, leaving suicide note: 'I hereby … proclaim my unmitigated hatred to Yankee rule.'

S

CARL SCHURZ (1829–1906) (Germany), journalist, politician, reformer Born near Cologne. After many adventures escaped Germany following crushing of 1848 revolution and in 1852 to the United States, settling in Wisconsin. Early supporter of **Frémont** and **Lincoln** and **Republican Party**. In 1860 appointed minister to Spain but 1862 returned to America and, as politically appointed general, fought at Second Bull Run, **Chancellorsville, Gettysburg** and **Chattanooga**. Sent by President **Johnson** to survey post-bellum south. Schurz's report advocated African American male suffrage and civil equality. Johnson shelved this report until Congress insisted upon its publication. From 1869 to 1875 Senator for Missouri. In 1870 helped establish **Liberal Republican Party** aimed at curbing **Grant**'s corrupt administration, peace with the South and civil service reform. In 1872 presided over convention which led to **Greeley**'s disastrous election as presidential candidate. Served from 1877 to 1881 as Minister of the Interior under **Hayes**, where he displayed an enlightened attitude to native Indians.

WINFIELD SCOTT (1786–1866) (Virginia), Union soldier   Saw action in 1812 war and, in 1838, helped move the Cherokees west beyond the Mississippi River. In 1841 put in command of the US army. In **Mexican War** captured Vera Cruz, March 1847 and, five months later, Mexico City. In 1852 stood as **Whig** presidential candidate against **Democrat Pierce** and lost (though gaining 35 per cent of popular vote). Was 74 when the Civil War broke out, suffering from dropsy, vertigo and gout, unable to mount his horse. Strongly criticised following defeat at **First Bull Run** and retired October 1861, being replaced by **McClellan**, but had outlined **Anaconda Strategy** – controlling Mississippi, blockading Southern coast and cutting South in two – which was finally to win war. Called 'Fuss and Feathers' because of obsession with military uniforms and decorum, Scott knew every president personally from **Jefferson** to **Lincoln**.

WILLIAM HENRY SEWARD (1801–72) (New York), politician   Graduated from Union College, Schenectedy in 1820 and, 1822, admitted to bar. Entered New York politics first on **Anti-Masonic** then **Whig** and **Republican** platform. From 1838 to 1840 Governor of New York. In 1848 entered Senate. Opposed **Compromise of 1850** on grounds that there was 'a higher law than the constitution' and, on 25 October 1858, spoke of an 'irrepressible conflict' between North and South at Rochester. Hope for Republican presidential nomination in 1856 and 1860 but considered too radical. Appointed **Lincoln**'s Secretary of State and in early struggle with President over control of cabinet, proposed abandonment of **Fort Sumter** and on 1 April 1861, in 'Some Thoughts for the President's

Consideration', proposed an aggressive policy against Britain, France and Spain to divert attention from domestic conflict. Ignored by Lincoln and, after Seward worked loyally to neutralise Europe, helped settle **Trent** and **Alabama** disputes and pressured France to evacuate Mexico in 1866. Supported **Johnson** during impeachment crisis and purchased Alaska from Russia, called 'Seward's Ice Box' and 'Seward's Folly', for $7.2 million. In 1869 he retired from politics.

ROBERT GOULD SHAW (1837–63) (Massachusetts), Union soldier   From prominent Bostonian **abolitionist** family. Served in 7th New York regiment and 2nd Massachusetts infantry and wounded at **Antietam**, when assigned by Governor John Andrew to raise and command first African American regiment in North – the 54th Massachusetts. Married 2 May 1863 and brief honeymoon before departure, 13 May, to South Carolina. After prior bombardment, launched assault on Fort Wagner, an earthwork battery on Morris Island. Repelled and Shaw and a quarter of troops killed. Confederate outrage at arming of African Americans and buried Shaw in common grave along with his dead soldiers. Father wanted no other monument, but memorial on Boston Common designed by Augustus St Gaudens, dedicated 1897. Robert Lowell's *For the Union Dead* portrays him as representative of lost republican virtues in midst of thermonuclear world, and Matthew Broderick played him in popular film, *Glory* (1989).

PHILIP HENRY SHERIDAN (1831–88) (New York), Union soldier   Family moved to Ohio. 'Little Phil' graduated from West Point 1853. Served on Rio Grande, North West, then **Halleck**'s Staff during Corinth Campaign. Cavalry engaged in Perryville and **Chickamauga** then came to **Grant**'s attention following daring cavalry charge on Missionary Ridge at Battle of **Chattanooga**. In April 1864 in charge of Cavalry Corps of Army of the Potomac and ravaged the Shenandoah Valley which had previously supplied **Lee**'s army and threatened Washington, and decisively checked Jubal Early at Cedar Creek. Cut off Lee's line of retreat, forcing his surrender at **Appomattox**. In 1867 Military Governor of the 5th Southern District with headquarters in New Orleans. Excessive harshness led to his removal to Missouri. Briefly replaced **Sherman** as Commander-in-Chief of US army. 'The people must be left nothing but their eyes to weep with over the war.'

WILLIAM TECUMSEH SHERMAN (1820–91) (Ohio), Union soldier   Known in family as 'Cump'. Graduated from West Point in 1840 and served in Florida and California until 1848. Superintendent of military college in Louisiana when war broke out. After sharing early reverse at **First Bull Run** was, in November 1861, on verge of nervous break-down and relieved of his Kentucky com-mand. But reputation redeemed at **Shiloh**, Corinth, **Vicksburg** and **Chattanooga**. Despite serious doubts entertained by many, set out, with lines extending back to Nashville, to march through Georgia to Atlanta, which was abandoned 1 September 1863. Then on to coast at Savannah, which was captured 21 December – a Christmas present for Lincoln – which helped immea-surably in his re-election in 1864. Then Sherman struck North, in an even more haz-ardous march through the Carolinas, often covering 12 miles per day, in a bid to reach the main theatre of war from behind. Columbia, the South Carolina state capital, was occupied 11 February and Charleston evacuated on 18 February. **Johnston**'s army surrendered 17 April 1865, eight days fol-lowing **Lee**'s surrender to **Grant**. Sherman's aim – physically to destroy, live off the land and demoralise the civilian population – was hugely successful. 'My aim then was to whip the rebels, to humble their pride, to follow them to their inmost recesses, and make them fear and dread us.' Privately, however, he entertained doubts: 'I am sick and tired of war. Its glory is all moonshine … War is

hell.' His Special Field Order No. 15 ceded Sea Islands and a swathe of land 30 miles inland from Charleston to Jacksonville, intended to provide land for the freedmen. President **Johnson** revoked this order. From 1869 to 1883 commander of the US army. In 1884 refused Republican candidacy for presidency. **Basil Liddell Hart** called him 'the first modern strategist'.

EDWIN MCMASTERS STANTON (1814–69) (Ohio), politician   An able lawyer who worked on California land cases until he moved to Washington in 1856. As **Democrat** and Attorney-General in **Buchanan**'s cabinet 1860, resigned on **Lincoln**'s election. Served Under-Secretary of War Simon Cameron and, in January 1862, replaced him. In a prickly Lincoln cabinet Stanton was one of the prickliest, but relations with the President mellowed and he proved a dynamic and enterprising War Secretary. Along with **Chase** put pressure on Lincoln to dismiss **McClellan**. Brilliantly managed demobili-sation of 800,000 Union soldiers at the war's end and remained in **Johnson**'s cabi-net. But identified with **Radical Republicans** and, having drafted Supplementary Recon-struction Act in 1867, over President's veto, Johnson requested his resignation in August 1867, under the Tenure of Office Act. He refused and barricaded himself in the War Department offices. He resigned on the same day Johnson was spared impeachment by one vote on 26 May 1868. December 1869 appointed by **Grant** to Supreme Court but died before taking seat.

ELIZABETH CADY STANTON (1815–1902) (New York), feminist and social reformer   In 1840 married **abolitionist**, Henry Brewster Stanton. At World's Antislavery Convention held in London 1840 was refused seating along with Lucretia Mott. In 1848 first female rights convention held at **Seneca Falls**, which resulted in famous Declaration. In 1860 left imprint on New York state laws giving women joint guardianship of children (she herself raised seven), female rights to sue in courts, receive and keep wages and other real and personal property. Also urged birth control measures and relaxing strict divorce laws. Objected to first constitutional use of 'male' in **14th Amendment** and objected to the **15th Amendment**, which precluded female suffrage. From 1868 to 1870 edited *The Review* with **Susan Anthony**; president of National Women's Suffrage Association 1869–90. Conceded that 'the social and political condition of women was largely changed by our Civil War'.

ALEXANDER STEPHENS (1812–83) (Georgia), Confederate politician In 1843 elected to Congress as **Whig** but, as Unionist, converted to **Democrats** following **Scott**'s rejection of the **Compromise of 1850**. Initially opposed to secession but succumbed when Georgia voted in favour and elected Vice President of Confederacy on 9 February 1861, which rested 'upon the great truth that the negro is not equal to the white man; that slavery ... is his natural and normal condition. This, our new government, is the first in the history of the world based upon this great, physical, philosophical and moral truth.' At loggerheads with President **Davis** throughout war, opposing conscription, the suspension of *habeas corpus* and the imposition of martial law. In February 1865 headed abortive peace talks at Hampton Road. Arrested and temporarily imprisoned in Boston for six weeks. His political apologia *A Constitutional View of the Late War between the States* appeared (1868–70), insisting the South fought not for **slavery** but to maintain **states' rights**.

THADDEUS STEVENS (1792–1868) (Vermont), politician Graduated from Dartmouth College 1814 and admitted to bar in 1816, then iron manufacturer in Pennsylvania. In 1848 elected to Congress as **Whig** and then, 1861, Chairman of House Ways and Means Committee. A **Radical Republican** with lifelong devotion to African American cause. In 1865 leader of House Republicans and member of Joint Committee on Reconstruction. Urged radical reconstruction which must 'revolutionize southern institutions, habits and manners. The foundation of their institutions ... must be broken out and relaid, or all our blood and treasure have been spent in vain.' Considered secession 'state suicide' and ex-Confederate states were to be treated by Congress as conquered territory. Urged adoption of **14th Amendment**, **Reconstruction Acts of 1867**, **Freedmen's Bureau** Bill and Tenure of Office Act and – most controversial of all – '**40 acres and a mule**' for freedpersons from sequestration of 400 million acres of land belonging to wealthiest 10 per cent of slaveowners in South. Pushed for impeachment of **Johnson** with his dying breath. Chose to be buried in black section of Lancaster graveyard, Pennsylvania, 'that I might illustrate in my death the principles which I advocated through a long life – Equality of Men before his Creator'.

HARRIET BEECHER STOWE (1811–96) (Connecticut), author Accompanied father, Lyman Beecher, to Lane Seminary, Ohio, then the centre of **abolitionist** agitation in the North-West. Visited Kentucky plantations. In 1836 married Calvin Stowe, a fellow professor at Lane, and returned to the East and Bowdoin College in 1850. *Uncle Tom's Cabin* published 1852 and sold 2,000,000 copies in first ten years. Lord Palmerston shed tears on reading it and **Lincoln** famously informed her: 'So you're the little lady who wrote the book that made this great war.' Uncle Tom is depicted as a Christ-like figure whose suffering redeems mankind, and Simon Legree is an evil sadistic Yankee overseer who implicates the north in the national shame of slavery. *Key to Uncle Tom's Cabin* appeared in 1853 to substantiate the factual basis of her fiction and refute her critics. Sister, Catherine, became a writer on domestic economy and social reform, and brother, Henry Ward Beecher, an eminent preacher, who urged the advocacy of

'Beecher's Bibles', i.e. rifles, in the fight against pro-slavery forces in Kansas.

JAMES EWELL BROWN 'JEB' STUART (1833–64) (Virginia) Confederate soldier To West Point 1850. Cavalry officer during Indian wars and engaged in Kansas. In 1859 assisted in arrest of **John Brown** at Harper's Ferry. Initially served under **Joseph Johnston** in Shenandoah Valley. Engaged in most battles, including – June 1863 – largest cavalry engagement of the war at Brandy Station. Took over from Albert Sidney Johnston following his death at **Shiloh**. Failed to get vital intelligence through to **Lee** at **Gettysburg** and **Sheridan** succeeded in separating him from Lee thereafter. Killed at Yellow Tavern 10 May 1864.

CHARLES SUMNER (1811–74) (Massachusetts), politician Graduated from Harvard 1830 and Harvard Law School 1834. Three years travelling in Europe. In 1851 elected Senator for Massachusetts. First 'conscience' **Whig**, then **Republican**. Opposed Fugitive Slave acts and excoriated the evil collaboration between 'the lords of the lash and the lords of the loom' (Southern slaveowners and Northern cotton manufacturers). On 19–20 May 1856 'Crime against Kansas' speech critically singling out Senator Butler, South Carolina, for his pro-slavery sentiments. Two days later Butler's nephew, Preston Brooks, avenging the insult, ferociously attacked Sumner on the floor of the Senate with his cane, severely injuring him. After three years' convalescence outraged Massachusetts constituents re-elected him to an empty seat. In 1860 Republican Senate leader and, March 1861, Chairman of Senate Foreign Relations Committee. Urged **Lincoln** to release two Confederate diplomats, Mason and Slidell, thus defusing the Anglo-American crisis over the **Trent Incident**. Major **Radical Republican** during **Reconstruction**, urging ballot, free schools and homesteads for freedpersons. In 1870 opposed **Grant**'s bid to annex Santo Domingo and urged heavy, indirect **Alabama Claims** against Britain,

hinting at acquisition of Canada as possible compensation, but deposed from Senate Chairmanship in 1871. **Civil Rights Act 1875** passed in his memory, but this was overruled by the Supreme Court in 1883. Lincoln said Sumner was his idea of a bishop.

T

ROGER B. TANEY (1777–1864) (Maryland), politician and jurist Slaveowner. Graduated from Dickinson College in 1795 and, 1799, admitted to bar. Initially a Federalist, he became an ardent **Democrat** and helped, as **Jackson**'s Attorney-General, to draft the bank veto message of 1832. Secretary of the Treasury, William Duane, refused to withdraw federal deposits from the Bank of the United States, so Jackson appointed Taney instead in September 1833. Censured by Senate. In 1835 Jackson appointed him Chief Justice of the Supreme Court to replace John Marshall. Charles River Bridge decision (1837) imposed narrow construction on charters granted by state and placed the rights of communities before that of corporate monopolies. Fateful and controversial decision in **Dred Scott Decision** (1857) denied Scott citizenship and declared **Missouri Compromise** unconstitutional. It followed, theoretically, that slavery could be established throughout the territories. The last controversial decision, **Ex parte Merryman**, 1861, overruled military suspension of *habeas corpus* in Baltimore without Congressional authority. Freed his slaves by his will.

ARTHUR (1786–1865) AND LEWIS (1788–1873) TAPPAN (Massachusetts), philanthropists and abolitionists Had dry goods business in Boston; became leaders of New York wing of

abolitionist movement. From 1827 to 1831 Arthur established *Reformist*, New York journal of commerce, supported **Charles Finney** and helped construct Broadway Tabernacle for him. Also instrumental in founding Kenyon College, Auburn and Lane Theological Seminaries and, 1833, Oberlin, the first college to admit African Americans. In 1833 Arthur first president of the American Antislavery Society. Lewis's house sacked by anti-abolitionist mob, 1834. Early collaboration with **Garrison** but split over Garrison's growing radicalism and, 1840, Arthur president of American and Foreign Antislavery Society.

ZACHARY TAYLOR (1784–1850) (Virginia), soldier and 12th President of the United States Joined the army 1808, and served under General **Harrison** during 1812 war. January 1846 ordered to Rio Grande by **Polk** and, 27 February 1847, decisive victory over Mexicans at Buena Vista. Never voted or belonged to political party, but as military hero, 'Old Rough and Ready', made him **Whig** candidate in 1848 in presidential election against **Lewis Cass** (**Democrat**). Believed, as a Louisiana slaveowner and father-in-law to Jefferson **Davis**, to be pro-Southern, but his broad nationalism made him refuse to reject the **Wilmot Proviso**, and the influence of **Seward**, and his hope that California and New Mexico would enter the Union as free states, alienated the South. Disdainful of the 'Omnibus Bill' the great **Compromise of 1850** was only passed following Taylor's death in office and with the support of the new president, **Millard Fillmore**.

HENRY DAVID THOREAU (1817–62) (Massachusetts), naturalist, writer Graduated from Harvard 1837, taught briefly, but resigned, refusing to impose corporal punishment. Turned to family industry of pencil making, then ran private school with brother, John, and organised nature field trips. Until 1841 lived and served as **Emerson**'s handyman in Concord. In 1845 went to Walden Pond for two years, building hut, experimenting in self-sufficiency, contemplating and 'driving life into a corner'. In 1845 refused to pay poll tax which financed **Mexican War** and expansion of slavery. Resulted in *Resistance to Civil Government* or *On the Duty of Civil Disobedience* (1849). Huge influence on Pacifist struggles of Gandhi and Martin Luther King Junior. *Walden, or Life in the Woods* (1854) opposed to materialism, aggressive individualism and commercialism. In 1857 met and admired **John Brown** at Emerson's. In 1859 deification of Brown following his failed raid on Harper's Ferry. Has himself become patron saint of anti-establishmentarians and environmentalists in contemporary America.

SAMUEL JONES TILDEN (1814–86) (New York), politician In 1841 admitted to New York bar, serving rail interests. Democratic Unionist during Civil War. From 1866 onwards chaired Democratic state commission exposing financial corruption of New York Tweed Ring and Erie Canal Ring. Reforming reputation gained him Democratic nomination 1876, which he lost in disputed election to **Hayes**. Compromise over the election led to the formal ending of **Reconstruction** in 1877.

ALEXIS HENRI CHARLES MAURICE CLEREL DE TOCQUEVILLE (1805–59) (France), writer Norman aristocrat. In 1830 assistant magistrate. In 1831 went to USA for ten months with Gustave de Beaumont, ostensibly to investigate American prisons and penitentiaries. Resulted in two parts *Democracy in America* (1835 and 1840). Saw American democratic mores as the future and object lesson for volatile French politics. 'A new science of politics is needed for a new world ... I have endeavoured to abate the claims of the aristocrats, and to make them bend to an irresistible future; so that the impulse in one quarter and resistance in the other being less violent, society might march on peaceably towards the fulfilment of its destiny.' Subtle socio-political insights into

Jacksonian America, liberalism, equality, the American spirit of association and the potential for majoritarian tyranny. Sat in French parliament 1839–51 and briefly Minister of Foreign Affairs. Retired from public life following **Louis Napoléon**'s *coup d'état*. *Ancien Régime* published 1856.

LYMAN TRUMBULL (1813–96) (Connecticut), politician   In 1837 moved to Illinois. In 1848 appointed to Illinois Supreme Court. Strong **Free Soiler** and **Republican**. With **Lincoln**'s assistance served in Senate, 1855–73, but, as Chairman of Senate Judicial Committee, critical of President's suspension of *habeas corpus*. During **Reconstruction** carried through **13th Amendment**, strengthened and funded **Freedmen's Bureau** Bill and organised Civil Rights Bill of 1866 guaranteeing 'full and equal benefit of all laws and for the security of person and property', both vetoed by **Johnson**. Also invalidated racially discriminatory laws in north. As Moderate opposed Johnson's impeachment.

SOJOURNER TRUTH (*c.* 1797–1883) (New York), abolitionist, reformer and feminist   Born slave, Isabella, in New York state. In 1828 freed by state law and successfully sued for return of son, Peter, sold illegally into slavery in Alabama. On 1 June 1843, on Pentecostal Sunday, underwent transformation by Holy Spirit, changing her name and becoming itinerant preacher. Three years in community in Northampton, Massachusetts, preaching feminism and anti-slavery. Met **Garrison** and **Douglass** and, in 1864, **Lincoln**, for whose re-election she campaigned. *Narrative of Sojourner Truth* published in 1850.

HARRIET TUBMAN (*c.* 1820–1913) (Maryland), abolitionist   Born into slavery in Maryland and, 1844, forced into marriage with John Tubman by master. In 1849 escaped north to Philadelphia. Changed slave name, 'Araminta', to Harriet. 'I looked at my hands to see if I was the same person now I was free. There was such glory over everything, the sun came like gold through the trees, and over the fields, and I felt I was in heaven … I had crossed the line of which I had so long been dreaming. I was free' (1886). Thereafter with aid of Quakers, made nineteen trips to the south to help up to 70 slaves escape. First to North then, with tightening of Fugitive Slave laws, to Canada. Became 'Moses of her people' and **John Brown** referred to her as 'General Tubman', but Maryland offered large reward for her capture. During Civil War in South Carolina served Union forces as cook, laundress, nurse, guide and spy. In later years purchased home and land in Auburn, New York, to care for aged freed persons.

NAT TURNER (1800–31) (Virginia), slave insurrectionist   Taught to read and write – illegally – by first master, Benjamin Turner. Sold temporarily to illiterate farmer, which proved traumatic. Given to hearing voices and seeing visions – 'white spirits and black spirits engaged in battle, and blood flowing in streams'. Saw providential role to lead slaves out of bondage. Solar eclipse in 1831 was signal to arise: recruited over 60 slaves during two days in Southampton county, Virginia, massacred 59 whites. Evaded capture for two months, then arrested, found guilty and hanged 11 November 1831. Dictated *The Confessions of Nat Turner*. Rebellion struck fear into Southern whites. Virginia legislature debated gradual emancipation, but finally rejected it and **Black Codes** tightened.

JOHN TYLER (1790–1862) (Virginia), 10th President of the United States   Graduated from William and Mary College in 1807. Originally a Jeffersonian strict Constructionist and **states rights** supporter. From 1825 to 1826 Governor of Virginia. In 1827 in Senate. Opposed **Jackson**'s 1828 and 1832 tariffs and only Senator to vote against Jackson's Force Bill. Changed from **Democrat** to **Whig** and elected Vice President to **Harrison**, 1840. Death of Harrison, 4 April 1841, led to 'his accidency' becoming

President. Struggle with **Clay** over Bank of the United States, leading to resignation of all the cabinet except **Webster** who, after negotiating Anglo-American Webster–Ashburton Treaty on Maine boundary dispute, followed in 1843. Pressed annexation of Texas with **Calhoun**. Expected slavery to wither away, but opposed to all federal regulation on the matter including the **Missouri Compromise** of 1820. Tried to broker peace in secession winter, 1860–61, but finally supported secession and elected to Confederacy of the House of Representatives. Died before taking seat.

CLEMENT VALLANDIGHAM (1820–71) (Ohio), politician In 1842 admitted to Ohio bar. From 1856 to 1862 Congress where, although he opposed slavery, urged the end of sectionism and highly critical of **Lincoln** and **Radical Republicans**. Became vociferous leader of Peace Democrats or '**copperheads**'. In 1862 lost Congressional seat and returned to Ohio, speaking against war. Arrested in Dayton, Ohio, and imprisoned by Burnside's forces and refused writ of *habeas corpus*. **Lincoln** commuted sentence of imprisonment to banishment to Confederacy. Instead Vallandigham escaped into exile in Canada. February 1864 tested constitutionality of presidential and military suspension of *habeas corpus* in *Ex parte Vallandigham* but Supreme Court insisted it did not possess appellated jurisdiction. Was Lincoln's 'fire in the rear'.

MARTIN VAN BUREN (1782–1862) (New York), 8th President of the United States Created Albany Regency, a powerful **Democratic** force in New York state politics. In 1821 to New York Senate; in 1828 Governor of

New York State. 'The sly fox' and 'little magician' was a new breed of politician, to whom politics was a profession entailing bartering and compromise. In 1828 responsible for passage of tariffs through Congress. As Jacksonian Democrat entered **Jackson**'s cabinet, 1829, as Secretary of State and, with Jackson's breach with **Calhoun**, Van Buren became Vice President and heir apparent. In 1836 casting vote in favour of **gag rule** and opposition to slavery in federal capital were unavailing attempts to keep Northern and Southern sections within the Democratic fold. Renominated in 1840 but lost to **Whig**, **Harrison**'s, 'hard cider' campaign. In 1844 opposition to the annexation of Texas led to Southern Democratic nomination of expansionist **Polk** instead. In 1848 nominated as **Free Soil** candidate at Buffalo, with Charles Francis Adams as Vice President, advocating non-extension of slavery. Won no electoral college votes, but popular vote was almost 300,000, and precursor to the **Republican Party** of 1854.

BENJAMIN FRANKLIN WADE (1800–78) (Massachusetts), politician In 1821 went to Ohio frontier. From 1831 to 1837 law office partner with Joshua Giddings – eminent antislavery leader. 'Conscience' **Whig**, 1851–69, then **Republican** in Senate. In 1861 helped establish Joint Committee on Conduct of War, critical of **Lincoln** and radical approach to South, urging immediate emancipation and arming of slaves, execution of Southern leaders and confiscation of Southern property. Countered Lincoln's moderate reconstruction plans of December 1863 with harsher **Wade–Davis Bill**, 1864, which Lincoln refused to sign. As President of Senate, *pro tem*, would have become

President if **Johnson** were successfully impeached, leading many to vote against impeachment.

DANIEL WEBSTER (1782–1852) (New Hampshire), politician Graduated from Dartmouth College 1801, first active Federalist then **Whig**, and staunch Nationalist. In 1818–19 argued as legal advocate for his old college in *Dartmouth College v. Woodward* and 1824 in favour of the Bank of the United States in *McCulloch v. Maryland*. From 1827 to 1841 and from 1843 to 1850 in the Senate. In 1833 joined **Clay** and **Whigs** in opposition to **Jackson**'s destruction of the Bank of the United States. Opposed also to **Calhoun**'s doctrine of **states' rights** and **nullification**. 'Liberty and Union, now and forever, one and inseparable.' In 1840 appointed **Harrison**'s Secretary of State and continued under **Tyler**, remaining to sign Webster–Ashburton Treaty, 1842, settling Anglo-American differences over Maine. Thereafter resigned in opposition to Tyler's states' rights principles. Also served as **Fillmore**'s Secretary of State. Upholder of high tariffs to protect native New England industry. Opposed slavery, but against federal interference. Conceded on tighter Fugitive Slave laws in order to achieve **Compromise of 1850**. Along with Clay and Calhoun, one of the three great statesmen of the mid-century who failed to gain the presidency. Held up to scorn by **Thoreau** as archetypal trimming politician in his *Civil Disobedience*.

THEODORE WELD (1803–95) (Connecticut), abolitionist Moved to upstate New York. Under **Charles Finney**'s influence in Utica trained for ministry. Joined Lane Theological Seminary, Ohio, but, 1834, forced out because of his radicalism. In May 1838 married **Angelina Grimké**. Strong advocate of moral suasion for slavery which was 'preeminently a moral question, arresting the conscience of the nation'. In 1839, produced *Slavery As It Is*, reprinting newspaper advertisements for recapture of fugitive slaves to emphasise plainly the horrors of 'peculiar institutions'. Great influence on Charles Dickens, among others.

GIDEON WELLES (1802–75) (Connecticut), US Secretary of the Navy Early journalism as a Jacksonian **Democrat**. In 1845 Polk appointed him Chief of Naval Bureau of Provisions and Clothing during **Mexican War**. Tightened Fugitive Slave laws and **Kansas–Nebraska Act** turned him into one of the founders of **Republican Party**. From March 1861 to March 1869 Secretary of Navy, which had to be built from scratch. With sudden defection officer class only half strength. Only 90 ships, but of these only 42 in commission and many in foreign stations. Established new Navy yard in Philadelphia, pushed through programme for twenty 'ironclads', tightened **naval blockade** and recruited African Americans into Navy – a quarter of the total by 1865. Overall personnel grew from 7,600 to 51,500 during war and by 1865 the US Navy was second only to that of the United Kingdom. A moderate Reconstructionist, he supported **Johnson** and, 1872, **Liberal Republicans**. Fascinating three-volume *Diary* (first published 1911) revealed inner workings of **Lincoln**'s and Johnson's cabinet.

WALT WHITMAN (1819–92) (New York), poet Started in journalism. From 1846 to 1848 editor of *Brooklyn Daily Eagle* – anti-slavery and **free soil**. *Leaves of Grass* (1855) – the great poem of Democratic America – enlarged and revised in twelve editions up to 1892. Wrote of himself as 'of pure American breed, large and lusty … a naïve, masculine, affectionate, contemplative, sensual, imperious person'. In 1862 went to Washington to nurse wounded brother and stay ten years as nurse, dresser and clerk. Dismissed by Harlan of Interior Department when discovered that Whitman was author of immoral verse (especially advocacy of same-sex 'adhesiveness' of *Calamus* poems). *Drum Taps* (1865) included moving elegies to Lincoln – 'Oh captain! my captain!' and 'When lilacs last in the door yard bloom'd'. Prose work,

Democratic Vistas (1871), excoriated crass materialism of post-Civil War America. In 1873 a stroke led him to spend last days with his brother in Camden, New Jersey.

HENRY WILSON (1812–75) (New Hampshire), writer and politician   Humble origins, a shoemaker. Witnessed slave auction in Washington. One of the founding members of **Free Soil Party** and presiding officer at National Convention in Buffalo 1852. From 1855 to 1873 Senator. During American Civil War chairman of Senate Military Commission and then strongly opposed **Andrew Johnson**. Served as **Grant**'s vice president during his second term but died before completion of term. In 1872–75 published three-volume *History of the Rise and Fall of the Slave Power in America.*

Northern values. In 1833 returned to South. In 1835 married wealthy heiress and, 1836, moved to large plantation in Alabama. From 1844 to 1846 in House of Representatives. Advocate of **states' rights** and federal protection of slavery. Opposition to **Compromise of 1850** and argued for **secession**. Led breakaway from **Democratic** Convention at Charleston which supported **Douglas** and at Baltimore urged nomination of **John Breckinridge**. In January 1861, introduced secession in Alabama and, March 1861, to Britain but failed to gain formal recognition for Confederacy. 'Our poetry is our lives; our fiction will come when truth has ceased to satisfy us; and, as for our history, we have made about all that has glorified the United States.'

Y

WILLIAM LOWNDES YANCEY (1814–63) (Georgia), Confederate politician   With mother's second marriage moved north to Troy, New York, and grew to dislike

GLOSSARY

A

ABOLITIONISM Movement dedicated to the ending of slavery and, more far-reaching, the establishing of racial equality. Jefferson, in his Declaration of Independence (1776), declared that 'all men are created equal' and slavery, beginning with Rhode Island in 1774, was illegal in all Northern states by 1846. In the South, however, slavery remained an integral part of the social and economic fabric (Jefferson was himself a Virginia slaveowner) and by 1860 fifteen Southern and **border states** imposed **Black Codes** which enforced the 'peculiar institution'. The aim of abolitionism was simple – emancipation: the means of achieving this end more difficult and complicated. Early abolitionists' aims relied on colonisation as a solution, along with compensation for the master, and the American Colonisation Society was established in 1816. Jefferson, Monroe, **Clay** and **Lincoln** as late as 1862 supported this movement. Monrovia (later Liberia) was established on the West African coast in 1822 and 10,000 freed African Americans settled there. Many returned home after the Civil War. But gradualism and compensation eventually gave way to immediatism, influenced by the second great religious awakening and the example of the British Empire's abolition of slavery and of the slave trade in 1833. The American Anti-Slavery Society was founded in 1833 with an alliance between **Garrison** and the **Tappan** Brothers. A new moral urgency entered the debate. The Garrisonian wing, centred in Boston, advocated moral suasion – an appeal to the sovereign conscience resulting in the recognition of sin in holding humans in bondage and atonement thereof – in the pages of *The Liberator* (1831–66). The New York wing, led by the Tappan brothers, was more moderate and willing to work through political parties (the **Liberty Party**, **Free Soil** and **Republican Party**) and petition Congress. In upstate New York and the north-west the movement was more rooted in evangelical religion and led by **Charles Finney** and **Theodore Weld**. Abolitionism was unpopular in a largely negrophobe North (where **Tocqueville** observed that racial prejudice was stronger than in the South): it has been estimated that only about 1 per cent of the Northern population were dedicated abolitionists who found their earliest martyrs in Elijah Lovejoy, who was killed trying to protect his abolitionist printing press in Alton, Illinois, in 1837, and Garrison, who was almost killed by anti-abolitionist mobs in Boston in 1835. The American Anti-Slavery Society had 200,000 members by 1840, but Garrison's growing radicalism and lurch towards Christian anarchy split the movement in 1840 into Garrisonian and a more pragmatic anti-Garrisonian wing which established the American and Foreign Anti-Slavery Society. The World Anti-Slavery Congress in London, 1840, refused to seat **Elizabeth Cady Stanton** and Lucretia Mott and throughout the crusade women played a vital role and drew parallels with slavery and the inferior role of women, urging feminism and female suffrage at the **Seneca Falls Convention** of 1848. African Americans too, such as **Frederick Douglass** and **Sojourner Truth**, played a crucial role, though they were often met by white condescension. **Thoreau** in his *Civil Disobedience* called for passive resistance in opposition to slavery and the **Mexican War**. Others urged economic sanctions. **John Brown**, notoriously, resorted to violence in his raid on Harper's Ferry (1859) intended as a prelude to slave insurrection. With Brown's execution the movement found yet another martyr–hero. **Lincoln**'s tardy progress towards emancipation during the war received heavy criticism until the **Emancipation Proclamation** of 1863 was followed by the passage of the **13th Amendment**, 1865, which freed all slaves. In that year Garrison resigned and **Wendell Phillips** took over as president of the American Anti-Slavery Society until 1870 and the passage of the **15th Amendment**, which granted suffrage to all African American males. Much criticism has been levelled against abolitionists, and it was Lincoln, the politician, not the agitators who finally freed the slaves. In measuring their achievement it is important to bear in mind the strength of opposition they were up against – in the form of the Constitution, the Union, the intransigence of the **slave power** in the South and endemic indifference in the North.

AFRICAN AMERICAN SOLDIERS Before the **Emancipation Proclamation** an informal system was established whereby black **'contraband'** acted as back-up to Union forces. **Lincoln** grasped the military importance of black soldiers: 'I believe it is a resource which, if vigorously applied now, will soon close the contest. It works doubly, weakening the enemy and strengthening us.' By 1865 over 190,000 black troops, constituting 10 per cent of the total Union forces, One-fifth of the male black population under 45 had joined 166 different regiments involved in 40 major battles, with a further 10,000 in the navy. In 1862 Governor Andrew of

Massachusetts raised two black regiments, the 54th and 55th Massachusetts, which fought heroically at Fort Wagner. Many, including white officer **Robert Gould Shaw**, were killed and, as a Southern officer commented, 'buried with his niggers'. Shaw's father said this was entirely appropriate. The black Union soldiers were segregated from the white and were paid less. Many captured African American soldiers executed. In last, desperate, days of war **Davis** and **Lee** decided to arm African Americans in the Confederate cause. But opposition came, including that of Howell Cobb of Georgia: 'If slaves will make great soldiers our whole theory of slavery is wrong.' August 1865 President **Johnson** removed all African American units from the South and, two years later, out of the army altogether. But African Americans had actively contributed to the liberation of their race.

ALABAMA CLAIMS Britain declared official neutrality towards American conflict on 14 May 1861. In May 1862, James Bulloch, Confederate naval envoy, commissioned building of vessels in Liverpool shipyard, notably *Alabama*, *Shenandoah* and *Florida*. Under Captain Raphael Semmes, *Alabama* destroyed or captured 64 Union vessels before being sunk herself June 1864. Following war **Seward** and **C.F. Adams** demanded damages of $19 million plus and, **Charles Sumner**, Chairman of Senate Foreign Relations Committee, made large and indirect claims and demanded Canada in compensation. With outbreak of Franco-Prussian War and Granville as Foreign Secretary, Treaty of Washington, May 1871, established five arbitrators who, in 1872, awarded $15.5 million to the United States in compensation.

AMERICAN SYSTEM **Whig** economic strategy advocated by Madison and Monroe, **John Quincy Adams** and **Henry Clay**. High tariffs would protect America's infant industry from foreign competition and raise revenue, federal government would finance internal improvements to aid West and establish transport infrastructure, and national banking system would stabilise economic growth. Opposed by *laissez-faire* **Jacksonian Democrats**, who saw it as too élitist and interventionist and benefiting the mainly wealthy and privileged.

AMISTAD CASE   On 1 July 1839 50 slaves mutinied on Spanish vessel, *Amistad*, off Cuban coast. Intercepted off Long Island and imprisoned. Spanish authorities and many Southerners wanted them tried for piracy and murder, but 1840 **abolitionists** took case to the Supreme Court, where **John Quincy Adams** argued for their release and freedom. In March 1841, slaves set free and 35 sent back to Africa.

ANACONDA STRATEGY   Overall Union strategy initially devised by General **Scott** deploying Eastern Army to protect federal capital, naval blockade of Confederacy to starve it, and capture and control of the Mississippi to cut Confederacy in two. This strategy was considered too slow and passive by Northern public opinion, which demanded decisive victories, but, essentially, in modified form, this was the plan carried out to subdue the South and achieve Northern victory.

ANDERSONVILLE PRISON   Notorious Confederate prison camp in Georgia. In summer of 1864 more than 100 deaths a day. In total some 13,000 out of 45,000 prisoners died (29 per cent), although Salisbury Camp in North Carolina had a worse mortality rate (34 per cent). The highest death rate in Union prisoner-of-war camps was Elmira (24 per cent). In total 15.5 per cent died in Southern camps and 12 per cent in Northern. Henry Wirz, the commander of Andersonville, was the only Confederate prisoner executed after the war.

ANTIETAM   Decisive Civil War battle. Buoyed up by Confederate victory at Second Bull Run, **Lee**'s Army of North Virginia crossed the Potomac and invaded Maryland, pursued by **McClellan**'s Army of the Potomac. Lee planned this audacious offensive to draw Union troops from Virginia, take the war into the enemy's camp, hope to encourage the **Northern Peace Democrats**, influence the mid-term Congressional elections and possibly gain European recognition of the Confederacy. Despite the Union's capturing details of Lee's movements, **Jackson**'s escape from Harper's Ferry to join up with Lee led Lee to take stand at Antietam Creek, Sharpsburg, and face army twice his size led by McClellan, **Hooker** and Burnside. That day, 17 September 1862, bloodiest day of Civil War with over 23,000 dead or wounded (over a quarter of Lee's army), but though severely battered Lee stood ground and on 19 September retreated across Potomac. McClellan failed to pursue Lee rigorously or make victory decisive. The impact of battle was incalculable. The Confederacy was thereafter on the defensive, and Lincoln grasped the opportunity to declare a preliminary **Emancipation Proclamation** five days later.

APPOMATTOX   COURT   HOUSE   Situated south-east of Lynchburg, Virginia, where **Lee** formally surrendered to **Grant** on 9 April 1865. On 2 and 3 April Lee was forced to evacuate **Petersburg** and attempted to join up with **Joseph Johnston** for last-ditch stand. But harried throughout, and retreat cut off, Lee forced to admit defeat. Grant's terms were generous: parole for Southern soldiers, immunity from prosecution for treason, officers to retain side arms, troops could keep horses to help plant spring crops, and three days' rations provided for 25,000 soldiers. Grant: 'I felt … sad and depressed at the downfall of a foe who had fought so long and valiantly, and had suffered so much for a cause, though that cause was, I believe, one of the worst for which a people ever fought.'

B

BLACK CODES Laws, varying from Southern state to state, legally enforcing aspects of slavery. Prohibited reading, writing and all aspects of education, restricted movement (passes were usually required to leave the plantation), forbade possession of weapons. Marriages forbidden and status and name of children derived from mother overcoming problem that father could be white and slaveowner. Strict vagrancy laws and compulsory apprenticeships vigorously applied. Hunting, shooting, fishing, free grazing of cattle forbidden and punishment by imprisonment, flogging, selling and breaking up of informal families, even killing of slaves, accepted occasionally, if consequence of 'moderate correction'.

BLACK CODES (1865–66) Series of Southern state laws rapidly implemented following end of war and emancipation of slaves as means of controlling freedpersons. Marital relations legalised but interracial marriage forbidden. Freedpersons excluded from juries and from voting; could testify in court but only against other freedpersons. Draconian labour laws – enforced contracts, harsh vagrancy laws – and apprentice laws which hired out orphans and the destitute seemed to Northerners to be almost tantamount to slavery. Radicalised North and **Republican Party**, who were determined to end them, and fuelled opposition to President **Johnson**, who was willing to accept them. Codes modified by 1866 Civil Rights Act.

'BLEEDING KANSAS' Phrase coined by **Greeley** to describe confused and confusing five-year guerilla warfare between pro- and anti-slavery factions in Kansas following **Kansas–Nebraska Act** of 1854. Majority of inhabitants anti-slavery but Southern 'border ruffians' crossed into territory and fraudulently elected pro-slavery Constitution and Convention at Lecompton without referendum in November 1857. Anti-slavers abstained and elected anti-slavery delegates to state legislature in Topeka in May 1857. Into this anarchic violent scene the North poured 'Beecher's Bibles' (rifles) and **John Brown** led a raid at Pottowatomie Creek (24–25 May 1856) in which five settlers were massacred and, 21 May 1856, anti-slavery centre of Lawrence sacked. February 1858, President **Buchanan**'s acceptance of Lecompton Constitution led to split and crippling of **Democratic** Party, opposition led by **Douglas**, and 22 Northern **Democrats** joined the **Republicans** in voting against it in House of Representatives. Kansas remained territory till entering Union as free state in January 1861. This was civil war in miniature.

BORDER STATES Of great political and strategic significance. As Lincoln said: 'I hope to have God on my side, but I must have Kentucky.' Four were slave states – Maryland, Virginia, Kentucky, Missouri – though only Virginia seceded, while West Virginia broke away to become a separate, free state in 1863. About 200,000 border whites fought for the Union and 90,000 for the Confederacy.

C

CALIFORNIA GOLD RUSH Gold was discovered near Sutter's Fort in January 1848 and confirmed by President **Polk** in December, just before California's transfer from Mexico to the United States. Many heeded **Greeley**'s challenge to go West and make a fortune – though few did – and the state's non-Indian population rose from 14 to 224,000 between 1848 and 1852. San Francisco, hitherto a small Spanish mission, was transformed into a major metropolis and port. California entered the Union in September 1850 as a non-slave state.

CARPETBAGGERS A Southern term of abuse aimed at Northern politicians, the dregs of Northern society who, with empty carpet bags, took advantage of the South following the war and cooperated with 'scalawags' and freedpersons to plunder and exploit South for personal economic gains. This is essentially Southern mythology; their crime to support black suffrage. The majority of 'carpetbaggers' were well-educated professionals, talented, ambitious and young, serving the **Republican Party**'s cause in the South. There was some venality and corruption (Henry Warmoth of Louisiana, for example), but then Louisiana was notoriously corrupt and most left the South in debt following the collapse of cotton prices after 1873. Never more than 2 per cent of the population in South. Played large role in state constitutional conventions, 1867–68, included Adelbert Ames (Mississippi), James Alcorn (Mississippi), Albion Tourgee (North Carolina) and William Brownlow (Tennessee).

CHANCELLORSVILLE Second resounding Unionist defeat, 1–4 May 1863, following **Fredericksburg**, December 1862. **Hooker**, having replaced Burnside as commander of the Army of the Potomac, 25 January 1863, crossed Rappahannock river, 27 April, while **Lee**, leaving Jubal Early with 10,000 troops at Fredericksburg to protect lines to Richmond, marched 10 miles and planned for **Jackson** to outflank Hooker's right flank under General **O.O. Howard**, and attack from rear. Lee held front line with 20,000 against double his numbers. Jackson attacked 2 May, inflicting great damage, but was himself mortally wounded by Confederate sniper. Hooker remained tentative and indecisive. On 3 May Hooker withdrew across river and, 5 May, with further Lee advance, retreated. North demoralised, especially with **Vicksburg** still untaken.

CHATTANOOGA Between August and November 1863, **Grant**, having captured **Vicksburg**, moved east to relieve Rosecrans's Army besieged at Chattanooga. Supported by further Union troops under **Sherman** and **Hooker**, Grant able to provide lines of supply and Confederacy further weakened by Longstreet being despatched to attempt to recapture Knoxville. Hooker captured Lookout Mountain and Grant broke through Missionary Ridge, 23 October, where South positioned. Confederacy managed orderly retreat to Georgia, but President **Davis** replaced **Bragg** by **Joseph Johnston**.

CHICKAMAUGA On 19–20 September 1863 **Bragg** (Confederate) retreated from Chattanooga pursued by Rosecrans's Union Army of the Cumberland. Longstreet attacked Union's right and broke through but Thomas (Union) – 'the Rock of Chickamauga' – managed to hold line and secure orderly retreat. Bragg failed to pursue Union troops. A tactical triumph for the Confederacy, but North held on to Chattanooga. Rosecrans was replaced by **Hooker**.

CIVIL RIGHTS ACT, 1875 Passed by Congress, in part as tribute to Senator **Sumner**, who died 1874. Declared that freedmen should be granted all privileges and immunities of citizens of the United States irrespective of race or colour. **Ben Butler**'s controversial clause for integrating schools was dropped. Declared unconstitutional by the Supreme Court in 1883 by insisting that segregation was not a badge of slavery (thus not contravening **13th Amendment**) and the guarantees granted them by the **14th Amendment** applied not to discrimination by individuals, and were to be enforced by the state and not the federal government.

CIVIL RIGHTS CASES, 1883 Second Civil Rights Act, 1875, attempted to ensure equality of all male citizens and stop racial segregation known as 'Jim Crow laws'. **Slaughterhouse Decision** had already undermined federal commitment of **14th Amendment**, which was to be enforced by state rather than federal authorities, and was unable to interfere in areas of private discrimination. Justice Joseph Bradley refused to accept that segregation constituted a badge of slavery or servitude and was, therefore, not unconstitutional under the **13th Amendment**. Justice Marshall Harlan entered his dissent: 'I cannot resist the conclusion that the substance and spirit of the recent amendments of the Constitution have been sacrificed by a subtle and ingenious verbal criticism.' Henceforth freedpersons could appeal neither to the 13th nor 14th Amendments to sustain their civil liberties.

COMMITTEE ON THE CONDUCT OF THE WAR Established October 1861 in wake of Union defeat at Ball's Bluff and **First Bull Run** to oversee more active prosecution of war and urge ending of slavery. Under chairmanship of Senator **Benjamin Wade** of Ohio, it was dominated by **Radical Republicans**, including Zachariah Chandler and George W. Julian. Accused of partisan political interference and 'Jacobin' tendencies by enemies.

COMPROMISE OF 1850 Resulting from seven months' heated debate, combining five acts and initially introduced by **Clay**, 29 January, as omnibus bill, which had to be voted on collectively. California was to enter Union as free state (ending free/slave balance of 15 states each), the remaining territory (Utah and New Mexico) to decide question by '**popular sovereignty**', Texas to drop outstanding territorial claims on Mexico in return for federal assumption of Texan debt, slave trade to be banned in Washington, DC, and, most controversial of all, Fugitive Slave laws of 1793 to be tightened and enforced by federal commissioners. Clay, supported by **Cass**, **Webster** and **Douglas**, supported bill against strong opposition from North and South including **Taylor**, **Chase**, **Davis**, **Seward**, **Sumner** and **Calhoun**. Calhoun died on 31 March, and President Taylor on 9 July, to be succeeded by Vice President **Fillmore**, who supported it. Essentially a truce and armistice, not a final settlement, and sectional tension intensified throughout the 1850s.

CONFEDERACY South Carolina was the first Southern state to secede, 20 December 1860, following on upon Lincoln's election. Six other states – Florida, Georgia, Alabama, Mississippi, Louisiana and Texas – followed up until 1 February 1861. On 4 February fifty delegates met at Montgomery, Alabama, to establish a **Confederate Constitution** and appoint provisional president and vice president (**Davis** of Mississippi and **Stephens** of Georgia respectively). The **Fort Sumter** crisis led to the secession of four further states – Virginia, Arkansas, Tennessee and North Carolina – making a total of eleven. On 29 May 1861 the capital was moved to Richmond, Virginia, and general elections took place in November 1861. Howell Cobb (Georgia) was elected President of Congress and Davis had a cabinet of six. The practical, constitutional dilemma Davis faced was holding together a new nation which was dedicated to **states' rights**, and despite suspending *habeas corpus*, imposing martial law, expropriating property and enforcing military conscription, he met opposition throughout the war from such governors as Joseph Brown of Georgia and Zebulon Vance of North Carolina, who obstructed the draft and hoarded food and supplies. It has been argued that the Confederacy suffered by not having a legitimate party opposition, unlike the North. Certainly the Confederacy organised its war **finances** less efficiently and its diplomatic strategy of gaining formal recognition and support from Europe by means of '**King Cotton**' failed entirely. The Southern white male made a huge blood sacrifice in his bid for independence. A total of 260,000 soldiers died, one-fifth of the Confederate adult male population, and three-quarters of all white males between the ages of 18 and 50 served. On 2 April 1865 Davis abandoned Richmond and was captured on 10 May and imprisoned for two years. It is only recently that Gary Gallagher has turned the traditional historical question of why the Confederacy lost to enquire, rather, how and why it held out for so long. While **Lee**'s army survived, so did the Confederacy. When Lee's army was defeated, so was the Confederacy.

CONSCRIPTION   The North had 3.5 times more whites of military age in 1860 than the South, but if disloyal excluded, plus those unavailable in the West and the Pacific, and the fact that slavery released more manpower for fighting in the Confederacy, the figure is probably closer to 2.5:1. The South represented some 39 per cent of the total US population, but if **border states** are subtracted the figure falls to 27 per cent and, when African Americans excluded, only 15.5 per cent. Four-fifths of Confederate able-bodied between ages 18 and 50 conscripted, as against 50 per cent of the North. On 28 March 1862 President **Davis** the first to introduce conscription. Able-bodied white males 18–35 years to serve for three years; existing one-year volunteers to remain two more years. Substitutes and exemptions were allowed – Confederate officials and (most unpopularly) one white for every twenty slaves, which was about 5 per cent of the Southern population. By the end of 1862 the Confederate army had risen from 325,000 to 450,000 (50 per cent volunteers to avoid the stigma of facing conscription). In 1864 Davis ended substitution and expiring three-year enlisters to remain and age was extended from 18- to 50-year-olds. After an initial call for 75,000 militia, and following retreat from the **Peninsula Campaign**, **Lincoln** called for 300,000 three-year recruits and 300,000 nine-month militiamen. By the end of the year the Union had 421,000 volunteers and 88,000 militia. On 3 March 1863 federal draft called on all males 20–45, though commutation fee of $300 gave exemption or substitutes could be brought, which was highly unpopular and repealed 1864. A total of 207,000 were drafted, while 87,000 paid for and 74,000 provided substitutes. With expiry

of three-year volunteers in 1864, Lincoln did not insist they stay but offered inducements – 30 days' furlough, $400 bounty – for those who did. Altogether 136,000 re-enlisted and 100,000 did not. In total the Union lost 16 per cent of its able-bodied men in the conflict: the South 20 per cent.

CONTRABAND   Three escaping fugitive slaves sought shelter at Fort Monroe, Virginia. The Confederacy demanded their return. General **Ben Butler** declared that Confederacy out of the Union, and, therefore, slaves' 'contraband' of war, who would not be returned but instead aid Union forces.

'COPPERHEADS'   Northern Peace **Democrats** opposed to **Lincoln**'s war strategy. Named after venomous snake, though often a term of opprobrium used by **Republicans** against all Democrats, who represented 44 per cent of the votes in the North in 1860 and 45 per cent in 1864. Sought peace terms with the Confederacy without black emancipation, and specifically accused Lincoln of despotism, suspending *habeas corpus*, conscription and the **Emancipation Proclamation**. **Vallandigham** a particular source of irritation to Lincoln. Concentrated in northwestern states of Ohio, Indiana and Illinois.

CRITTENDEN AMENDMENT   Introduced by Senator **Crittenden** of Kentucky, 18 December 1860. Staunch Unionist, chairing Committee of Thirteen attempting final compromise to avoid Civil War. Essentially restored **Missouri Compromise** line of 36°30' which would run west to the Pacific. South of this line slavery, the interstate slave trade, and compensation for unrecovered fugitive slaves would protect the 'peculiar institution'. The amendment introduced the word 'slavery' into the Constitution for the first time. These constitutional amendments were to be submitted to a national referendum and, if passed, were not themselves subject to amendment. All **Republican** members of the Commission rejected it, as did two Southerners, Robert Toombs and

Jefferson Davis, and the Senate also rejected it by 25 to 23 on 22 December 1860. Lincoln himself could not yield as it would destroy the vital Republican plank on the non-extension of slavery.

D

DAVIS BEND A 10,000-acre plantation on the Mississippi River, south of Vicksburg. Joseph and **Jefferson Davis** experimented in model slave community influenced by Robert Owen, the English Socialist. A degree of self-government, yearly labour contracts, slave jury system, own elected judges and sheriffs to impose discipline. In 1862 Joseph Davis had to flee. Reverted to Joseph 1865, who sold it to African American leader, Benjamin Montgomery, and making profits of $160,000 per annum. But 1878 restored to Davis family, which ended this 'negro paradise'.

'DOUGHFACES' Pejorative Northern term, first used by John Randolph to identify pro-Southern Northern **Democrats** before Civil War who tended to favour Southern territorial expansion and **slavery**. **Pierce** and **Buchanan** were presidents accused of this tendency.

DRED SCOTT DECISION, 1857 In 1830s a slave, Dred Scott, taken by master, John Emerson, north to Illinois and territory which is now Minnesota. On his return lawyers claimed that Scott, having been in free territory, was free. Denied, 1854, by Missouri Circuit Court, case reached Supreme Court in 1857, which addressed the following: was Scott a citizen with rights to sue in Federal Court? Did prolonged residence in free territory free Scott? Did Congress have right to ban slavery in territories in the first place as it had in the **Missouri Compromise** of

1820? Five members of the court were **Democratic** Southerners (**Taney**, the Chief Justice, was a Maryland slaveowner), two were Northerners and two (Nelson and Grier) from Pennsylvania. Taney initially intended a narrow interpretation on citizenship, but fissures forced him to attempt to widen a more definitive interpretation. First, Scott as slave was not a citizen of the United States. African Americans 'had for more than a century before been regarded as being of an inferior order, and altogether unfit to associate with the white race, either in social or political relations; and so far inferior that they had no rights which the white man was bound to respect; and that the negro might justly and lawfully be reduced to slavery for his benefit'. Taney went further. Scott could not claim freedom because the Missouri Compromise, passed by Congress in 1820, was unconstitutional in that it substantively denied the 5th Amendment to the Constitution, which insisted that citizens could not be deprived of life, liberty or property (i.e. black slaves) either north or south of the Missouri Compromise line. Undue pressure was placed on Grier to join majority opinion. Three other Northerners dissented. The political consequences of this decision – the split in **Democratic** ranks and united opposition of the **Republicans** to their '**free soil**, free labour, free men' dogma – were disastrous and hastened the Civil War. On 26 May 1857 Scott was granted manumission by his owner, and he lived for one year as a freedperson.

E

ELECTORAL COLLEGE Founding fathers, with their suspicion of popular opinion, established indirect method of electing president. Number of specially chosen electors in each state (number equalling the sum of two senators per state plus the number of state representatives in the House of Representatives) would vote for candidate, with the highest number becoming president and second highest vice president. In 1804, following tied vote election between Jefferson and Burr in 1800, 12th Amendment to the Constitution recognised the existence of party, and insisted on separate votes for president and vice president. Time, new conventions and growing democratisation led to informal modifications. By 1860 universal white male suffrage voted directly for presidential party candidate (whose vice-presidential running mate was appointed by presidential candidate at party convention). The winner in each state, however closely, took all that state's Electoral College votes. This is called the 'unit rule'. Various anomalies can arise from this system. In 1860, for example, **Lincoln (Republican)** gained 180 Electoral College votes to **Douglas**'s (**Democrat**) 12. Converted into popular voting, the figures were 1.8 million and 1.4 million respectively. It is also possible for a candidate to win the popular vote but lose the Electoral College vote, such as happened with Gore versus Bush in 2000.

EMANCIPATION PROCLAMATION   As late as 1862 **Lincoln** still advocating colonisation: 'There is an unwillingness on the part of our people, harsh as it may be, for you free coloured people to remain among us.' On 6 March 1862 Lincoln offered gradual, compensated emancipation in **border states** but rejected by all. Northern backlash against the ferocity of the **New York City Draft Riots**, African American heroism and their assault on Fort Wagner and, most significantly, Union military success at **Antietam**, led five days later to the preliminary Proclamation, 22 September 1862. Those states still in rebellion against Union would have slaves freed, 1 January 1863, the day the Emancipation Proclamation came into force. Proclamation not a ringing rhetorical declaration (**Hofstadter** refers to document as having

'all the moral grandeur of a bill of lading') but grounded on military necessity: slaves were freed in remaining Confederate areas, but not where Union troops in control. Led London *Spectator* to observe: 'The principle asserted is not that a human being cannot own another, but that he cannot own him unless he is loyal to the United States.' But the war effort, hitherto seen as fight for Union, now also fight for black freedom, and paved way for **13th Amendment** of 1865 which formally freed slaves.

F

FILIBUSTERING   Military adventurers invading Central American countries for profit and extension of slave empire. Most notably William Walker, who exploited Civil War in Nicaragua and made himself its president, 1856–57. August 1860 invaded Honduras. Executed 12 September 1860.

FINANCE   In August 1861, and for the first time in American history, an income tax of 3 per cent over $800 p.a. incomes was imposed on the North to finance the war. By 1864 this had risen from 5 per cent on incomes over $600 to 10 per cent on incomes over $10,000 p.a. Excise taxes and higher tariffs brought in a further $600 million in the last three years of the war. One in four families in the North purchased $1.5 million of war bonds, which combined profits with patriotism to help sustain the war effort. **Chase** at the Treasury suspended payment of bills in 'specie' (that is, without gold or silver backing) on 30 December 1861, and issued $447 million 'greenback' dollar notes as legal tender. In February 1863 and again in June 1864 Chase passed **National Bank Acts** which began the process of centralising a banking system splintered and decentralised by Jacksonians.

Banks could acquire federal charters and issue national bank notes up to 90 per cent of the value of US bonds they held. By the end of the war, after the imposition of a 10 per cent tax on state bank notes, there were 1,294 national as against 349 state banks. The Confederacy paid its war bills by taxes, printing paper money and borrowing. Hoping for a short war, the Confederacy was wary of imposing taxes. A small direct property tax was mainly paid for by state loans and raised only 7 per cent of total revenue. On 24 April 1863 a graduated income tax of 15 per cent on incomes over $10,000 p.a. was introduced, but there was much evasion, it was difficult to collect and paid for in depreciated currency which only yielded $119 million in two years. Sixty per cent of the total raised was through printing money which led to high inflation: 1865 prices were 92 times above pre-war levels and this hit the poor hardest because wages lagged behind prices. This contributed generally to Southern discontent and, specifically, to the Richmond bread riots which broke out in the spring of 1863, news of which was suppressed by the Southern press. Impressment of provisions was also deeply unpopular. War bonds, as in the North, were more successful, though at only two-fifths of the total raised did not equal the Northern figure, which was close to two-thirds. Comparison shows, on the whole, that the North coped better in financial matters. Income tax in the North raised 21 per cent as against only 5.6 per cent in the South, while inflation, which ran at 60 per cent in the South, was only 13 per cent in the North. The war transformed a traditionally *laissez-faire* economy: by the war's end federal expenditure represented 15 per cent of total Gross National Product.

FIRE EATERS Vociferous Southern extremists advocating aggressive extension of **slave power**, **secession** and independent **Confederacy**, and, implicitly, the superiority of a semi-feudal caste system over the rampantly egalitarian, atomistic, materialist and reformist North. Included **Thomas Ruffin**, **William Yancey** and Robert Butler Rhett.

FIRST BULL RUN First major military engagement of war at Manassas Junction, only 30 miles from Washington. General McDowell, hoping to march to Richmond, met **Beauregard**'s smaller numbers. General **Joseph Johnston**, managing to elude General Patterson in Shenandoah Valley, travelled 60 miles by train to reach battlefield on afternoon of 21 July 1861 with 11,000 troops and make forces more equal. Union attack initially successful, but Confederate counterattack about 4.00 p.m. led to Northern rout and retreat to Washington. General Bee witnessed **Jackson**'s assault: 'There is Jackson standing like a stone wall. Rally behind the Virginians.' Hence, thereafter, 'Stonewall' Jackson. Chaos captured graphically by London *Times*'s war correspondent, William Howard Russell, had considerable impact. But curiously Northern demoralisation activated **McClellan**'s formidable organisation of the Army of the Potomac while the Confederacy suffered a degree of hubris and a false sense of superiority.

FORTS HENRY AND DONELSON **Grant** and Foote set out from Cairo, 5 February 1862, on Mississippi with 15,000 troops to attack Confederate General Albert Johnston's weak point at Fort Henry (on Tennessee River) and Donelson (Cumberland River). Fort Henry taken 6 February and Donelson 16 February, when 13,000 troops, one-third of Johnston's army, surrendered. This, and the opening it gave Northern troops to penetrate deep into Southern territory – Nashville, Tennessee, the first Confederate state capital to fall – followed on 23 February, made this first decisive Union victory in the West and added to Grant's growing reputation.

FORT SUMTER Federal fortress at mouth of Charleston Harbor, South Carolina. Immediate cause of Civil War. President **Buchanan** had procrastinated, but **Lincoln**, in Inaugural of 4 March 1861, insisted: 'The power confided to me will be used to hold, occupy and possess the property and places belonging to the government.' Despite **Seward** giving impressions to the contrary, Lincoln and cabinet decided to reprovision rather than send troop reinforcements. Fort held by General Anderson and, 6 April, Lincoln ordered Fox's expedition to sail. **Davis**, aware of this, made decision to fire on fort, 9 April, before Fox's expedition arrived, and, 12 April, **Beauregard** unleashed 34-hour bombardment. On 13 April Anderson surrendered, and on 14 April Confederate flag raised over fort. On 15 April Lincoln issued first proclamation for 75,000 militia for 90 days to put down the insurrection.

'40 ACRES AND A MULE' Along with freedom and education, the greatest desire of freedpersons was for land ownership. **Sherman**'s Order 15 had granted 40,000 freedpersons conquered land beyond Charleston (but rescinded later by President **Johnson**). **Stevens** urged the confiscation of former slaveowners' lands to be given to freedpersons, but this rejected as too radical an attack on property rights. The **Freedmen's Bureau** controlled 850,000 acres of land, some of which was sold to freedpersons. By 1880 up to 5 per cent of farmed Southern land was owned by freedpersons. By 1910 that figure had reached 25 per cent.

FREDERICKSBURG On 7 November 1862, **Lincoln** replaced **McClellan** with Burnside as commander of the Army of the Potomac, which moved towards Richmond. Burnside suffered delays in crossing the Rappahannock River before engaging **Lee** on 13 December. **Meade** managed to breach gap in Confederate ranks, but this was repelled and on 15–16 December Burnside retreated back across Rappahannock. This Union defeat encouraged France to take Mexico City six months later and Lincoln – 'If there is a worse place than Hell, I am in it' – replaced Burnside by **Hooker**.

FREE SOIL The principle of 'free soil, free labour, free men' galvanised Northern electorate and, beginning as platform in **Liberty** and **Free Soil parties**, successfully captured presidency for **Lincoln** and **Republican Party** in 1860. Encapsulated in Lincoln's message to Congress, 4 July 1861: 'This is essentially a people's contest. On the side of the Union is a struggle for maintaining in the world that form and substance of government whose leading object is to elevate the condition of man – to lift artificial weights from all shoulders, to clear the paths of laudable pursuits for all; to afford all an unfettered start, and a fair chance in the race of life.' In determining whether territories of West – America's future – should be slave or free, 'free soil' embraced a wide spectrum of opinion from negrophobe to abolitionist, with promise of geographical and social mobility and ultimately self-employment. Lincoln: 'When one starts poor, as most do in the race for life, free society is such that he knows he can better his condition; he knows there is no fixed condition of labor for his whole life.' The West also operated as safety valve for social unrest and, racially, land free of African Americans as well as slavery. Ironically post-war economics tended to lock working class into permanent wage labour.

FREEDMEN'S BUREAU Established March 1865 under General **O.O. Howard** to deal with immediate and pressing social and economic conditions in South. First task to distribute daily rations (150,000 daily between 1865 and 1870), one-third of which went to white refugees. No separate budget but dependent upon War Department. Funds vetoed by **Johnson**, July 1866, but Congress overruled him and renewed funding for two years. A total of 550 local agents, but never more than 900 altogether. Possessed 850,000 acres of abandoned land in 1865, but mainly returned to pardoned owners. Paternalistic on labour, imposing labour contracts and paid wages to freedpersons. Greatest success, and $5 million out of its total $9 million budget, went into educating whites and blacks. By 1870, 4,000 freedmen schools, 9,000 teachers and 200,000 pupils (though only 12 per cent of total). Reduced black illiteracy from 80 per cent (1870) to 70 per cent (1880) and by 1880 three-fifths of white children and two-fifths of black children in schools. There was no interracial schooling. Bureau ceased to function June 1872.

G

GADSDEN PURCHASE   In 1854 the Treaty of Guadaloupe Hidalgo did not settle all outstanding US–Mexican questions, including Article 11 of the treaty, which concerned Mexican protection from native Indians. July 1853, James Gadsden, Minister to Mexico, was instructed by President **Pierce** to settle with Santa Anna administration and secure territory for Pacific Railroad by the Southern route. After much opposition from antislavery forces, and much questionable lobbying and speculation, purchase was ratified 25 April 1854. Mexico was paid $10 million for over 45,000 square miles of what is now part of Arizona and New Mexico.

GAG RULE   First used by Congress, 1836, to treat anti-slavery petitions, 'without being either pointed or referred, be laid on the table and that no further action whatever shall be had thereon'. Congress had received 415,000 petitions, many from women, by 1838. Strong Northern opposition: seen as trampling on civil liberties and interfering in legitimate political protest. Overruled in 1844.

GETTYSBURG   Emboldened by victory of **Chancellorsville**, **Lee** invaded Pennsylvania and threatened Harrisburg. Minor skirmish when Union forces met Confederate troops by chance turned into major conflict. **Meade**, having replaced **Hooker**, 28 June 1863, arrived on scene on 1 July. On 2 July **Lee** ordered two frontal attacks – Longstreet on left and Ewell on right – but uncoordinated. On 3 July, Lee tried again with full attack on Meade's centre. Pickett led famous charge on Cemetery Ridge, and, though losing half his men, almost succeeded. On 4 July Lee began his retreat and, 13 and 14 July, recrossed Potomac. Longstreet criticised by Confederates and Meade in North for not pursuing Lee. Total casualities, over 50,000, horrifying, and Lee had lost one-third of his army. Along with fall of **Vicksburg**, also on 4 July, this battle was the turning point in war.

H

HOMESTEAD ACT   Integral part of **Republican Party**'s economic strategy to realise '**free soil**, free labour, free men' doctrine. Passed 20 May 1862. Free title given to 160 acres of land worked and improved after five years (by male or female) with small registration fee. A total of 15,000 settled 3 million acres of land during Civil War alone. Ultimately Act gave 80 million acres to half a million settlers. Not always successful. Speculators and rail companies tended to get best land, and 160 acres unsustainable on poor soil.

K

KANSAS–NEBRASKA ACT (see Map 2)   Initially urged by Senator **Stephen Douglas** and representative William Richardson (Chairman of Senate and House Committees on Territories respectively) to organise territory on lines of '**popular sovereignty**' as prelude to railway from Chicago to San Francisco. Both Kansas and Nebraska were north of **Missouri Compromise** line of 1820, but support of congressional Southern votes demanded this. Signed by President **Pierce**, 22 May 1854. Opposition from **Sumner**, **Chase**, **Seward**, etc., solidified in new **Republican Party** opposed to extension of slavery and struggle between pro- and anti-slavery forces in '**Bleeding Kansas**'. The Act was a vital prelude to Civil War.

KING COTTON Economic strategy employed by Confederacy to put pressure on Europe, and Britain in particular, by starving it of raw cotton and forcing formal recognition or aid. The South produced about 80 per cent of the world's raw cotton in the 1850s and 75 per cent of Britain's supplies. By 1862 Confederate embargo reduced supply to Britain by two-thirds. But strategy failed. Between 1857 and 1860 Britain had acquired large surpluses, new supplies were opening up in Egypt and India and, with a series of disastrous harvests in Europe, 'King Corn' forced Britain to import 50 per cent of her grain supplies from Union. Diplomatically, Palmerston was far more concerned with Europe and Bismarck, feared for the vulnerability of Canada, and desired a stable western hemisphere free of possible future Confederate adventurism.

KU KLUX KLAN Informal group of white males, often Confederate veterans, whose aim was to intimidate by violence or threat of violence white **Republicans** ('**scalawags**') or African Americans, especially when trying to exercise their right to vote. Founded in Pulaski, Tennessee, 1866, it peaked 1867–71, particularly during presidential elections of 1868, and operated over about a quarter of the South, more so in racially mixed hill country. In Louisiana alone in 1868 they were responsible for the killing of from 800 to 1,000 individuals. On 20 April 1871 the Enforcement Acts further tightened by Ku

Klux Klan Bill on felony and conspiracy. President could employ the army, suspend *habeas corpus*, outlaw the Klan itself, purge the Klan from juries, and impose stiff penalties for perjury, stop discrimination in voting on grounds of race, and elect supervisors to oversee fair elections. In October 1871 **Grant** declared a state of lawlessness in nine up-country South Carolina counties and, though few Klansmen were indicted or convicted, did aid in assisting order.

L

LINCOLN–DOUGLAS DEBATES Seven joint debates between 27 August and 15 October 1858 in campaign for Illinois's Senate. Format of first speaker talking for one hour; one and a half hour reply by opposite number, closing with another half hour, making three hours in all. **Lincoln** argued eloquently for **free soil**, the non-extension of slavery and for peaceful change leading to its ultimate extinction. 'If slavery is wrong, then nothing is wrong. I cannot remember when I did not so think and feel.' But this was far short of recognising or accepting racial equality: 'There is a physical difference between the races which I believe will forever forbid the two races living together on terms of social and political equality.' On 27 August, at Freeport, put question to **Douglas** – identified with '**popular sovereignty**' doctrine – whether territory could exclude slavery prior to formation of state constitution. This faced Douglas with dilemma of reply of 'yes', which would alienate South, or 'no' and alienate Northern wing of the **Democratic Party** and expose the overall weakness of 'popular sovereignty', particularly in light of **Dred Scott**. Douglas answered yes: 'Slavery cannot exist a day in the midst of an unfriendly people with unfriendly laws.' Douglas played racial card in central and southern Illinois, accusing Lincoln of being 'Black Republican', to which Lincoln replied by exposing Douglas's moral indifference to the issue and 'cares not whether slavery be voted down or voted up'. Douglas won the Senate seat, but debates made hitherto unknown Lincoln a national political figure and helped gain him presidency two years later.

M

MANIFEST DESTINY Phrase first used by newspaper editor, John O'Sullivan, July 1845, in favour of **Polk**'s expansionist campaign for presidency. 'The American claim is by right of our manifest destiny to overspread and to possess the whole of the continent which Providence has given us for the development of the great experiment of liberty and federative self-government entrusted to us.' Embodied in Polk's dispute with Britain over **Oregon**, the annexation of Texas and the **Mexican War**, which together added more territory, half a million square miles, to the United States than under any other president. But overshadowed by sectional struggle over whether this expansion would be free or slave.

EX PARTE **MERRYMAN** Constitution (Article 1, Section 9) stated that *habeas corpus*, legal right protecting individual being detained without charges, 'shall not be suspended unless when, in case of rebellion or invasion, the public safety may require it'. John Merryman, Baltimore secessionist, imprisoned by military in Fort McHenry. Lincoln had suspended *habeas corpus* in Maryland in April but, 28 May 1861, Chief Justice **Taney**, acting in his capacity as senior judge of Maryland Circuit Court, insisted Congress, and not President alone, could suspend

writ and that civilians could not be arrested by military without sanction of civil government. Lincoln ignored decision, deriving powers as Commander in Chief and justifying himself before Congress, 4 July 1861: 'Are all the laws, *but one*, to go unexecuted and the government itself go to pieces, lest that one be violated?' Merryman released after seven weeks and case never came to trial.

MEXICAN WAR, 1846–48 Annexation of Texas led to US–Mexican dispute over territory. Clash on River Rio Grande, 25 April 1846, led to President **Polk** declaring war 12 May. **Zachary Taylor** defeated Santa Anna's forces at Buena Vista in February and, with support of **Frémont**, the Bear Flag revolt led California to declare her independence from Mexico in June. Still Mexico refused to negotiate and in March 1847 General **Winfield Scott** landed his troops at Vera Cruz and, 14 September, occupied Mexico City. Treaty of Guadaloupe Hidalgo, 2 February 1848, added 900,000 square miles and a Pacific outlet for the United States, but domestic repercussions as to whether acquired territory was to be free or slave led to great upheaval and helped precipitate war. **Emerson**: 'Mexico will poison us.'

EX PARTE **MILLIGAN, 1866** Lambdin P. Milligan (Indiana, '**Copperhead**') arrested 1864 and sentenced to death by military tribunal for collaborating with Confederacy. Supreme Court held, 1866, that as civilian and outside war zone where civil courts available, Milligan had been unconstitutionally tried by martial law and was released after 18 months' imprisonment. Rejecting presidential or congressional right to establish military tribunals, this decision undermined **Radical Republican** plans for **Reconstruction**.

MISSISSIPPI PLAN, 1875 Techniques of intimidation and ostracism, threats, social and economic pressures, widespread stuffing of ballot boxes, to force statewide

Republicans (10–12 per cent of voters) back into **Democratic Party** and stop African Americans from voting. September 1875 Governor Adelbert Ames appealed to **Grant** for troops, but refused fearing anti-Republican negrophobe repercussions in North. Democrats gained 30,000 majority and Ames forced to resign and leave state rather than face impeachment. Ames: 'a revolution has taken place – by force of arms and a race are disfranchised – they are to be returned to a condition of serfdom – an era of second slavery'. Similar techniques used in other Southern states to establish Democratic Party 'Solid South' and effectively disfranchise African Americans.

MISSOURI COMPROMISE, 1820 There were 11 free and 11 slave states in 1819. In 1820 Maine was admitted as the twelfth free state and Missouri as the twelfth slave, with an amendment introduced by Senator J.B. Thomas (Illinois) that in the remaining Louisiana Purchase territory slavery was to be prohibited above the geographical line 36°30′. There was a sense that this delicate balancing act could not last indefinitely. To President Jefferson it sounded 'like a fire bell in the night … A geographical line, coinciding with a marked principle, moral and political, once conceived and held up to the angry passions of men, will never be obliterated; and every new irritation will mark it deeper and deeper'. To **J.Q. Adams** it was 'a mere preamble – a title page, to a great tragic volume'. The Compromise was congressionally annulled in **Douglas**'s **Kansas–Nebraska Act** of 1854 and constitutionally by the Supreme Court in **Taney**'s **Dred Scott Decision** of 1857.

MORRILL LAND GRANT ACT, 1862 First advocated in Congress, 1857, by Justin Morrill (Vermont, **Whig**), 'to promote the liberal and practical education of the industrial classes in the several pursuits and professions in life'. Vetoed by **Buchanan** but approved by **Lincoln**, 2 July 1862. Each state received 30,000 acres of federal land for each state member of Congress to establish funds and endow colleges of agricultural and mechanical arts. Led to creation of 70 institutions including, for example, Berkeley, California, and the University at Madison in Wisconsin.

MUDSILL Poor white farmers of South. So called by wealthy slaveowner, James Hammond, of South Carolina. 'In all social systems there must be a class to do the manual duties, to perform the drudgery of life … it constitutes the very mudsill of society.' But while their economic and social status was below that of the slaveowner, it was racially above that of the slave. Senator **Calhoun** (South Carolina) stated in 1848: 'With us the two great divisions of society are not the rich and poor, but white and black; and all the former, the poor as well as the rich, belong to the upper class, and are respected and treated as equals.' This encouraged mudsill's class fight against invading Union troops during Civil War.

N

NATIONAL BANKING ACT **Salmon Chase**'s wartime regulation, February 1863, of currency and banking. Unregulated since the time of **Jackson**, over 1,600 different banks existed with 12,000 different bank notes. Banks granted charter to buy US bonds up to one-third of total capital of bank and issued federal bank notes – 'greenbacks' – up to 90 per cent of value of bonds. A 10 per cent tax levied on state bank notes drove them out of circulation, establishing a more stable and uniform currency.

NAVAL BLOCKADE Though only 5 per cent of Northern armed forces, **Gideon Welles**'s navy played vital role in blockade of 3,500 miles of Southern coast in support of land armies. **Lincoln** proclaimed naval blockade against Confederacy, 19 April 1861, and, although five out of six blockade runners got through, the majority of vessels were small and imports fell by one-third. In all, 500 Union vessels captured or destroyed about 15,000 blockade runners. In early days of war, a sunken ship, *Merrimack*, raised by Confederacy, iron-clad and re-named *Virginia*. Sunk two Union vessels, *Cumberland* and *Congress*, off Hampton Roads, but stand-off with Union *Monitor* and thereafter scuttled. By end of war Union possessed 58 'iron-clads' and Confederates 21. Northern blockades slowly took hold. North's early lack of sea control hampered **McClellan**'s **Peninsula Campaign** against Richmond. In April 1862, **Farragut** captured New Orleans (Louisiana) and, August 1864, Mobile (Alabama), leaving only Wilmington (North Carolina) and Charleston (South Carolina) as major open Southern ports. Wilmington fell January 1865. Farragut's control of mouth of the Mississippi aided **Grant**'s capture of **Forts Henry and Donelson** and aided final capitulation of **Vicksburg**, 4 July 1863. The **Anaconda Strategy** had finally succeeded.

NEW YORK CITY DRAFT RIOTS Following Conscription Act, March 1863, which enabled wealthier to pay commutation fee of $300 or provide substitute (about $1,000). Also working-class male fears of being swamped in labour market by freedpersons. Rioters targeted draft headquarters and African Americans, 11 out of total of 105 dead during five days of riot, 13–17 July 1863. Unofficial estimates put the figure as high as 1,000. Put down by detachment from **Meade**'s army and city paid many commutation fees for workmen. Worst city riot in American history.

NULLIFICATION Constitutional principle that the sovereign state can nullify laws it deems unconstitutional within its own borders: closely allied to **states' rights**. First employed by Republicans, Madison and Jefferson, 1798, in their Virginia and Kentucky Resolutions aimed at the Federalists' president, John Adams's prosecution of the Alien and Sedition Acts, 1798, which were interpreted as being aimed at the Republican opposition. In 1814 Federalists at the Hartford Convention nullified Jefferson's Embargo Act of 1807, which they argued damaged New England trade and industry. The principle was perfected by John **Calhoun** in his *South Carolina Exposition* and *Disquisition on Government*. States retained their ultimate sovereignty: a numerical majority electing a convention within the state could legitimately nullify federal laws: a concurrent majority representing a particular interest could exercise a veto over government action. These principles were put to the test in 1832–33 when South Carolina nullified the 1828 'Tariff of Abominations' and the modified tariffs of 1832 and went on to nullify **Jackson**'s Force Bill of 1833, which was only repealed when Congress adopted a compromise tariff. Nullification was increasingly seen as a Southern doctrine protecting that section from federal intervention in slavery, but 14 Northern states passed Personal Liberty Laws which implicitly nullified the Fugitive Slave laws of 1850. The doctrine was finally laid to rest by the Civil War.

OREGON DISPUTE Anglo-American dispute over US–Canadian border between Rocky Mountains and Pacific. In 1818 settlement agreed to 10-year joint occupation, but mass immigration following establishment of Oregon Trail after 1840 led to demands that Oregon territory become American. **John Quincy Adams**'s proposal of the 49th Parallel was initially rejected by Britain and **Polk** won the presidential election of 1844 in particular with the popular cry of '**Manifest Destiny** – 54°40′ or Fight'. In fact the United States did not fight but ratified the 49th Parallel on 15 June 1846.

OSTEND MANIFESTO **Polk** had tried to purchase Cuba in the 1840s. In 1854 **Pierce**'s secretary of state, William Marcy, sent **Buchanan** to UK, John Mason to France and Pierre Soulé to Spain to negotiate offer. If rebuffed, US claimed that 'by every law, human and divine, we shall be justified in wresting it from Spain if we have the power'. Marcy repudiated Manifesto when made public and Soulé forced to resign.

P

PACIFIC RAILROAD ACT Promoted as military as well as economic measure, **Lincoln** signed Act 1 July 1862 to connect Omaha, Nebraska, to San Francisco in California to be financed by loans and generous land grants (120 million acres in total). Northern route also planned from St Paul, Minnesota, to Seattle, Washington. Project commenced 1865 and, 10 May 1869, Central and Union Pacific lines met at Promontory Point, Utah, creating trans-Continental Railroad.

PANIC OF 1857 Economic bust after initial boom following **Mexican War**. Inflation following **Californian Gold Rush**, intensive land speculation and weak banking system contributed. Collapse of Ohio Life Assurance and Trust Company in Cincinnati, 24 August 1857, triggered off depression which effected railways, manufacture and wheat production in West but left cotton relatively unscathed. By mid-October banks forced to suspend specie payment and the conversion of bank notes into gold and silver coin. Helped shape politics of 1860 presidential election with **Republicans** offering economic solution of high tariffs, sound banking, free soil and homesteads to offset decline.

PENINSULA CAMPAIGN Spring 1862, attempt by Union to capture Confederate capital, Richmond. **Lincoln** wanted direct assault by land but **McClellan**, commander of the Army of the Potomac, decided on indirect approach by sea, landing on Yorktown Peninsula and proceeding 70 miles to Confederate capital. Lincoln insisted, however, on retaining 40,000 troops to protect Washington, DC. McClellan set out April 1862 with 110,000 troops and, 3–4 May, captured Yorktown and Williamsburg and reached James River only nine miles from Richmond. The Confederate, **Johnston**, retaliated at Fair Oaks (31 May–1 June), was wounded and replaced by **Lee**, who repelled McClellan, while **Jeb Stuart**'s cavalry encircled Union army, gathering information and destroying extended supply routes. McDowell's forces, when not defending Washington, were engaged against **Jackson** in Shenandoah Valley and unable to come to the aid of McClellan, whose army had retreated to James River. In Seven Days' battle (26 June–2 July) Lee took offensive, but Union forces held him at bay at Malvern Hill (1 July) while McClellan reached safety of Harrison's Landing. Lee withdrew and campaign came to end. Lee had saved Richmond and repelled Army of the Potomac but achieved no outstanding victory.

PETERSBURG, SIEGE OF Petersburg was important rail centre 20 miles from Richmond. **Grant**'s aim was to cut three rail links to town and explode mines beneath Southern earthworks. Siege lasted 15 June 1864 to 2 April 1865. **Lee** hoped to break out and join up with **Johnston**'s army in North Carolina, and destroy **Sherman**'s troops before they met up with Grant's. Failed, and on 2 April evacuated with 35,000 troops. Richmond surrendered following day and Lee a week later.

PLESSY V. FERGUSON, 1896 This case tested the constitutionality of an 1890 Louisiana law which racially segregated its railway carriages. Justice Henry Brown, in majority decision, conceded that **14th Amendment** was intended to enforce racial equality, 'but in the nature of things it could not have been intended to abolish distinctions based upon color, or to enforce social, as distinguished from political, equality, or a commingling of the two races on terms unsatisfactory to either'. Brown cited racial segregation in schools and state laws against interracial marriage to reinforce his contention and proposed the principle of 'separate but equal' facilities. Justice Marshall Harlan entered a vigorous dissent, 'in the view of the Constitution, in the eye of the law, there is in this country no superior, dominant ruling class of citizens. There is no caste here. Our Constitution is color-blind'. The 'separate but equal' doctrine was only overturned in 1954 by Chief Justice Warren's Supreme Court, which declared in *Brown v. Board of Education of Topeka* that 'separate educational facilities are inherently unequal' and therefore unconstitutional. This landmark decision inaugurated the second Reconstruction or Civil Rights Movement of the twentieth century.

POPULAR SOVEREIGNTY OR 'SQUATTER SOVEREIGNTY' Allowing inhabitants of territory to decide by voting whether to enter Union free or slave. First proposed by Senator **Lewis Cass** (Michigan), 1847, as political solution to slavery question as applied in **Great Compromise of 1850** to Utah and New Mexico. But in giving neither North nor South cast-iron guarantee, served to exacerbate question and lead to '**bleeding Kansas**'. Opposed by **Lincoln**: 'That if any one man choose to enslave another, no third man shall be allowed to object.' Also uncertainty over timing of vote; whether during territorial stage or when adopting a state constitution and entering Union. Adopted by **Douglas** in **Kansas–Nebraska Act**, 1854, which repealed **Missouri Compromise** and rejected by Supreme Court ruling in **Dred Scott**, 1857.

PRESIDENTIAL VETO Executive power to prevent enactment of congressional legislation. President can refuse to sign, or pocket (delay) it but veto can be overruled by two-thirds of both Houses of Congress. **Jackson**, the first to use it extensively (12 vetoes), **Tyler** (10), **Polk** (3), **Pierce** (9), **Buchanan** (7), **Lincoln** (6) (including the **Wade–Davis Bill**) and **Johnson** (28), reflecting the tense constitutional struggle between President and Congress over **Reconstruction**.

PRIGG V. PENNSYLVANIA **(Supreme Court case), 1842** 1832 female slave, Margaret Ashmore, and children fled from Maryland to Pennsylvania. Five years later Edward Prigg, agent, seized her and returned her to owner. Pennsylvania statute of 1826 prohibited kidnapping without requisite state certificate and this upheld by Pennsylvania Supreme Court, 1840. In a decision written by Justice Joseph Story, Pennsylvania law declared unconstitutional because 1793 federal Fugitive Slave Act put slaveowners' rights to property above state laws. But future enforcement to be federal not state responsibility. Nine Northern states passed Personal Liberty Laws between 1842 and 1850 when laws further tightened under Great **Compromise of 1850**.

R

RADICAL REPUBLICANS Major leaders in Senate included **Charles Sumner** (Massachusetts) and **Henry Wilson** (Massachusetts), **Ben Wade** (Ohio) and Zachariah Chandler (Michigan). In House of Representatives, **Thaddeus Stevens** (Pennsylvania), George Boutwell (Massachusetts) and George Julian (Indiana) called for emancipation and arming of slaves during Civil War and urged radical **Reconstruction** in

South as against **Lincoln**'s moderate Reconstruction. Lincoln: 'They are nearer to me than the other side, in thought and sentiment, though utterly hostile to me personally. They are utterly lawless and the unhandiest devils in the world to deal with – but after all their faces are set Zionwards.' Came into their own with swelling of **Republican** ranks in 1866 mid-term elections and constitutional struggle with President **Johnson** when their ranks were reinforced by moderate Republicans. Sumner declared Confederate states had committed 'state suicide' by secession and reverted to territory under full congressional control. Stevens argued that Confederate states were 'conquered provinces' and should be treated accordingly. With the failure of Johnson's impeachment and **Grant**'s election in 1868 their influence waned.

RECONSTRUCTION Name given to various methods adopted to deal with **Confederacy** following defeat in Civil War. Complex and containing multiplicity of conflicts and clashing principles: sectional, North versus South plus widely different attitudes within these sections, politically **Republican** versus **Democrat**, and, constitutionally, with the President fighting Congress for control of the Reconstruction process. The Presidents – **Lincoln**, **Johnson** and **Grant** – tended to pursue moderate policies emphasising swift return of ex-Confederacy to Union over radical change in South. The majority of Republicans were moderates too, but President Johnson's obstinacy and clumsy mishandling of the process swung many to more radical solutions. Johnson is the only president in American history to be impeached, and it failed by only one vote. The Republican Party genuinely wished to aid freedpersons, but vociferous Southern opposition and a negrophobe Northern electorate set limits to its achievements. Male freedpersons supplied a new source of loyal Republican voters. Eighty per cent of Southern Republicans were black and they held about 20 per cent of public posts. In September 1867 there were 735,000 African American voters as against 635,000 whites (10–15 per cent having been disfranchised and 25–30 per cent not registering out of protest). But informal intimidation and violence and corruption plus formal procedures (poll tax, literacy tests, grandfather clauses) increasingly disfranchised freedpersons and segregation – 'Jim Crow laws' – reinforced the invisibility of black minority. **Frederick Douglass** highly critical: 'Yes, let us have peace, but let us have liberty, law and justice first.' The three Civil War amendments are testimony to high ideals of Reconstruction, but the fact that the second Reconstruction and Civil Rights were required in the twentieth century indicates its contemporary failure in practice.

RECONSTRUCTION ACT, MARCH 1867 Ten Southern states which refused **14th Amendment** divided into five military districts and military rule to set up state constitutional conventions that would ratify 14th Amendment and write new constitution which would gain approval of majority of registered voters and establish freedmen's suffrage. Passed over President **Johnson**'s veto. Resultant constitutional conventions, 1867–69, often progressive and introduced funded public education, poor relief and land taxes. Allowed freedpersons to vote in constitutional conventions.

RELIGION America is predominantly a Protestant republic rooted in the original Puritan mission of exceptionalism – America as a beacon upon a hill and example to the rest of the degenerate world – personal transcendence and obedience to God's divine will. The Constitution, however, reflected an enlightened eighteenth-century rationalist world view which separated church from state: 'Congress shall make no law respecting an establishment of religion, or prohibiting the free exercise thereof' (1st Amendment, 1791). Increasingly strict Calvinistic predestinarianism yielded to a more tolerant and positive assumption of a benign God and the possibilities of human perfectionism, and the immense impulse of the Second Great Awakening of the 1830s was the seedbed of mid-nineteenth century reformism – education, female rights, improvements in prisons and hospitals, and **abolitionism**. It also fed the philosophy of **Transcendentalism** and utopian experimentation. Religion and politics were intimately connected and extremely polarised. Modern research reveals that ethno-cultural factors such as prohibition, sabbatarianism, naturalisation, denominational education and anti-Catholicism were, in part, a nativistic response to mass European immigration in the 1840s and 1850s, and were vital in voting patterns. Pietistic churches (Episcopalian, Presbyterian, Congregationalism) were closely identified with the **Whig**, **'Know-Nothing'** and **Republican** parties, and the ritualistic, Catholic and new immigrant usually identified with the **Democratic Party**. Just as slavery split the nation, so it split the churches. Quakers rejected slavery as early as 1787, the Methodists separated, North from South, in 1844 and the Baptists in 1845. Lutherans, Episcopalians and Catholics sidestepped the issue and only separated with secession. Opposed to the abolitionists' theological fervour which advocated 'moral suasion' was the opposite conviction that slavery and submission was sanctified by the Bible. In 1860 there were *c*. 292,000 Presbyterians, 1,661,000 Methodists and 650,000 Southern Baptists. Religious faith proved a great solace for both sides of the Civil War and **Lincoln**, in his Second Inaugural, suggested that a divine will had led America into war as a means of extirpating the sin of slavery: 'The Almighty has His own purposes.' Religious fervour was a solace, too, for the African Americans during these dark and difficult years and a major source of their spiritual survival when secular support faltered. As **DuBois** wrote: 'The Preacher is the most unique personality developed by the Negro on American soil.'

S

'SCALAWAGS' Term of abuse used in South against 'white negroes' who remained loyal to Union and collaborated with **Republican Party** during **Reconstruction**. Calculated at about 20 per cent of Southern population. Formally **Whigs** and **Unionists** opposed to **secession** many upcountry farmers who were resentful of wealthy slaveowning **Democratic** class. Moderates, they desired no radical change in Southern race relations.

SECESSION The US Constitution has nothing to say on the right of secession – it would be strange for a Constitution to codify its own demise – but **states' rights'** advocates appealed to the legitimacy of revolution derived from the Declaration of Independence (1776), the fact that chronologically state sovereignty existed before federal sovereignty, that the Constitution was a voluntary compact made between states and ratified by state conventions which, having been made, could be unmade. **Lincoln** rejected this interpretation in 1860 (as **Jackson** had before him during his conflict with South Carolina over tariffs and **nullification** in 1832), forcefully reasserting the indissolubility of the Union in his first inaugural: 'The union of these states is perpetual … Plainly the central idea of secession is the essence of anarchy.' Triggered by Lincoln's election to the presidency in November 1860, Southern secession began in two waves. The first, from the lower South, began with South Carolina, 20 December 1860, with six others following in January–February of 1861. These seven states met at Montgomery, Alabama, to formulate a new **Confederate Constitution** and elect president and vice president. Arkansas at first rejected secession, as did Virginia, vitally, on 4 April 1861. The **Fort Sumter** crisis and Lincoln's call for volunteers led to a second wave with Virginia, North Carolina,

Tennessee and Arkansas seceding, making a total of 11 to form the **Confederacy**. Most ordinances of secession were passed by state legislatures or specially convened conventions. Only Texas submitted secession to a popular referendum. The Union held on to the four vital **border states** of Maryland, Kentucky, Missouri and Delaware.

SENECA FALLS CONVENTION About 200 delegates, mainly women (40 men), met on 19–20 July 1848 to urge Women's Rights Movement. Grew out of anti-slavery crusade. Abby Kelley: 'In striving to cut [the slaves'] irons off, we found most surely that *we* were manacled ourselves.' Declaration of Sentiments, modelled on Jefferson's **Declaration of Independence**: 'We hold these truths to be self-evident: that all men and women are created equal ... Such has been the patient sufferance of the women under this government, and such is now the necessity which constrains them to demand the equal station to which they are entitled.' **Elizabeth Cady Stanton** and **Frederick Douglass** went further and urged female enfranchisement. Convention met with ridicule and contempt, but annual women conferences met thereafter. Vote not given until the 19th Amendment, ratified 1920.

SHARECROPPING Economic compromise between former slaveowners and freedpersons in South after Civil War. In return for land, housing, fuel, tools, feed, seed, etc., provided by landlord, tenant farmer and family would labour on land and take share of crop at harvest – usually 30–50 per cent, in place of cash payment. Led to growing indebtedness in time of poor harvest, but preferred to wage or gang labour.

SHILOH On 6–7 April 1862 **Grant**'s capture of **Forts Henry and Donelson** and Buell's occupation of Nashville forced Confederacy to retaliate and try to regain initiative in West. Albert Sydney Johnston's aim to strike Grant before he joined up with Buell and, on 6 April, launched surprise

attack and forced them back to Tennessee River. On 7 April Grant and Buell counter-attacked, and Johnston was killed. **Beauregard** assumed command but forced to retreat to Corinth. Beauregard replaced by **Bragg**. Over 20,000 killed or wounded. Decisive battle of Western theatre, giving North the initiative.

SLAUGHTERHOUSE CASE, 1873 First test case of 'privileges and immunities' clause of **14th Amendment**. In 1869, Louisiana legislature gave monopoly grant to one livestock slaughterer in New Orleans. Others, excluded, appealed on grounds that loss of business violated their privileges and immunities as citizens. Justice Samuel Miller, in majority decision, held there was a dual citizenship – of the state, and of the United States – that the 14th Amendment did not give blanket coverage to US citizens who must look to states from which individual civil rights came. The consequence for freedpersons was the catastrophic removal of total federal commitment to equal civil liberties intended by the 14th. **Frederick Douglass**: 'Two citizenships means no citizenship. The one destroys the other ... The nation affirms, the state denies, and there is no progress. The true doctrine is one nation, one country, one citizenship, and one law for all the people.'

SLAVE POWER The considerable political power exercised by South in promoting pro-Southern interests in national politics and to obstruct any opposition to its growing strength. This, to most Northerners, more threatening than the institution of **slavery** itself because of its ability to control national politics and threaten extension of **free soil** and free labour to west. The acquisition of further slave states translated, economically, into land and the production of slave labour, and, politically, to greater representation in Congress. The **three-fifths rule** gave greater Southern representation in the House of Representatives and, given their smaller population, slave states (15 in 1850 equal to 15 free) also over-representation in Senate. This also gave South over-weighted **Electoral College** votes. In 1850 it is estimated the South had 30 more Electoral College votes than its voting population entitled it to. This imbalance helped election of both **Jefferson** in 1800 and **Jackson** in 1828 – both slave-owners – and between 1788 and 1861 slave-holder presidents were in control for two-thirds of this time. Twenty-four of the 36 presidents of the Senate represented Southern states, as did 23 Speakers of the House of Representatives. The South also tended to dominate the judiciary as well as the executive. **Taney**'s Supreme Court had a pro-Southern majority and 20 of the 35 Associate Justices before the war were from the slave states. There was, therefore, some proof in the North's accusation and **Lincoln**, in the 'House Divided speech' of 1858, discerning Southern conspiracy, seemingly confirmed by events favourable to South: the annexation of Texas, the **Mexican War**, the **Fugitive Slave Act** of 1850, the **Kansas–Nebraska Act**, and the **Dred Scott Decision** of 1857.

SLAVERY The first Africans were transported to Jamestown, Virginia, in 1619. Although only 4.5 per cent of the total transatlantic slave trade sent to the Western hemisphere settled in the US (the slave trade ceased in 1808), the slave population by 1776 was about 500,000 out of a total of 2,500,000 settled overwhelmingly in what were to become the 15 Southern slave states. By 1860 slave numbers had reached four million, one third of the total Southern population and 20 per cent of the total US population, ranging from 1.6 per cent in Delaware (a **border state**) to a black majority in South Carolina and Mississippi in the deep South. Six per cent of the black population was free, two-thirds in the border states of Delaware, Maryland and Virginia, but manumission – the freeing of individual slaves – became increasingly rare. African Americans, like white indentured servants, initially served a limited term by contract before achieving their freedom, but increasingly the fatal conjunction of race and status – the insistence that a dark skin signified inferiority and was synonymous with slavery – was established and legally codified. Essentially slaves were 'chattels personal', an owned property who served his or her master or mistress for life. Slavery was involuntary – who would choose to be a slave? – thus had, ultimately, to be based on coercion. The legal implications of this were confronted clearly by Judge Ruffin of North Carolina in 1829: 'The power of the master must be absolute to render the submission of the slave absolute.' The **Black Codes** which systematically controlled and exploited slave labour varied from state to state but generally the teaching of reading and writing was forbidden (illiteracy was about 90 per cent), as was formal marriage; slaves could not be party to a suit or contract, bear witness against whites in court and were required to carry passes if they travelled beyond their immediate surroundings. Offspring took the name of their slave mother to avoid the sometimes embarrassing recognition that the slave's father might be white (there were about half a million mulattos in 1860). Punishments ranged from short rations, to jail, whipping, branding, gelding or selling, for slavery was a mobile labour system and the Southeastern states increasingly became the source of an internal slave trade where slaves were sold in markets such as New Orleans and Natchez to work on an expanding Western frontier. It has been estimated that one family in three in the upper South was broken up and that 50 per cent of children were separated from at least one parent. Economically the system was profitable and buttressed by a master class ideology of semi-feudal paternalism. With the invention of Eli Whitney's Cotton Gin and Jefferson's Louisiana purchase of 1803 slavery became identified with '**King Cotton**', with roughly 1.8 million slaves engaged in cotton production. A total of 3.8 million bales were produced in 1860 – two-thirds of all American exports. Tobacco, sugar, race, hemp and indigo were other staples of an overwhelmingly rural system, though approximately 10 per cent worked in urban centres. One in four Southern whites owned slaves, though large plantations were exceptional: only 12 per cent owned more than twenty slaves and only 3 per cent owned fifty slaves or more. In return for living quarters, food, clothing and rudimentary health care, house slaves worked indoors as domestics while field hands laboured in gangs under the supervision of an overseer from dawn to dusk, which could mean a sixteen-hour day during harvests. Sundays and various holidays were allowed for rest and recuperation. Infant mortality was high – roughly two out of three children died – and the average life span was only 21 years (though only slightly higher, 26, for whites). There were minor revolts led by Gabriel Prosser in Richmond in 1800 and Denmark Vesey in Charleston in 1822: the largest was led by **Nat Turner** in Southampton County, Virginia, in 1831 in which about fifty-nine whites were murdered. As a consequence **Black Codes** were tightened. More typically malingering, deliberate incompetence, self-mutilation and sabotage created what **Kenneth Stampp** called 'a troublesome property' and John Blassingame a 'sullenly obedient and hostilely submissive' body. Despite all this a creative African American culture survived and flourished, mainly through dance, music and religion.

SLAVERY AS A POSITIVE GOOD Thesis argued increasingly and vociferously in South that, beyond mere economic expediency and financial profit, slavery was a positive good both for the slave and the slaveowner. Upheld by James Hammond, **Calhoun, Edmund Ruffin** and, succinctly, by Thomas Dew in *Review of the Debate in the Virginia Legislature* (1832) following the **Nat Turner Revolt**. Slavery was unequivocally sanctioned by the Bible, present throughout ancient and modern history, a means of social control and, given the slave's inherent childlike inferiority, masters could act as paternal trustees and inculcate training into civilised values.

STATES' RIGHTS The United States' Constitution is a federal constitution made up of independent states which came together to establish a central federal government: it is a balancing, deliberately ambiguous act, carefully distributing power between states and federal government. Struggles within the Philadelphia Constitutional Convention of 1787 continued with the federalists and anti-federalists emphasising central and state government respectively. Federalists, and Hamilton in particular, gave a 'loose construction' to the Constitution, which granted the federal government wide powers and enabled it to establish a Bank of the United States (which was not specified in the Constitution) and, along with Jay and Madison, wrote *The Federalist Papers*, a classic of political theory urging powerful central controls to offset endemic anarchy. Federalists also got 'We, the people of the United States' written into the constitutional preamble rather than 'We, the States of the United States' in order to bypass the states and emphasise a direct compact between individual citizens and their federal government. Marshall's long tenure of the Supreme Court (1801–35) entrenched Federalists' principles in the Supreme Court into the Jacksonian era. In 1819, in *McCulloch v. Maryland*, he insisted that a state, Maryland, could not tax the Bank of the United States. But a counter tradition also flourished. The 10th Amendment of the Bill of Rights (1791) insisted that all powers not specifically granted to the federal government remained with the state governments. Madison and Jefferson's Kentucky and Virginia Resolutions of 1798 raised the spectre of state nullification of federal laws, in this case John Adams's Alien and Sedition Acts of 1798. **Calhoun** perfected the theory of state nullification and ultimately secession from the Union, and South Carolina's opposition to the tariffs of 1828 and 1832 was a testing ground for these colliding principles. The final testing grounds were the battlefields of the Civil War itself. States' rights were identified with the South's defence of slavery against federal intervention, but the Confederate Constitution's emphasis on states' rights hampered **Davis**'s presidential duties, and states' rights' principles were entirely ignored by the South, when she insisted in 1850 in imposing stricter national Fugitive Slave laws on a deeply reluctant North. Following their defeat, Confederate writers such as Davis and **Stephens** claimed the war was fought to defend the principle of states' rights, not slavery – what James McPherson calls the 'virgin birth' theory of the war's origins. In fact states' rights, though they can be claimed to be a check on federal authority, are essentially a means not an end, an oppositional tool aimed at limiting federal authority. Throughout the war **Lincoln** talked increasingly of mystical nationhood rather than a union of states and the three **Civil War Amendments** extended federal authority through its commitment to African Americans. But the doctrine never entirely dies and during the 1950s and 1960s it was again resurrected in the South to halt the extension of the Civil Rights Movement.

T

THREE-FIFTHS RULE Cynical sectional compromise by founding fathers at Philadelphia, 1787, concerning taxation and representation. Each slave to count as three-fifths of a person in calculation of tax (which satisfied North) and representation (which satisfied South). This gave South over-weighting both in House of Representatives and Electoral College, which elected president. This was abolished with the **13th Amendment** of 1865.

TRANSCENDENTALISM A rather inchoate but influential philosophy derived from informal Transcendental Club meetings at **Emerson**'s Concord home – including the **Alcotts**, W.E. Channing, **Margaret Fuller**, Orestes Brownson, **Thoreau**, **Hawthorne**, Elizabeth Peabody and **Theodore Parker** – 1836–44, and publicised through its chief organ, *The Dial* (1840–44). Its source in the writings of the German Idealist school (especially Kant, Fichte, Hegel and Schelling) and transmuted by British romantic poets, particularly Coleridge and Wordsworth, in their call to 'plain living and high thinking'. Kant: 'I call all knowledge transcendental which is concerned not with objects, but with our mode of knowing objects so far as this is possible *a priori*.' In its rejection of eighteenth-century rationalism and empiricism personified in John Locke and the restrictive orthodoxy of preordained Calvinism, it preached the significance of individual intuition, perception and imagination in grasping essential spiritual truths and rejecting material values. There was a monistic unity in the world held together by the indwelling imminence of God. Intensely individualistic stress on the sovereign conscience, this spiritual renaissance fed into mid-nineteenth-century reformism, **abolitionism** and feminism, Utopian community experimentation (Brook Farm and Fruitlands) and verged towards philosophical anarchy. Emerson: 'To educate the wise man, the State exists; and with the appearance of the wise man, the State expires. The appearance of character makes the State unnecessary. The wise man is the State.'

TRENT INCIDENT James Mason (Virginia) and John Slidell (Louisiana) left Charleston on board British vessel *Trent* as Confederate envoys hoping to engage Britain and France in recognition of Confederacy. Captain Charles Wilkes on *San Jacinto* boarded *Trent* and arrested them as contraband of war when they were imprisoned in Fort Warren in Boston Harbour. Storm of European diplomatic protest led **Seward**, Secretary of State, to declare that Wilkes had violated international law and should have taken *Trent* into port for adjudication before Prize Court. Both released, January 1862. **Lincoln** declared – 'one war at a time'.

typhoid, pneumonia, dysentery. Grant: 'The fate of the Confederacy was sealed when Vicksburg fell.' **Lincoln**: 'The Father of Waters again goes unvexed to the sea.'

U

UNDERGROUND RAILROAD A loose network of supporters, mainly African American, aiding escape of fugitive slaves providing food, transport, safe shelter to North or, following tightening of Fugitive Slave laws in 1850, to safety of Canada. About 1,000 a year.

UNION LEAGUE Founded in North as anti-**Copperhead** organisation. Educated and organised African Americans into ranks of **Republican Party**, achieving high turnouts at elections. Faced stern opposition of **Democratic Party** and most Southerners.

V

VICKSBURG Six-week siege ending in surrender of Pemberton and 30,000 Confederate troops in 1863. Confederates still controlled 200 miles of Mississippi River from Vicksburg to Port Hudson. President **Davis** ordered **Joseph Johnston** to relieve Vicksburg, but **Grant** marched his Army of Western Tennessee 180 miles in seventeen days, winning five engagements on the way. Final surrender on 4 July 1863, same day **Lee** retreated from **Gettysburg**. High mortality rate on both sides: starvation, scurvy,

W

WADE–DAVIS BILL Introduced by **Benjamin Wade** (Ohio) in Senate and Henry Davis (Maryland) in House of Representatives to stall **Lincoln**'s moderate 10 per cent plan. Passed July 1864. Preconditions for entering Union required end of military resistance, majority of white electorate to take oath of allegiance to Union, provisional government to oversee state constitutional convention where voting for delegates or sitting in convention itself required 'ironclad oath' that individual had never voluntarily aided **Confederacy**. The constitutional conventions, in turn, were required to end slavery, repudiate Confederate war debt and disqualify leading rebels from voting or holding office. Lincoln imposed a pocket veto on this bill.

WILDERNESS CAMPAIGN Final, bloody and indecisive stage of war following **Gettysburg** and fought in impenetrable area west of Fredericksburg, Virginia, between **Grant** and **Lee**. On 3–4 May, Grant crossed Rapidan River engaging Lee, Ewell, Hill and Longstreet. On 5–6 May Hill's troops destroyed, but impasse followed. Grant repulsed at Spotsylvania (8–12 May) but thereafter, with diminished troops, Lee was on defensive and Grant determined to cut off his retreat to Richmond, which he achieved at Cold Harbor, 1–3 June. Grant crossed James River (12–14 June) determined to lift the siege of **Petersburg**. Casualties were huge – approximately 60,000 for Union and over 20,000 for Confederacy.

WILMOT PROVISO Proviso added to $3 million Appropriation bill to cover costs of **Mexican War**. Introduced by representative David Wilmot (Pennsylvania), 8 August 1846, stating 'that, as an express and fundamental condition of the acquisition of any territory from the Republic of Mexico … neither slavery nor involuntary servitude shall ever exist in any part of said territory'. Slavery had been ended in Mexico in 1825. After much heated debate, passed in House of Representatives by 80:64 but rejected in Senate, which had a Southern majority. Ominously, debate divided not on partisan lines of **Whig** versus **Democrat** but North (83 versus 12 in favour) versus South (67 versus 2 opposed).

ANNOTATED BIBLIOGRAPHY

Abbreviations:

JAH – *Journal of American History*
JSH – *Journal of Southern History*
AHR – *American Historical Review*

Peter Novick, *That Noble Dream: The 'Objectivity Question' and the American Historical Profession* (Cambridge, 1988), is invaluable although its comprehensive treatment does not concentrate exclusively on the Civil War era. Other books on the historical profession in America include August Meier and Elliott Rudwick, *Black History and the Historical Profession, 1915–1980* (Urbana, 1986), Richard Hofstadter, *The Progressive Historian* (New York, 1970), Marcus Cunliffe and Robin Winks (eds), *Pastmasters* (New York, 1969), Michael Kraus and Davis Joyce, *The Writing of American History* (Norman, Oklahoma, 1983), Harvey Wish, *The American Historian* (New York, 1960), John Hope Franklin, 'Afro-American History: State of the Art', *JAH* (74, 1988) and James McPherson and William J. Cooper Jr (eds), *Writing the Civil War: The Quest To Understand* (Columbia, S. Carolina, 1998).

For general surveys aimed at a British readership students should consult Hugh Brogan, *Longman History of the United States of America* (London, 1988), also available in Penguin paperback, and Maldwyn Jones, *The Limits of Liberty: American History, 1607–1980* (Oxford, 1983). Four outstanding histories on aspects of the era are Eugene Genovese, *Roll Jordan Roll* (New York, 1976); David Potter, *The Impending Crisis, 1848–1861* (New York, 1976); James McPherson, *Battle Cry of Freedom* (Penguin, 1988), and Eric Foner, *Reconstruction: America's Unfinished Revolution, 1863–1877* (New York, 1988). McPherson is also the author of *The Struggle for Equality: Abolitionists and the Negro in the Civil War and Reconstruction* (Princeton, 1964) and 'Slavery and Race' in *Perspectives in American History* (3, 1969).

Useful collections of material can be found in Charles Crowe (ed.), *The Age of Civil War and Reconstruction, 1830–1900* (Homewood, Ill., 1975), Gerald Grob and George Billias (eds), *Interpretations of American History: Patterns and Perspectives*, I (New York, 1972), William Cartwright and Richard Watson Jr (eds), *The Reinterpretation of American History and Culture* (Washington, 1973), Frank Gatell and Allen Weinstein (eds), *American Themes: Essays in Historiography* (London, 1968), John Garraty (ed.), *Interpreting American History* (London, 1970), John Higham (ed.), *The Reconstruction of American History* (London, 1972),

William Brock (ed.), *The Civil War* (New York, 1969), Robert Swierenga (ed.), *Beyond the Civil War Synthesis* (Westport, Conn., 1975), Arthur Link and Rembert Patrick (eds), *Writing Southern History* (Baton Rouge, 1965), Richard Leopold *et al.* (eds), *Problems in American History*, I (New Jersey, 1966), and Paul Escott and David Goldfield (eds), *Major Problems in the History of the American South*, I (Lexington, 1990). Among the liveliest collections of essays by Civil War historians are: George Fredrickson, *The Arrogance of Race* (Middletown, Conn., 1988), Staughton Lynd, *Class Conflict, Slavery and the U.S. Constitution* (Indianapolis, 1967), James McPherson, *Abraham Lincoln and the Second American Revolution* (Oxford, 1991), and the same author's *Drawn With the Sword* (Oxford, 1996), Herbert Aptheker, *Essays in the History of the American Negro* (New York, 1964), Don Fehrenbacher, *Prelude to Greatness: Lincoln in the 1850s* (Stanford, 1962), and *Lincoln in Text and Context* (Stanford, 1987), David Donald, *Lincoln Reconsidered* (New York, 1969), John Hope Franklin, *Race and History* (Baton Rouge, 1989), C. Vann Woodward, *The Burden of Southern History* (Baton Rouge, 1974), and *American Counterpoint* (New York, 1971), William Freehling, *The Reintegration of American History: Slavery and the Civil War* (Oxford, 1994), Eric Foner, *Politics and Ideology in the Age of the Civil War* (Oxford, 1980), David Potter, *The South and the Sectional Conflict* (Baton Rouge, 1968), and *History and American Society* (Oxford, 1973), Willie Lee Rose, *Slavery and Freedom* (Oxford, 1982), Eugene Genovese, *In Red and Black* (New York, 1972) and Benjamin Quarles, *Black Mosaic* (Amherst, Mass., 1988).

There is a vast literature on the character of the ante-bellum South, among which see: David Potter, *The South and the Sectional Conflict* and his 'The Historical Use of Nationalism' in *History and American Society*, the Nashville Agrarians' *I'll Take my Stand*, edited by Louis Rubin Jr (New York, 1962), essays by Franklin and Donald in Charles Sellers Jr (ed.), *The Southerner as American* (Chapel Hill, 1960), C. Vann Woodward's Introduction in his edition of George Fitzhugh, *Cannibals All, or Slaves Without Masters* (Cambridge, Mass., 1960), and his *Burden of Southern History*, Eugene Genovese, *In Red and Black* and *The Southern Tradition: The Achievement and Limitations of an American Conservatism* (Cambridge, Mass., 1996), Michael O'Brien, *The Idea of the American South, 1920–1941* (Baltimore, 1979), the same authors, *Conjectures of Order: Intellectual Life and the American South, 1810–60*, 2 vols (Chapel Hill, 2005), and James McPherson, *Drawn With the Sword*. The crucial concept of male honour has been explored by Bertram Wyatt-Brown, *Southern Honor: Ethics and Behavior In The Old South* (New York, 1982) and Kenneth S. Greenberg, *Honor and Slavery* (Princeton, 1996).

Useful collections of essays on slavery are: Allen Weinstein and F.O. Gatell (eds), *American Negro Slavery: A Modern Reader* (Oxford, 1974), and J. William Harris (ed.), *Society and Culture in the Slave South* (London, 1992). Other general studies include Peter Kolchin, *American Slavery* (Penguin, 1993), and his 'American Historians and Antebellum Southern Slavery, 1959–1984' in William J. Cooper *et al.* (eds), *A Master's Due: Essays in Honor of David Donald* (Baton Rouge, 1985), 'The Historiography of Slavery' in George Fredrickson, *The Arrogance of Race*, David

Brion Davis, 'Slavery and the Post World War Two Historians' in his *From Homicide to Slavery* (New York, 1986), Peter Parish, *Slavery: History and Historians* (New York, 1989), which also has an excellent bibliography. Ulrich Bonnel Phillips's main publications are *American Negro Slavery* (New York, 1918), *Life and Labour in the Old South* (Boston, 1929), and *The Slave Economy of the Old South: Selected Essays in Economic and Social History* (Baton Rouge, 1968), introduced and edited by Eugene Genovese. Genovese also writes on Phillips in *In Red and Black*, and Wendell Holmes Stevenson devotes a chapter to him in *The South Lives in History* (New York, 1955). Kenneth Stampp's 'The Historian and Southern Negro Slavery', *AHR* (63, 1958) was followed by his booklength *The Peculiar Institution* (New York, 1956) which was, in turn, criticised as a neo-abolitionist tract by Robert Fogel and Stanley Engerman, *Time on the Cross* (2 vols, London, 1974). Stanley Elkins, *Slavery: A Problem in American Institutional and Intellectual Life* (Chicago, 1959) was assessed in Ann Lane (ed.), *The Debate Over Slavery* (Urbana, Ill., 1971), in Genovese, *In Red and Black*, and Stampp, *The Imperiled Union* (Oxford, 1980). A.H. Conrad and J.R. Meyer, 'The Economics of Slavery in the Antebellum South' is reprinted in Peter Temin (ed.), *New Economic History* (Penguin, 1973). Fogel and Engerman, *Time on the Cross* was assessed in Paul David *et al.* (eds), *Reckoning with Slavery* (Oxford, 1976), Stampp, *The Imperiled Union* and Frank Tipton Jr and Clarence Walker in *History and Theory* (14, 1975). Robert Fogel, *Without Consent or Contract* (New York, 1989) is a later and more balanced study. Genovese's main works include *The Political Economy of Slavery* (New York, 1967), *The World the Slaveowner Made* (London, 1970), *Roll Jordan Roll* (New York, 1976), *The Slaveholder's Dilemma* (Columbia, S. Ca., 1992), and *The Southern Tradition: The Achievement and Limitations of an American Conservatism* (Cambridge, Mass., 1996). Appraisals of Genovese appear in C. Vann Woodward, *The New York Review of Books* (21 (5), 1974), David Brion Davis, *The New York Review of Books* (42 (15), 1995) and George Fredrickson, *The Arrogance of Race*. Herbert Gutman, *The Black Family in Slavery and Freedom, 1750–1925* (Oxford, 1976) was subject to criticism by Dan Carter in *Reviews in American History* (5, 1977). Cultural studies of the slave community include John Blassingame, *The Slave Community: Plantation Life in the Antebellum South* (New York, 1972), George Rawick, *From Sundown to Sunup: The Making of the Black Community* (Westport, Conn., 1972), Leslie Owens, *This Species of Property: Slave Life and Culture in the Old South* (New York, 1976), Albert Raboteau, *Slave Religion: The 'Invisible Institution' in the Antebellum South* (New York, 1978), Lawrence Levine, *Black Culture and Black Consciousness* (New York, 1977) and Sterling Stuckey, *Slave Culture* (New York, 1987).

Women and slavery are analysed in Stephanie M.H. Camp, *Closer To Freedom: Enslaved Women and Everyday Resistance in the Plantation South* (Chapel Hill, 2004), Sally G. McMillen, *Southern Women: Black and White In The Old South* (Wheeling, Ill., 1992), Wilma A. Dunaway, *The African-American Family in Slavery and Emancipation* (Cambridge, 2003), Victoria E. Bynum, *Unruly Women: The Politics of Social and Sexual Control in the Old South* (Chapel Hill, 1992), George Rables, *Civil Wars: Women and the Crisis of Southern Nationalism* (Urbana, 1989),

Deborah Gray White, *Ar'n't I A Woman?* (New York, 1985), Drew Gilpin Faust, *Mothers of Invention: Women Of The Slaveholding South in the American Civil War Era* (Chapel Hill, 1996), Anne Firor Scott, *The Southern Lady: From Pedestal to Politics* (Chicago, 1970), Catherine Clinton and Nina Silber (eds), *Divided Houses: Gender and the Civil War* (New York, 1992), Catherine Clinton, *The Plantation Mistress* (New York, 1982) and Elizabeth Fox-Genovese, *Within the Plantation Household*. Other aspects of slavery are covered in Jonathan D. Martin, *Divided Mastery: Slave Hiring in The American South* (Cambridge, Mass., 2004), Marie Jenkins Schwartz, *Born in Bondage: Growing Up Enslaved in the Antebellum South* (Cambridge, Mass., 2000), Walter Johnson, *Soul by Soul: Life Inside the Antebellum Slave Market* (Cambridge, Mass., 1999), John Hope Franklin and Loren Schweringer, *Runaway Slaves* (New York, 1999), John W. Blassingame, *Black New Orleans, 1860–1880* (Chicago, 1973), John B. Boles, *Black Southerners, 1619–1869* (Lexington, Kentucky, 1984), Michael Tudman, *Speculators and Slaves: Masters, Traders and Slaves in the Old South* (Madison, Wisconsin, 1989), Leon Litwack, *North of Slavery: The Negro in The Free States, 1790–1860* (Chicago, 1961), Ira Berlin, *Slaves Without Masters: The Free Negro in the Antebellum South* (Oxford, 1981), Adam Rothman, *Slave Country: American Expansion and the Origins of the Deep South* (Cambridge, Mass., 2005) and Steven Hahn, *A Nation under our Feet: Black Political Struggles in the Rural South from Slavery to the Great Migration* (Cambridge, Mass., 2005).

Comparative studies in slavery include George Fredrickson, *White Supremacy: A Comparative Study in American and South African History* (New York, 1981) and 'From Exceptionalism to Variability: Recent Development in Cross-National Comparative History', *JAH* (82 (4), 1995), Peter Kolchin, *Unfree Labor: American Slavery and Russian Serfdom* (Cambridge, Mass., 1987) and 'Comparing American History', *Reviews in American History* (10, 1982) and Shearer Bowman, *Masters and Lords: Mid Nineteenth Century U.S. Planters and Prussian Junkers* (New York, 1993), Herbert Klein, *Slavery in the Americas: A Comparative Study of Virginia and Cuba* (Chicago, 1967), Carl Degler, *Neither Black nor White: Slavery and Race Relations in Brazil and the United States* (New York, 1971) and Orlando Patterson, *Slavery and Social Death: A Comparative Study* (Cambridge, Mass., 1982).

On abolitionism Hugh Hawkins, *The Abolitionists* (Boston, 1964), and with additional material (Lexington, Mass., 1972), and Richard Curry (ed.), *Abolitionists* (New York, 1965) are excellent compilations. Other general surveys include: Merton Dillon, *The Abolitionists: The Growth of a Dissenting Minority* (New York, 1974), his 'The Abolitionists: A Decade of Historiography, 1955–1969', *JSH* (35, 1969), and 'The Failure of the American Abolitionists', *JSH* (25, 1959), David Brion Davis, 'Antebellum Reform' reprinted in Gatell and Weinstein (eds), *American Themes: Essays in Historiography* and his 'The Emergence of Immediatism in British and American Antislavery Thought', *Mississippi Valley Historical Review* (48, 1962), Donald Mathews, 'The Abolitionists on Slavery', *JSH* (33, 1967) and the important collection, *The Anti-Slavery Vanguard* edited by Martin Duberman (Princeton, 1965). Classic early studies include Gilbert Barnes, *The Anti-Slavery Impulse*

(New York, 1933; reprinted in 1964), Dwight Dumond, *Anti-Slavery Origins of the Civil War in the United States* (Ann Arbor, Michigan, 1939; reprinted in 1960 with an Introduction by Arthur Schlesinger Jr) and his *Antislavery: The Crusade for Freedom in America* (Ann Arbor, Michigan, 1961). Merton Dillon assesses these two historians in *Reviews in American History* (21, 1993). David Donald's essay, 'Towards a Reconsideration of Abolitionists' is reprinted in *Lincoln Reconsidered* and questioned by Gerald Sorin, *The New York Abolitionists* (Westport, Conn., 1971) and Robert Skotheim, 'A Note on Historical Method', *JSH* (25, 1959). Useful articles include: Martin Duberman, 'The Abolitionists and Psychology', *Journal of Negro History* (47, 1962), Richard Hofstadter on Wendell Phillips in *The American Political Tradition* (London, 1967), C. Vann Woodward, 'The Northern Crusade Against Slavery' in *American Counterpoint*, and Eric Foner's section on 'Ambiguities of Anti-Slavery' in his *Politics and Ideology in the Age of the Civil War*. George Fredrickson had edited a collection of writings, *William Lloyd Garrison: A Profile* (Englewood Cliffs, New Jersey, 1968). The standard biographies are: Walter Merrill, *Against Wind and Tide* (Cambridge, Mass., 1963) and John Thomas, *The Liberator: William Lloyd Garrison* (Boston, 1963), and Garrison is central to Aileen Kraditor, *Means and Ends in American Abolitionism* (New York, 1969), as is the crusade for female equality. A more recent study is Henry Mayer, *All On Fire: Garrison and the Abolition of Slavery* (New York, 1998). Benjamin Quarles has written on *Black Abolitionists* (New York, 1969). There is an excellent life of Frederick Douglass by William S. McFeely (New York, 1991) and the *Narrative* he wrote has been edited by John W. Blassingame *et al.* (New Haven, 2001). Women's contribution to the movement is treated in Mark Perry, *The Grimké Family's Journey from Slaveholders to Civil Rights Leaders* (New York, 2001), Jean Yellin and John Van Horne (eds), *The Abolitionist Sisterhood: Women's Political Culture in Antebellum America* (Ithaca, 1994) and Wendy Hammond Venet, *Neither Ballots nor Bullets: Women Abolitionists and the Civil War* (Charlottesville, 1991). For John Brown see Stephen Oates, *To Purge This Land with Blood* (New York, 1970), his *Our Fiery Trial* (Amherst, 1979), and 'John Brown and his Judges' in Robert Swierenga (ed.), *Beyond the Civil War Synthesis*, Bertram Wyatt-Brown, *Yankee Saints and Southern Sinners* (Baton Rouge, 1985), C. Vann Woodward, 'John Brown's Private War' in *The Burden of Southern History*, Willie Lee Rose, 'Killing for Freedom' in *Slavery and Freedom* and the chapter on Harper's Ferry in David Potter, *The Impending Crisis*. More recently, David S. Reynolds, *John Brown, Abolitionist* (New York, 2005), Merrill D. Peterson, *John Brown: The Legend Revisited* (Charlottesville, 2005) and Peggy A. Russo and Paul Finkelman (eds), *Terrible Swift Sword: The Legacy of John Brown* (Columbus, Ohio, 2005) where we learn that Brown probably suffered from bipolar disorder. Elkins's thesis on abolitionists in *Slavery* was responded to by Aileen Kraditor in Lane (ed.), *The Debate Over Slavery*, and Wyatt-Brown in *Yankee Saints and Southern Sinners*. Two recent important works by British historians are Richard Carwardine, *Evangelicals and Politics in Antebellum America* (New Haven, 1993) and John Ashworth, *Slavery, Capitalism and Politics in the Antebellum Republic*, I (Cambridge, 1995). More general surveys include John

Stauffer, *The Black Hearts of Men: Radical Abolitionists and the Transformation of Race* (Cambridge, Mass., 2002), David Brion Davis, *Challenging the Boundaries of Slavery* (Cambridge, Mass., 2003), Lawrence Friedman, *Gregarious Saints: Self and Community in American Abolitionism, 1830–1870* (Cambridge, Mass., 1982), Ronald Walters, *The Antislavery Appeal* (Baltimore, 1976), Lewis Perry, *Radical Abolitionism: Anarchy and the Government of God in Antislavery Thought* (Ithaca, 1973), James Brewer Stewart, *Holy Warriors: The Abolitionists and American Slavery* (New York, 1997), and Larry Gara, *The Liberty Line: The Legend of the Underground Railroad* (Lexington, Kentucky, 1961).

Two helpful collections of documents on Civil War origins are Kenneth Stampp (ed.), *The Causes of the Civil War* (Englewood Cliffs, New Jersey, 1963) and Edwin Rozwenc (ed.), *The Causes of the American Civil War* (Boston, 1961), Thomas Pressly, *Americans Interpret their Civil War* (New York, 1962) is a general survey of the historiography. Other surveys include David Potter, 'The Literature on the Background of the Civil War' in *The South and the Sectional Conflict* (Baton Rouge, 1968), Arthur Schlesinger, 'The States' Rights Fetish' in *New Viewpoints in American History* (New York, 1922), Gabor Boritt (ed.), *Why the Civil War Came* (Oxford, 1996), Kenneth Stampp, 'The Irrepressible Conflict' in *The Imperiled Union*, James McPherson, 'The War of Southern Aggression' in *Drawn With the Sword*, and Eric Foner, 'The Causes of the American Civil War: Recent Interpretations and New Directions' and 'Politics, Ideology and the Origins of the American Civil War' in *Politics and Ideology in the Age of the Civil War*. General narratives include: Kenneth Stampp, *And the War Came* (Chicago, 1980), David Potter, *Lincoln and his Party in the Secession Crisis* (New Haven, 1962) and his *Impending Crisis*, James McPherson, *Battle Cry of Freedom*, Brian Holden Reid, *The Origins of the American Civil War* (London, 1996) and Robert Cook, *Civil War America: Making A Nation, 1828–1877* (London, 2003). The impact of the slave power in domestic politics has been investigated by Leonard Richards, *The Slave Power: The Free North and Southern Domination, 1780–1860* (Baton Rouge, 2000), Don E. Fehrenbacher, *The Dred Scott Case: Its Significance in American Law and Politics* (New York, 1978) and his *The Slaveholding Republic: An Account of the United States Government's Relations to Slavery* (Oxford, 2001) and Richard Sewell, *Ballots for Freedom: Antislavery Politics in the United States, 1837–60* (Oxford, 1976). The secessionist movement is explored in William W. Freehling, *The Road to Disunion: Secessionists at Bay, 1776–1854* (New York, 1990), William L. Barney, *The Secessionist Impulse: Alabama and Mississippi in 1860* (Princeton, 1970), Steven A. Channing, *Crisis of Fear: Secession in South Carolina* (New York, 1970) and Charles Dew, *Apostles of Disunion: Southern Secession Commissioners and the Causes of the Civil War* (Charlottesville, 2001). The Progressive line is best captured in Charles and Mary Beard, *The Rise of American Civilisation* (New York, 1930) with commentaries on this approach by Richard Hofstadter, *The Progressive Historian* and Staughton Lynd, *Class Conflict, Slavery and the U.S. Constitution*. Revisionist texts include Avery Craven, *The Coming of the Civil War* (Chicago, 1957), his *An Historian and the Civil War* (Chicago, 1967) and his 'Coming of the War between the States: An

Interpretation', *JSH* (2, 1936), J.G. Randall, 'A Blundering Generation' reprinted in Stampp (ed.), *The Causes of the Civil War*, and Randall's 'The Civil War Restudied', *JSH* (6, 1940), Roy Nichols, *The Disruption of American Democracy* (New York, 1948) and David Donald, 'An Excess of Democracy: The American Civil War and the Social Process' reprinted in *Reconsidering Lincoln* (New York, 1969) and Stampp, *The Causes of the Civil War*. Critical readings of the revisionist interpretation can be found in Thomas Bonner, 'Civil War Historians and the "Needless War" Doctrine', *Journal of the History of Ideas* (47, 1986), Peter Geyl, 'The American Civil War and the Problem of Inevitability' in *Debates with Historians* (New York, 1962), and Arthur Schlesinger Jr, 'The Causes of the Civil War: A Note on Historical Sentimentalism' in *The Politics of Hope* (London, 1964) and also reprinted in Rozwenc, *The Causes of the American Civil War*. The consensus school is best represented by Daniel Boorstin, 'The Civil War and the Spirit of Compromise' in *The Genius of American Politics* (Chicago, 1953). The new political history approach can be found in Lee Benson, *Towards the Scientific Study of History* (Philadelphia, 1972), Michael Holt, *Forging A Majority* (New Haven, 1969), Holt, *Political Parties and American Political Development: From the Age of Jackson to the Age of Lincoln* (Baton Rouge, 1992), Holt, *The Rise and Fall of the American Whig Party: Jacksonian Politics and the Onset of the Civil War* (Oxford, 1999), Joel Silbey, *The Partisan Imperative: The Dynamics of American Politics before the Civil War* (Oxford, 1985), Robert Swierenga (ed.), *Beyond the Civil War Synthesis* (Westport, Conn., 1975), Silbey, *A Respectable Minority: The Democratic Party in the Civil War Era, 1860–1869* (New York, 1997) and William Gienapp, *The Origins of the Republican Party, 1852–1856* (New York, 1987). This new approach has been examined critically by Don Fehrenbacher in *Lincoln in Text and Context*, Eric Foner in *Politics and Ideology in the Age of the Civil War*, in Swierenga, and by Morgan Kousser in *Reviews in American History* (4, 1975; and 21, 1993).

The Lincoln literature is vast. John Nicolay and John Hay's *Life* can be read in a condensed form with an Introduction by Paul Angle (Chicago, 1966). J.G. Randall, *Lincoln: The President* is in four volumes, completed by Richard Current (London, 1945–55). The best one-volume biographies are: Benjamin Thomas, *Abraham Lincoln* (New York, 1952), Stephen Oates, *With Malice Towards None* (New York, 1977), David Donald, *Lincoln* (London, 1995), William Gienapp, *Abraham Lincoln and Civil War America* (Oxford, 2002), Richard Carwardine, *Lincoln: Profiles In Power* (Harlow, 2003) and Philip Shaw Paludan, *The Presidency of Abraham Lincoln* (Lawrence, Kansas, 1994). See also David Donald, *Lincoln Reconsidered*, Mark Neely Jr, *The Fate of Liberty: Abraham Lincoln and Civil Liberties* (Oxford, 1991), Richard Current, *The Lincoln Nobody Knows* (New York, 1988), Don Fehrenbacher, *Prelude to Greatness: Lincoln in the 1850s* (Stanford, 1962) and *Lincoln in Text and Context*, James McPherson, *Abraham Lincoln and the Second American Revolution* (Oxford, 1991), Gabor Boritt (ed.), *The Historian's Lincoln* (Urbana, 1988), Hofstadter's essay on Lincoln in *The American Political Tradition*, Merrill Peterson, *Lincoln in American Memory* (Oxford, 1994), and Cullom Davis *et al.* (eds), *The Public and Private Lincoln* (Carbondale, Ill., 1979) with its suggestive essay which compares Mrs Lincoln with her female contemporaries, Grant's and Sherman's *Memoirs* are available in the Library of America editions (New York, 1990). On the early writings of Henderson see Jay Luvass (ed.), *The Civil War: A Soldier's View: A Collection of Civil War Writings by Col. G.F.R. Henderson* (Chicago, 1958), J.F.C. Fuller, *Grant and Lee: A Study in Personality and Generalship* (London, 1933) and *The Generalship of Ulysses S. Grant* (Bloomington, Indiana, 1929). More recent studies include Josiah Bunting III, *Ulysses S. Grant* (New York, 2004), Brooks Simpson, *Ulysses S. Grant* (Boston, 2000) and Geoffrey Perret, *U.S. Grant: Soldier and President* (New York, 1997). Basil Liddell Hart's *Sherman: Soldier, Realist, American* (London, 1929) is a classic study. John F. Marszalek, *Commander of All Lincoln's Armies: A life of General Henry W. Halleck* (Cambridge, Mass., 2004) is the first major biography of a neglected general. There are two excellent biographies of these influential military historians: Brian Holden Reid, *J.F.C. Fuller: Military Thinker* (London, 1987), and Brian Bond, *Liddell Hart* (London, 1977). Jefferson Davis's *The Rise and Fall of the Confederate Government*, in two volumes, has been reprinted with a Preface by Bell Wiley (New York, 1988) and extracts from Alexander Stephens's *A Constitutional View of the late War between the States* are available in both Rozwenc and Stampp, *The Causes of the Civil War*. Lives of Davis include Hudson Strode, *Jefferson Davis* (3 vols, New York, 1955–64), Clement Eaton, *Jefferson Davis* (New York, 1977), Paul Escott, *After Secession: Jefferson Davis and the Failure of Confederate Nationalism* (Baton Rouge, 1978), William Cooper Jr, *Jefferson Davis: American* (New York, 2001) and William C. Davis, *Jefferson Davis: The Man And his Hour* (New York, 1991). On Lee there is the classic four-volume *Robert E. Lee: A Biography* (New York, 1934–1935) by Douglas Freeman, supplemented by his *Lee's Lieutenants: A Study in Command* (3 vols, New York, 1942), 'Freeman: Historian of the Civil War: An Appraisal' is included in T. Harry Williams, *The Selected Essays* (Baton Rouge, 1983). Also Emory Thomas, *Robert E. Lee* (New York, 1995), Thomas Connelly, *The Marble Man: Robert E. Lee and His Image in American Society* (New York, 1977), Alan Nolan, *Lee Considered* (Chapel Hill, 1991), James McPherson, 'Lee Dissected' in *Drawn With the Sword*, Michael Fellman, *The Making of Robert E. Lee* (New York, 2000) and J. Tracy Power, *Lee's Miserables: Life In The Army of Northern Virginia from the Wilderness to Appomattox* (Chapel Hill, 1998). Among the plethora of military histories see Grady McWhiney (ed.), *Grant, Lee, Lincoln and the Radicals* (Northwestern, 1964) and McWhiney, *Southerners and Other Americans* (New York, 1973), Richard Beringer *et al.*, *Why the South Lost the Civil War* (Athens, Georgia, 1986), Herman Hattaway and Archer Jones, *How the North Won* (Urbana, 1983), Jay Luvass, *The Military Legacy of the Civil War* (Chicago, 1989), David Donald (ed.), *Why the North won the Civil War* (London, 1960), Bruce Collins, 'The Southern Military Tradition' in Brian Holden Reid and John White (eds), *American Studies: Essays in Honor of Marcus Cunliffe* (London, 1991), Gabor Boritt (ed.), *Why the Confederacy Lost* (Oxford, 1992), T. Harry Williams, *Lincoln and his Generals* (London, 1952), James McPherson, *Ordeal by Fire* (New York, 1982),

Gerald Linderman, *Embattled Courage* (New York, 1987), Kenneth Williams, *Lincoln Finds a General* (5 vols, New York, 1949–59), Archer Jones, *Confederate Strategy from Shiloh to Vicksburg* (Baton Rouge, 1961), Thomas Connelly and Archer Jones, *The Politics of Command: Factions and Ideas in Confederate Strategy* (Baton Rouge, 1973), Frank Vandiver, *Rebel Brass* (Baton Rouge, 1956), Warren Hassler Jr, *Commanders of the Army of the Potomac* (Baton Rouge, 1962), Gary Gallagher, *The Confederate War* (Cambridge, Mass., 1997), Marcus Cunliffe, *Soldiers and Civilians* (London, 1969). James McPherson, *What They Fought For* (New York, 1994) and *For Cause and Comrade* (New York, 1995) supplements the earlier writings on the common soldier by Bell Wiley. McPherson has also written a vivid survey of one of the most decisive battles of the conflict, *Crossroads of Freedom: Antietam* (Oxford, 2002). On neglected naval warfare, see John Niven, *Gideon Welles: Lincoln's Secretary of the Navy* (New York, 1973) and Kevin J. Weddle, *Lincoln's Tragic Admiral: The Life of Samuel Francis Du Pont* (Charlottesville, 2005). Stig Förster and Jurg Nageler (eds), *On the Road to Total War* (Cambridge, 1997) make interesting comparisons with the German wars of unification and Gabor Boritt (ed.), *War Comes Again* (New York, 1995) with the Civil War and Second World War. The black contribution is covered in Benjamin Quarles, *The Negro in the Civil War* (Boston, 1953), James McPherson, *The Negro's Civil War* (New York, 1965) and the same author's *The Struggle for Equality: Abolitionists and the Negro in the Civil War and Reconstruction* (Princeton, 1964), John Hope Franklin, *The Emancipation Proclamation* (New York, 1963). On the vexed question of morale, see Stanley Lebergott, 'Why the South Lost: Commercial Purpose in the Confederacy, 1861–1865', *JAH* (69, 1983), Emory Thomas, *The Confederate Nation, 1861–1865* (New York, 1979) and his *The Confederacy as a Revolutionary Experience* (Columbia, S. Ca., 1971), Charles Roland, *The Confederacy* (Chicago, 1960), E. Merton Coulter, *The Confederate States of America* (Baton Rouge, 1980), Frank Owsley, *State Rights in the Confederacy* (Chicago, 1925), Charles Ramsdell, *Behind the Lines in the Southern Confederacy* (Baton Rouge, 1944), Kenneth Stampp, 'The Southern Road to Appomattox' in *The Imperiled Union* and William W. Freehling, *The South v. The South: How Anti-Confederate Southerners shaped the Course of the Civil War* (New York, 2001). For the Union side, see Philip Paludan, *A People's Contest* (New York, 1988). For the rapidly changing Northern economic order, see Heather Richardson, *The Greatest Nation of the Earth* (Cambridge, Mass., 1997), and for the new social history Mavris Vinovski (ed.), *Towards a Social History of the American Civil War* (Cambridge, 1990), Joan E. Cashin (ed.), *The War Was You and Me: Civilians In The American Civil War* (Princeton, 2002), Paul A. Cimbala and Randall M. Miller, *An Uncommon Time: The Civil War and the Northern Home Front* (Fordham, 2002), Catherine Minton (ed.), *Southern Families At War: Loyalty and Conflict In The Civil War South* (Oxford, 2001), Iver Bernstein, *The New York City Draft Riots* (New York, 1990), Jeanie Attie, *Patriotic Toil: Northern Women and the American Civil War* (Ithaca, 1998), Susan-Mary Grant, *North Over South: Northern Nationalism and American Identity in the Antebellum Era* (Lawrence, Kansas, 2000), Randall M. Miller *et al.* (eds), *Religion and the American Civil War*

(Oxford, 1998), Agatha Young, *The Women and the Crisis: Women of the North in the American Civil War* (New York, 1959), Reit Mitchell, *The Vacant Chair: The Northern Soldier leaves Home* (New York, 1993) and Mary Elizabeth Massey, *Bonnet Brigade: American Women and the American Civil War* (New York, 1966). For cultural repercussions, see Edmund Wilson, *Patriotic Gore* (New York, 1962), F.O. Malthiessen, *American Renaissance: Art and Expression in the Age of Emerson and Whitman* (Oxford, 1941), George Fredrickson, *The Inner Civil War: Northern Intellectuals and the Crisis of the Union* (New York, 1965), Daniel Aaron, *The Unwritten War: American Writers and the Civil War* (Oxford, 1973) and Irving Howe, *The American Newness: Culture and Politics in the Age of Emerson* (Cambridge, Mass., 1986). On specific writers, Roy Morris, *The Better Angel: Walt Whitman in the Civil War* (Oxford, 2000), Richard B. Sewall, *The Life of Emily Dickinson* (2 vols, London, 1976) and Robert D. Richardson Jr, *Emerson: The Mind On Fire* (Berkeley, California, 1995) are outstanding. On the diplomatic aspects of the war, see E.D. Adams, *Great Britain and the American Civil War* (2 vols, New York, 1925), Frank Owsley, *King Cotton Diplomacy* (Chicago, 1931), H.D. Jordan and Edwin Pratt, *Europe and the American Civil War* (London, 1931), Harold Hyman (ed.), *Heard Round the World: The Impact of the Civil War* (New York, 1968), D.P. Crook, *The North, the South and the Powers* (New York, 1974), Brian Jenkins, *Britain and the War for the Union* (2 vols, Montreal, 1980), and Mary Ellison, *Support for Secession: Lancashire and the American Civil War* (Chicago, 1972). Works that discuss the impact of the Civil War on the American consciousness include David W. Blight, *Race and Reunion: The Civil War in American Memory* (Cambridge, Mass., 2001), Gary Gallagher and Alan Nolan (eds), *The Myth of the Lost Cause and Civil War History* (Bloomington, Indiana, 2000), Gaines M. Foster, *Ghost of the Confederacy: Defeat, the Lost Cause and the Emergence of the New South, 1863–1913* (New York, 1987), Tony Horwitz, *Confederates in the Attic* (New York, 1998) and Nina Silber, *The Romance of Reunion: Northerners and the South, 1865–1900* (Chapel Hill, 1993).

Staughton Lynd has edited a useful collection of documents on *Reconstruction* (New York, 1967), as has Richard Current, *Reconstruction* (Englewood Cliffs, New Jersey, 1965). William Dunning, *Reconstruction: Political and Economic, 1865–1877*, first published in 1907, has been reprinted (New York, 1962) and his *Essays on the Civil War and Reconstruction* (New York, 1965) has an Introduction by David Donald. See also Philip Miller, 'Look Back Without Anger: A Reappraisal of William A. Dunning', *JAH* (61, 1974–75). Richard Current has edited a series of articles on Reconstruction that appeared in *The Atlantic Monthly* in 1901, *Reconstruction in Retrospect* (Baton Rouge, 1969). W.E.B. DuBois, *Black Reconstruction in America, 1860–1880* (New York, 1969), DuBois's 1910 article on 'Reconstruction and its Benefits' is reprinted in Lynd, *Reconstruction*, as is his 'Of the Dawn of Freedom'. See also Meyer Weinberg (ed.), *W.E.B. DuBois: A Reader* (New York, 1970). Elliott Rudwick has written on DuBois in John Hope Franklin and August Meier (eds), *Black Leaders of the Twentieth Century* (Urbana, 1982), and Herbert Aptheker has written on

DuBois the historian in Rayford Logan (ed.), *W.E.B. DuBois: A Profile* (New York, 1971). Early revisionist writings include Vernon Wharton's survey in Link and Patrick, *Writing Southern History*, Howard Beale, 'On Rewriting Reconstruction History', *AHR* (46, 1940), and Francis Simkins, 'New Viewpoints of Southern Reconstruction', *JSH* (5, 1939). Kenneth Stampp, *The Era of Reconstruction* (London, 1965) and John Hope Franklin, *Reconstruction* (Chicago, 1961) represent this new viewpoint in book form, as do Willie Lee Rose, *Rehearsal for Reconstruction: The Port Royal Experiment* (Indianapolis, 1964), Michael Perman, *Reunion Without Compromise: The South and Reconstruction, 1865–1868* (New York, 1973), Leon F. Litwack, *Been In The Storm So Long: The Aftermath of Slavery* (New York, 1979) and James Alex Baggett, *The Scalawags: Southern Dissenters in the Civil War and Reconstruction* (Baton Rouge, 2003). Eric Foner's major study is *Reconstruction: America's Unfinished Revolution, 1863–1877*, but see also his *Politics and Ideology in the Age of the Civil War* (Oxford, 1980), *Nothing But Freedom: Emancipation and its Legacy* (Baton Rouge, 1983), 'Reconstruction Revisited' in *Reviews in American History* (10, 1982), and 'The Meaning of Freedom in the Age of Emancipation', *JAH* (81 (1–2), 1994). Other modern appraisals include: Philip Paludan, *A Covenant with Death* (Urbana, 1975), which deal with constitutional issues, as does Michael Vorenberg, *Final Freedom: The Civil War, the Abolition of Slavery and the Thirteenth Amendment* (Cambridge, 2001), Stanley Kutler, *Judicial Power and Reconstruction Politics* (Chicago, 1968) and Harold Hyman, *A More Perfect Union: The Impact of the Civil War and Reconstruction on the Constitution* (New York, 1973). Kenneth Stampp and Leon Litwack (eds), *Reconstruction: An Anthology of Revisionist Writings* (Baton Rouge, 1969), John Hope Franklin, *George Washington Williams* (Chicago, 1985), David Donald, *The Politics of Reconstruction* (Cambridge, Mass., 1984), La Wanda and John Cox, *Politics, Principle and Prejudice, 1865–1866: Dilemmas of Reconstruction America* (New York, 1963), Eric Anderson and Alfred Moss Jr (eds), *The Facts of Reconstruction: Essays in Honor of John Hope Franklin* (Baton Rouge, 1991), Harold Hyman (ed.), *The Radical Republicans and Reconstruction, 1861–1870* (Indianapolis, 1967), Richard Current, *Three Carpetbag Governors* (Baton Rouge, 1967) and *Those Terrible Carpetbaggers* (Oxford, 1988) and Gaines Forster, *Ghosts of the Confederacy* (New York, 1987) for the Southern legacy of Reconstruction. On Johnson see Hans Trefousse, *Andrew Johnson: A Biography* (New York, 1989) and Eric McKitrick, *Andrew Johnson and Reconstruction* (London, 1960). For Grant and the Freedmen, see Arthur Zilversmit in Robert Abzug and Stephen Maizlich (eds), *New Perspectives on Race and Slavery in America* (Lexington, Ky, 1989), Brooks Simpson, *Let Us Have Peace: Ulysses S. Grant and the Politics of War and Reconstruction, 1861–1868* (Chapel Hill, 1991) and Keith Polakoff, *The Politics of Inertia: The Election of 1876 and the End of Reconstruction* (Baton Rouge, 1973). The political and economic consequences of Reconstruction are analysed in Roger L. Ransom and Richard Sutch, *One Kind of Freedom: The Economic Consequences of Emancipation* (Cambridge, 1989), Richard Franklin Bensel, *Yankee Leviathan* (Cambridge, 1990), Morton Keller, *Affairs of State: Future*

Life in late Nineteenth Century America (Cambridge, Mass., 1977) and Heather Cox Richardson, *The Death of Reconstruction* (Cambridge, Mass., 2001).

Useful articles include: Thomas Pressly, 'Racial Attitudes, Scholarship and Reconstruction: A Review Essay', *JSH* (32, 1966). Peter Kolchin, 'The Business Press and Reconstruction, 1865–1868', *JSH* (33, 1967) and Stanley Coben, 'New England Business and Radical Reconstruction: An Examination', *Mississippi Valley Historical Review* (75, 1989) both refute Beard's thesis on Reconstruction. La Wanda and John Cox, 'Negro Suffrage and Republican Politics: The Problem of Motivation in Reconstruction Historiography' in Gatell and Weinstein (eds), *American Themes: Essays in Historiography*, Bernard Weisberger, 'The Dark and Bloody Ground of Reconstruction History', *JSH* (25, 1959), Larry Kincaid's 'Victims of Circumstance: An Interpretation of Changing Attitudes Towards Republican Policy Makers and Reconstruction', *JAH* (49, 1963). Allan Bogue, 'Historians and Radical Reconstruction: A Meaning for Today', *JAH* (69, 1983), David Donald, 'Scalawags in Mississippi Reconstruction', *JSH* (10, 1944), Allan Trelease, 'Who Were the Scalawags?', *JSH* (29, 1963), Armistead Robinson, 'Beyond the Realm of Social Consensus: New Meanings of Reconstruction for American History', *JAH* (68, 1981). C. Vann Woodward's thesis in *Reunion and Reaction: The Compromise of 1877 and the End of Reconstruction* (New York, 1956) was questioned by Allan Peskin, 'Was There a Compromise of 1877?', *JAH* (59, 1973), with a reply by C. Vann Woodward in the same issue.

Websites

Civilwarhome.com (includes battles, biographies, medicine, potpourri, Confederacy, essays, letters, naval war and other relevant websites).
Civilwar.net (links database, maps, official records, photographic database, detailed regimental histories, soldiers and sailors, 1860 census, state by state, etc.).

INDEX

Page numbers for figures have suffix **f** and those for tables have suffix **t**

Routledge History

American Civilization
An Introduction – 4th Edition

David Mauk and John Oakland

'The best friend for American Studies students' *Julio Canero Serrano, Alcala de Heneres University*

'Every chapter states the major issues and offers clear synthesis of the main interpretations' *Francesco Meli, IULM University*

'Excellent for current information about the US' *Felicity Hand, Universitat Autònoma*

American Civilization is a comprehensive introduction to contemporary American life. It covers the key dimensions of American society including geography and the environment, immigration and minorities, government and politics, foreign policy, the legal system, the economy, social services, education, religion, the media and the arts.

This fourth edition has been thoroughly revised and includes many updated diagrams, tables, figures and illustrations, as well as coverage of the George W. Bush presidency, the 2004 election, the manifold effects of the 9/11 terrorist attacks, the Iraq Gulf War and the war on terrorism. This new edition is accompanied by a companion website.

Hbk 0-415-35830-2 / 978-0-415-35830-9   Pbk 0-415-35831-0 / 978-0-415-35831-6

American Cultural Studies
2nd Edition

Neil Campbell and Alasdair Kean

This much-needed update of *American Cultural Studies* takes into account the developments of the last seven years and provides an introduction to the central themes in modern American culture and explores how these themes can be interpreted.

Chapters in the book discuss the various aspects of American cultural life such as religion, gender and sexuality, and regionalism, and updates and revisions include:

- a new introduction engaging with current debates in the field
- an all-new chapter on foreign policy
- thorough discussion of globalization and Americanization
- new case studies
- updated further-reading lists.

Following in the footsteps of its predecessor, *American Cultural Studies* will become a staple text on the reading lists of all American Studies students.

Hbk 0-415-34665-7 / 978-0-415-3465-8   Pbk 0-415-34666-5 / 978-0-415-34666-5

Available at all good bookshops
For ordering and further information please visit:

www.routledge.com

Routledge History

The Slavery Reader

Edited by Gad Heuman and James Walvin

The Slavery Reader brings together the most recent and essential writings on slavery. The focus is on Atlantic slavery – the enforced movement of millions of Africans from their homelands into the Americas, and the complex historical story of slavery in the Americas. Spanning almost five centuries the articles trace the range and impact of slavery on the modern western world. Key themes include:

- the origins and development of American slavery
- slave culture
- slave economy and material culture
- Africans in the Atlantic world
- race and social structure.

Together with the editors' clear and authoritative commentaries and substantial introductions to each part, this volume will become central to the study of slavery.

Hbk 0-415-21303-7 / 978-0-415-21303-5   Pbk 0-415-21304-5 / 978-0-415-21304-2

The Routledge Atlas to American History – 5th Edition

Martin Gilbert

This new edition of this invaluable reference guide presents a series of 157 clear and detailed maps, accompanied by informative captions, facts and figures, updated with additional maps and text to include the 2004 presidential election and recent events in Iraq. The complete history of America is unrolled through vivid representations of all the significant landmarks, including:

- Politics – from the annexation of Texas and the battle for black voting rights to the present day
- Military Events – from the War of Independence and America's standing in two world wars to the conflicts in Korea, Vietnam, and the Gulf up to the events of 9/11, the war in Iraq and its aftermath
- Social History – including the abolition of slavery to the growth of female emancipation and recent population movements and immigration
- Transport – from nineteenth-century railroads and canals to the growth of air travel and recent ventures into space
- Economics – from early farming and industry to urbanisation and the ecological struggles of the present day.

Hbk 0-415-35902-3 / 978-0-415-35902-3   Pbk 0-415-35903-1 / 978-0-415-35903-0

Available at all good bookshops
For ordering and further information please visit:

www.routledge.com